XIN LOI,
VIET NAM

XIN LOI, VIET NAM

Thirty-one Months of War:
A Soldier's Memoir

AL SEVER

PRESIDIO
PRESS

BALLANTINE BOOKS • NEW YORK

A Presidio Press Book
Published by The Random House Publishing Group

Copyright © 2002 by Al Sever

All rights reserved under International and Pan-American Copyright Conventions. Published in the United States by Presidio Press, an imprint of The Random House Publishing Group, a division of Random House, Inc., New York, and simultaneously in Canada by Random House of Canada Limited, Toronto. Originally published by Quiet Storm Publishing in 2002.

Presidio Press and colophon are trademarks of Random House, Inc.

www.presidiopress.com

ISBN 0-89141-856-3

Manufactured in the United States of America

First Presidio Press Edition: March 2005

OPM   9 8 7 6 5 4 3 2 1

DEDICATION

Upon arrival in Viet Nam, most troops were given a card titled "Standing Orders for Rogers' Rangers." Originally issued to troops in the French and Indian War, the Orders are good advice to soldiers of any war. The first Order is, "Don't forget nothing."

I didn't forget very much. Most of all I cannot ever forget the brave men who were with me in front of the guns of the NVA. I dedicate this book to them.

Roger Backes
Ronald Baker—KIA
Jim Barre
Dean Bolhouse—KIA
Eber Brown
Jim Crisp—KIA
Joe Deal
Lou Diantonio
Acevedo Garcia
Dale Gilchrest
Steve Herring—KIA
Scott Hesse
Richard Holman—KIA
Robert Jantz—KIA
Cecil Johnson

Mike Meagher
Melvin Morgan—KIA
Dave Nancarrow
Mike O'Conner
Pete Polak—KIA
Pat Ronan
Harry Rose—KIA
Taco Sayes
William Scott—KIA
Charles Sellner—KIA
Art Silacci
Joe Skarda
Mike Ward
Clifford Wright—KIA
Everett Wilsher—KIA

PROLOGUE

A boy I went to school with left his legs in Viet Nam. He once told me that, after most people got to know him, they would eventually ask, "What was it like in Viet Nam?"

What a question to ask! What was Viet Nam like? No one wants to learn about the geography or the topography when they ask that question. Their next question is always, "Did you kill anyone?"

"How the hell should I know," he'd answer, "I was only there eight days!"

Eight days. I can visualize exactly what he looked like then. Another FNG who didn't know anything. Everyone too busy or tired to show him anything. I imagine he looked like the young man portrayed as one of three infantrymen in the sculpture at the Vietnam Veterans Memorial. Most people who look at the sculpture don't realize what they are seeing. There is more there than three tired young men. When I first saw the statue, I just shook my head. I wondered why the artist had made such a glaring error—until I realized he had shown the truth. In the small group, the error of carrying a belt of ammunition with the cartridge bullet tips pointing toward his neck makes one man immediately recognizable as the typical expendable replacement, the new guy no one knows. And no one cares if he lives or dies. When I stood in front of the statue, like a lot of old soldiers, I felt the urge to reach out and twist the ammunition belt so the bullets wouldn't abrade his neck. Wearing a belt of ammunition backwards is a small mistake, but those little errors slow you down and can kill.

I never asked my friend how he happened to lose his legs and he never volunteered any information. I suppose we both knew if he had told me how it occurred, all I could say about his loss would have been *"Xin loi,"* the only Vietnamese words a lot of soldiers knew. But those two short words said it all. Just about everyone learned this phrase shortly after they arrived in country. They were the American soldier's generic answer to almost every problem.

Eight days in country were enough to learn these words, but even those of us who were there much longer knew very few other words of Vietnamese. Few of our soldiers even knew how to say, "Hello!" While we did use some local words and phrases from our infrequent contact with the Vietnamese, one has to wonder about our choices. The local words we all used from the Delta to the DMZ speak volumes about us: kill; crazy; go away fast; come here; stop. There must be some hidden reason we chose to use Vietnamese for these hard words. One reason, perhaps, was to ensure that there was no mistake in translation when we spoke these words. There was one expression, however, that we used daily in our conversations with each other which was perfect for our war: *Xin loi*. Depending on the tone of voice or how it was used in a sentence, it meant "Sorry about that," but could also mean "Fuck you." *Xin loi* was our way of sincerely expressing a complete lack of empathy. It is God's reply to the question asked by every casualty: "Why me?"

While my friend didn't serve much time in country, a pair of legs is a pretty steep price for a short trip to Asia. He was one of many, many young men who were finished with the war almost as soon as they walked into the rice. Prior to becoming resigned to our fate and losing our fear, most of us had occasionally envied those boys who were wounded soon after they arrived, considering them lucky. Their war was finished quickly, and while their bodies were torn, their souls had not been scarred. They had missed the day-after-day mind-numbing fear and brutality of guerrilla warfare that worked as a dull rasp to slowly wear away frivolous civilian emotions and fraudulent morals until nothing was left but the harsh truth. By leaving so fast, they missed learning something very subtle that only came with experience. There came a point when a person realized there was something sublime about being in contact with the enemy, and that there was much more to that inner feeling of well-being than just adrenaline. Only the new guys wondered why so many guys smile during a firefight.

After you have faced the enemy guns several times and realize the fight is a ceremony of life, not death, you tend to start thinking about what is happening. The lessons in the muzzle flashes show the way, the light, and the truth. The dead of both sides, sprawled in the dirt with limbs askew and leaking Rorschach blots of bright red blood, are omens to be divined. What do they say? They seem to scream out lessons that go unheard. You can read secrets in the alphabet of the dead. It's too easy to not see the forest for the trees. Combat is not about death, as there is a lot more death in peace than in war. The firefights become intoxicating and addicting. There is a lesson to be learned and, just when you start to think that you recognize the answer, you realize you don't know the question. The muzzle flashes of enemy guns wink like the eyes of the gods. Do you get what they mean? Bright tracers float toward you bringing messages from the angel of death. Bullets that miss were sent to tell you things not found in the Bible. Heavy contact with the enemy is more religious than a church service but you only realize it afterward. You know you just experienced something extremely important but you forget what it was. Your hands subconsciously pat your body, feeling for blood or wounds, while the euphoria of being shot at and missed fills your brain like heroin. You know something was shown to you. But then again, perhaps adrenaline fogged my brain and it was an illusion. I could have sworn there was something being given to us but we were too foolish to take it. Nonetheless, something drew us to the bright muzzle flashes of the enemy guns like moths to a flame.

Sometimes, however, those muzzle flashes left scars on our souls. There was never any honor or glory in anything we did, but some days broke our hearts. Even though combat made us hard as steel, there were on occasion incidents that were too tough for us to rationalize. Occasionally the chatter of automatic weapons uttered things about ourselves we didn't want to learn.

I once spent a bright sunny afternoon and the fading twilight of the same evening watching a young man die. A teenage soldier had been shot in front of a camouflaged enemy bunker. He was lying wounded under the muzzle blast of an NVA machine gun. His comrades were scattered behind him and lay on both sides of the trail as bullets shredded shrubs lining the trail. A small group of infantrymen, they had attempted to save their wounded point man by outflanking the bunker, but had received heavy fire from camouflaged fighting positions on its flanks. Neither artillery nor air strikes could be used on the enemy position without destroying the wounded boy with the bunker, so the infantry platoon leader had called for gunships. My platoon leader, Nine Six, received the order to fly over their position.

After being briefed on the mission, Nine Six, who was flying as aircraft commander (AC) on my ship, radioed our other two gunships, telling them to follow and help destroy a bunker. Heading northeast, skimming treetops of the Ho Bo Woods, in a few minutes we passed over a river and circled the area of the map coordinates given. After we made radio contact with the troops lying in the brush, the ground commander quickly explained the problem while we flew low circles above him to familiarize ourselves with the terrain. Listening to the conversation on the radio and looking down at the wounded boy sprawled in front of the bunker, I watched the muzzle blast of a machine gun dance from the bunker's firing port. Our infantry were pinned down. They wanted us to save their point man and to destroy the bunker with a rocket. Easier said than done. Our rockets weren't very accurate and we had to hit the bunker without killing the wounded soldier. Nine Six decided to send our other two ships to circle to the northeast while he tried to knock out the bunker with rockets.

My ship then left the infantry patrol, flew east to the nearby river to gain a little altitude, turned sharply and dove toward the bunker. Rolling in hot, Nine Six put rockets on the eastern side of the bunker, but the NVA machine gun continued to fire at the prone infantrymen sprawled in the dirt on both sides of the trail leading to the bunker. Flying as low and slow as possible, Nine Six tried to ensure that our rockets would not miss the bunker and hit the wounded soldier. Turning around, we made a second gun run. As our rockets impacted next to the bunker, enemy positions north of the bunker fired several rocket-propelled grenades at our ship. Flying through the dust and the smoke from our exploding rockets, I heard the infantry platoon leader screaming on the radio, "Cease fire! Cease fire! Stop your rockets, you're hitting us!"

"We're not even close to you!" Nine Six told him angrily. "RPGs are missing us and impacting around you." Our platoon prided itself on never hitting our own infantry, and I believe Nine Six took it as a personal insult that the ground commander thought he had fired a rocket into a friendly position.

Deciding our rockets weren't accomplishing anything except blowing the vegetation from the bunker, and to prove to the infantry that RPGs were hitting near them and not our rockets, Nine Six advised the ground troops we were going to knock the bunker out with hand grenades.

I knew we would be going in low and slow from east to west, flying level with the tops of the low shrubs screening the bunker, and that Nine Six expected me to put a hand grenade into the bunker.

Prior to dropping grenades, we made a practice run. As our skids knocked leaves from the shrubs, I machine-gunned every possible hiding place to the right and left of the bunker, hoping to hit any men hidden in spider holes on the flanks. While I sprayed the area a few meters under our left skid, our gunner sent a stream of tracers into the NVA positions firing RPGs and small arms from our right. After pass-

ing two meters above the bunker, we immediately made a
hard left, turning a semicircle toward the front of the bunker.

As soon as our turn brought us over the trail the bunker
guarded, the firing port of the bunker glowed bright yellow-
orange from the muzzle flash of the enemy machine gun. I
had never been so close to the wrong end of a machine gun;
it was fascinating watching the flame of the muzzle flash
pulsate and dance before my face. Gunships cannot hover,
but we seemed to be suspended over the infantry as our ship
crawled through the air above the trail until we passed two
meters above the heels of the wounded soldier. The pulsating, hypnotic glow of the NVA machine gun had made time
irrelevant and our ship inched its way through the thick gelatinous mass of semifrozen time over the bunker. With all
the time in the world, I leaned forward out the door and
poured machine gun rounds into the bright muzzle flash
throbbing from the gun port. Drifting toward the bunker, the
wind from our rotor blades and the muzzle blast of the NVA
machine gun combined to ripple the blond hair and clothing
of the wounded boy. The rippling made it appear he was trying to move. Only his hands or head moved, however, indicating he was hit in the spine. Without the use of his legs, he
wasn't going to crawl from the bunker. Keeping my rounds
from the wounded man, and ignoring the enemy entrenched
in the fighting positions north of the bunker, I concentrated
on putting bullets into the face of death, grinning at me in the
flame dancing out of the firing port. Our two other gunships
tried to cover our flank by firing rockets into the area where
we were receiving the RPG fire, but each time I glanced
north, the twinkling muzzle flashes of enemy guns sparkled
in the low brush.

After passing the bunker on our practice run, we flew east,
did a quick turn over the river, and with our skids in the
brush, headed back to kill the bunker. Going in on our first
grenade run, Nine Six told me to throw the grenade at my
discretion at the back of the bunker in an attempt to put it in
the rear entrance. Fatalistically taking a fragmentation grenade out of its black cardboard container, I wished for a

miracle—anything that would stop or change our attack. We fought bunkers until someone was dead—and sometimes it wasn't the occupants of the bunker. I would never have volunteered to throw grenades next to a wounded soldier, but I had no choice. I knew I would never forgive myself if I killed the young man. Leaning out of the open doorway to my left, grenade pin pulled, I held the spoon tightly and gazed at the wounded boy lying directly in front of my target and waited stoically for an NVA bullet to hit me. No matter what happened, I had to keep my grenades away from the front of the bunker and the wounded soldier. Forgetting everything else, I looked down through the smoke trails of RPG rounds and tried to judge our airspeed, the possible location of the bunker entrance, and the arc of a grenade thrown from a moving helicopter. As always, when trying to destroy a bunker, I felt vulnerable hanging out of the ship, holding a hand grenade. I would be unable to shoot back if an NVA soldier popped up the camouflage cover of his spider hole and emptied his AK-47 at me.

This can't be happening, I told myself, hoping to wake from a bad dream. *Why me?*

I didn't want the responsibility of knocking out this bunker. Not with the wounded boy so close to it. I was not confident I could keep a grenade from exploding near the wounded soldier, but I knew I had better not kill him. On the other hand, I realized I might be shot as we approached the bunker. The NVA soldiers in the nearby spider holes were not going to ignore me while I dropped grenades on their friends. I couldn't win. Releasing the grenade spoon, I held an armed grenade ready to explode in seconds. In those few seconds, I reminded myself that I had volunteered for this job and wondered why I had ever joined the Army.

■

Anthracite coal country, hard coal and hard times, Schuyl-kill County, Pennsylvania, is where I'm from. Not a prosper-ous place during my youth, it still isn't. Energy competition from fuel oil and natural gas had made most coal mines in the county uneconomical after World War II and Schuylkill County, instead of joining the country's postwar boom, slipped back toward the Depression. Growing up, it was rare to see neighbors buy new cars, eat in restaurants or take a va-cation. Our families seemed to just barely get by. But, since everyone was in the same economic boat, we young people felt the situation was probably the same everywhere. While television and movies indicated there was a prosperous life out there, we tended to regard such indications as fairy tales.

Our small town was a typical mining community, probably extinct in America today. It was a town of four thousand peo-ple with two movie theaters, two supermarkets, thirty-five bars and twenty-seven churches. Like other nearby mining towns, ours had a lot of bars because they were the social meeting places for neighborhoods. There were a lot of churches because no one would ever think of going to church with people of a different nationality. We might work to-gether, go to school together and drink together, but, whether Catholic or Protestant, church was for those of your own eth-nic group from the old country. We grew up hearing a dozen foreign languages spoken on our block, and being American kids, we learned none of them.

We didn't have many diversions growing up and were left to find our own amusements. Society catered to adults then, not children. Like all teenagers we talked about what we were going to do and where we would go, and we were all sure that we would never stay in Saint Clair. Judging from our environment, life was going to be a struggle to get by, but we realized the struggle probably would be easier somewhere else. There were quite a few boys in my high school class who looked to the military as a way of escaping the reality of closed coal mines.

The older males we knew were strictly blue-collar workers whose biggest adventure in life was to have served in the Big War, WWII. We grew up hearing stories of our relatives and neighbors conquering the Japanese and Germans. They had marched through Burma; sailed the Pacific and North Atlantic; parachuted into France; blown up a bank and filled knapsacks with jewels in Belgium; lost their booty in German counterattacks; were the Bulge at Bastogne; drove the first tank into Manila.

After WWII stories, it seemed that every adult's second favorite conversation was to complain about every level of government. Yet it was somehow understood that everyone was expected to back the government and its policies, no matter what their personal feelings might be about those policies. During the Viet Nam War years, adult discussions always generalized the conflict as a waste of time, money and lives, but there was never what would be called an anti-war mentality. Instead, conversations were slanted toward the stupidity of those in charge. It made no sense to our citizens that the government would expend such energy and funds on an unknown third world country like Viet Nam. Who cared if it went Communist? To those who had fought for continents, wasting years and men for rice paddies and jungle was incomprehensible. Where was the Paris to liberate? Where was the evil madman to destroy? Our television news programs showed American troops burning peasant homes and villages, not liberating them.

A stranger might have thought there was a lack of support in our country for the war in Viet Nam. Not true. In our communities, it was accepted that, if a young man was of military draft age, he should anticipate serving in the armed forces. There were very few draft dodgers in our county and no organized antiwar movement. If drafted, a young man was expected to serve honorably. There was no lack of support for the common soldier.

While the draft was accepted as part of our lives, it was also the local consensus that, while one might be drafted, no one would be so foolish as to actually join the U.S. Army. If you were going to volunteer, join the Navy, the Air Force or even the Marines. Any armed service but the Army. Most of the older men remembering World War II thought that the Army wasted its troops, using them as cannon fodder. In their opinion, the Army of World War II fought a war of attrition—the favorite tactic being a human wave attack. Joining the Navy or Air Force would at least mean a bed to sleep in and three hot meals a day. As for the Marines, our local veterans believed the Navy invented the Marines so that sailors wouldn't have to march in parades. Since most of our local veterans had served in the Army during World War II, they always rooted for Navy in the annual Army-Navy football game and strongly suggested that young men consider enlistment in other branches of the armed forces.

For those of us in high school in the 1960s, there didn't appear to be many choices for the future. I doubt if any of us really knew what we wanted to do with our lives; we had no awareness of choices available. The military seemed the only profession interested in us—they sent recruiters to the high school to talk to seniors. We were not the sons of doctors, lawyers or engineers and had no contact with people who were professionals. We were expected to find blue-collar work.

I think back on high school as a warehouse for teenagers rather than an educational institution. It's surprising more of us didn't quit school. Even though fighting was occurring in Viet Nam, most of us knew older boys in the military and knew that relatively few troops were sent to Viet Nam. Local boys were coming home on leave from Iceland, Spain, Germany, Korea and other countries, but I knew of only two local boys who had gone to Viet Nam in 1966. When I graduated in June 1966, approximately 25 percent of my senior class had enlisted in the military. I was the only one going into the Army.

Why did I join the Army? I viewed the military as an escape from small-town boredom and monotony. I wanted to experience adventure in capital letters. All through my senior year the news media were full of stories about the conflict in Viet Nam. I noticed most stories included helicopters. At eighteen, I wanted to experience war—and helicopters. The U.S. Army seemed to be the way to go. I couldn't understand how other eighteen-year-old boys could consider joining the military to drive trucks, type, cook, et cetera. I picked helicopter training, not to learn a trade, but to ensure that I would get into combat.

I doubt if very many boys of my age enlisted to purposely serve in Viet Nam. Many young men were doing everything they could to avoid serving anywhere. Quite a few of them would regret not having served with those who went. But we didn't really need them and they probably would have only slowed us down. I believe that Viet Nam was my generation's chance to do something unusual, and I had no intention of not participating in history. I was one of those boys of fighting age who were afraid to miss the action.

Eight days following my graduation from high school, I raised my right hand and vowed to protect and defend the Constitution of the United States. Ten minutes later, I was boarding a bus headed south to Fort Gordon, Georgia, for basic training. Two hundred and thirty-nine young men and I were to spend eight weeks in Georgia under a hot summer sun learning the basic skills expected of every soldier in the U.S. Army. Here we would learn Close Order Drill (march in formation everywhere); military courtesy (everyone who outranked us should be considered a god); first aid (never use *your* battle dressing to bandage anyone else; save your clean battle dressing for your own wounds); the M-14 rifle (it's heavy so that when we ran out of ammunition, we could use it to beat someone to death); bayonet drill (tai chi); squad tactics (the guy behind you is more likely to shoot you than the enemy).

We were welcomed to Fort Gordon by screaming drill sergeants who intimidated us before we even were out of our bus. Our first group activity was to march to the barber to get haircuts so that we would look alike. The military haircuts showed we had something in common—whether city boys or country, northern Yankees or southern rebels—scars on our heads from rock fights.

We were measured for clothes and boots and were soon issued our clean, bright olive drab fatigues and black combat boots. During the next two months we would turn our clothes white with salt deposits from our sweat, while our boots would shine like mirrors from constant "spit shining." All civilian clothes worn on our trip to Georgia were either shipped home or thrown away. We would be wearing nothing except green for a long time.

My new home in Georgia would be an old two-story barracks built as a temporary building in World War II. Thirty men to one large room on each floor with no privacy whatsoever. We slept in bunk beds and soon learned why, if given a choice, a soldier always took a top bunk. No one sat on it to mess it up. Our clothes were hung on the wall behind the bunks in a prearranged order—no fancy wall lockers here. Our footlockers sat in the barracks' center aisle and held small folded items like underwear and socks. The footlocker also held mandatory personal gear such as toothbrush and tooth powder (toothpaste was not allowed); shaving brush and shaving soap (no shaving cream allowed); a razor with five extra double-edge blades, no more, no less; comb (mandatory, even though we had no hair); cleaning items— shoe polish, brass polish, et cetera. One day in the future we would realize that barracks life was easy living.

Basic training was a combination of physical and mental brainwashing. We were no longer considered individuals; our squad, platoon and company were what mattered. Everyone was part of a team and we had better learn to function as a team. Mass punishment was the rule. If a squad member screwed up, the whole squad suffered. If a squad screwed up, the whole platoon suffered. An infraction by one person meant everyone would be doing push-ups.

Needless to say, mass punishment encouraged everyone in the squad or platoon to have their gear prepared. Group discipline seemed stupid and ridiculous to us; we thought it was unfair for everyone to be punished for another person's mistake. We didn't realize it but we were being trained to take care of each other. After a while, no one looked at his own uniform and gear without subconsciously watching what the other guys in the squad were doing. It was the old story of a chain being as strong as its weakest link. The system was going to force us to work as a team and was going to force the strong to help the weak. We slowly learned that if we helped each other and worked together, mass punishment became less frequent. If someone had a problem that caused us to suffer, it would benefit all of us to help that person meet the standards of our sergeants. We had no idea that our sergeants were manipulating us. We were the ones training our slowest learners, not the sergeants.

Several years later, when serving with men who had actually been drill instructors, I learned our treatment was part of the master training plan. While I hadn't really noticed it during basic training, the plan also allowed drill sergeants to disappear periodically to rest while their counterparts kept us too busy to notice their absence. They would then reappear refreshed and we would not even notice that they had been missing. No wonder they were able to run us into the ground. Another trick was to "pile on" any soldier who might question their power. At the first hint of possible insubordination from a trainee, two, three or four sergeants would immediately surround the perceived possible threat to their command and intimidate the trainee into submission. The sergeant originally challenged was the one who shouted loudest and who gave the final commands.

The first several weeks of training were spent learning dismounted drill (no one ever told us what mounted drill was), military courtesy, military justice, military this, military that. We could hardly wait to be through with the basic military subjects: we wanted our rifles. The highlight of basic was the day in the third week of training when we received our M-14 rifles. The rifle was a symbol of acceptance—the supreme tool of the trade. A weapon meant we were warriors. We smiled with joy when we walked away from the arms room, carrying our rifles and bayonets.

Even though we carried our rifles everywhere for five weeks, we only spent a week firing them. Rather than shoot at a fixed bull's-eye target as the Marines were trained to do, our training was based on the theory that any hit on a man was a good hit and that multiple targets at varied ranges had to be engaged instantly. Our targets were head or head-and-shoulder targets out to one hundred meters; half-torso with head at two and three hundred meters; three-quarter torso with head at longer distances. Targets were electronically controlled so that they could be made to pop up as singles, doubles or triples. As always, the military was training us to fight the last war. We were practicing for the human wave attacks of the Korean War. Each target had an electronic sensor that could register if a bullet had hit that target. When a bullet passed through the target, the sensor automatically folded down the target so that the scorer knew the target had been hit. When someone in Viet Nam described his job as being a "pop-up target," this is what he was talking about. Good description.

Of course, there were some people who just couldn't master the program. Every company had a few guys who were still going back to the range weeks after the rest of their unit had qualified with their weapons. These men would be shooting until they could hit something; the Army was not going to let them out of basic without the minimum skill necessary to shoot at a man and hit him. Our sergeants called it the "Lee Harvey Oswald theory." Oswald barely scored the minimum on his Marine Corps marksmanship test, but he hit a president, riding in a moving vehicle, in the head using a rifle known to be a piece of junk. Shows the value of good training.

While we spent a week on the ranges firing our weapons, we spent more than a week practicing to use our rifles as spears. That's what we had when we attached a bayonet to the end of a rifle. No matter how busy our day might be, our sergeants always found time for us to practice the slow "tai chi" movements and the traditional sacred mantra of bayonet practice. "What's the spirit of the bayonet?" a sergeant would yell periodically, and with religious fervor the troops would scream their reply, "To Kill! To Kill!" The monastic chant of bayonet drill was supposed to build "Spirit." I don't think that the Army does bayonet drill anymore. There might be a lesson there.

Most training stressed that we were to shoot or stab someone else, but we also had to realize that we might be the person shot or stabbed. Basic first aid training for combat wounds was given frequently and, while many of us had learned first aid in the Boy Scouts, the scoutmasters hadn't been too interested in teaching us how to treat sucking chest wounds. It seemed to be the favorite wound of the military, perhaps because the treatment worked if you or your buddy had been lucky enough to get a piece of shrapnel in the lung and not be literally vaporized into molecules of blood and flesh by high explosives. I recall being advised to avoid getting hit in the liver; it was extremely painful and always fatal. Probably good advice if one is being given a choice of where he will be shot, though I don't recall anyone ever asking my preference prior to shooting at me. What we really were taught was to do the best that we could to save our buddies: they were all we had. *Never* abandon your wounded! Stop the bleeding, clear the airway, protect the wound, treat for shock. In this game of high-velocity bullets and high explosives, you may be next. Take care of your friends and they will take care of you. It all seemed very important and everyone paid attention.

In retrospect, the Army probably did a good job of training us. But there was one item of warfare that was neglected. The whole issue of taking enemy prisoners was never mentioned. We were told what to do if we were captured: give our name, rank and serial number. But I cannot recall anyone ever teaching us how to take and secure enemy prisoners. I know that when we practiced assaulting bunkers, we fired our blank ammo into the occupants of the bunker. In bayonet practice, we were never told to stop the thrust of the blade if an opponent surrendered. First aid specifically taught how to treat our own wounded. While nothing was ever actually said, it seemed to be understood that prisoners were not a priority. I think we learned this lesson very well.

Eventually basic training ended. We could march, salute, shoot, bayonet, pull KP and generally function in the U.S. Army. It was an experience we would always remember. After basic, we were probably in better physical condition than we would be in Viet Nam; we ate better and had more rest. Mentally, we were still soft clay needing the heat of combat to form us into soldiers. Those of us who survived a year of combat in Viet Nam were going to be hardened to a degree unimaginable to most civilians.

Leaving Fort Gordon and basic training, I was off to Fort Eustis, Virginia, to learn about helicopters. We were taught a lot about helicopters, but the pace was fast. We probably forgot most of what we learned as quickly as it was taught to us. Almost all of our instructors had been in Viet Nam and they would constantly reassure us that we were only being given a basic mechanical understanding of helicopters. Probably the first thing we learned was what to call a helicopter. It was always referred to as a "ship," which was short for "airship," and I still cringe when I hear someone call a helicopter a "chopper." As in any profession, we had to learn the jargon of the job. Even though we spent long hours becoming familiar with helicopters, we couldn't expect to become expert mechanics as a result of our training. When we were sent to Viet Nam, we'd be so busy working that we'd soon know how to take a helicopter apart and put it back together in our sleep. I can't honestly say that our training was very helpful, but I would later learn that our instructors were right about learning things when we were working on the flight line. Actual experience would be our best teacher.

Most of the men in our class didn't care much about learning how to fix helicopters. While a few had enlisted specifically to become helicopter mechanics, with the idea of converting their military schooling into a future career, the majority of us were trying to use helicopter repair school as a means to an end. For most of us, helicopter school meant becoming a crew chief on our own "ship": the crew chief flew as the left-door gunner. Door gunner was the coolest job in the Army. Say Viet Nam and you think helicopter. Say helicopter and you think door gunner.

There was no military occupational specialty (MOS) specifically designating a soldier to be a door gunner; therefore, no one was trained to be a helicopter door gunner. The crew chief, however, automatically became the man at the left-door gun whenever his ship flew. If you wanted to fly with a machine gun, the best way to do it was to go to school to become a crew chief/mechanic.

The right-door gunner usually came from whatever troops happened to be available when a door gunner was needed. Helicopter door gunners not only flew but also used the best work of art in the U.S. Army, the M-60 machine gun. A perfect meld of form and function that sent 750 rounds per minute to a target, it was the one weapon that all troops truly loved; every other weapon was merely a tool. Whether in the air, on the ground or on an armored vehicle, the M-60 was the weapon of choice. Sitting on a helicopter with an M-60 allowed one to travel fast in relative comfort, heavily armed. A high percentage of American casualties would be helicopter crewmembers, but we didn't know or care. Since the only guaranteed way to be a door gunner was to become a crew chief, we were going to be crew chiefs.

For the most part, training was tedious and boring, but our last week of training was fun and exciting. For a week we practiced helicopter assaults into Virginia swamps. We fired away with blank ammunition, conducted ground sweeps of mock Vietnamese villages where we stepped on mines and were shot by troops dressed as Viet Cong, and listened to our instructors tell their war stories of 1965 and 1966. We should have paid attention and noticed how we were slaughtered in our war games. Just because our instructors faced poorly equipped guerrillas in their war was no reason to believe that we would. A lot of us were going to face disciplined North Vietnamese soldiers who were equipped with weapons as good as or better than ours. While the instructors laughed about jumping into bunkers to escape 60mm mortar fire, we'd hide from 122mm rockets that leveled bunkers. Our instructors didn't give us the impression that the war was going to be either difficult or dangerous. They made it sound easy, the classic fight of Elhanan against Goliath. And we were Goliath. We had no idea that things were going to be a hell of a lot different for us in the land of rice and opportunity.

Following my training at Fort Eustis in early December of '66, I returned home to Schuylkill County for a two-week leave prior to reporting for my next duty assignment in Texas. On leave I was surprised by the lack of interest my old friends had about the war in Viet Nam. The conflict had been discussed daily in the barracks. Back on the block, no one seemed to give the subject much thought until they were drafted. My two-week leave went fast and, several days prior to Christmas, I traveled to Fort Hood, where I was assigned to an air cavalry troop. This unit was air cavalry in name only, however. Stateside units were very low on the priority list to receive helicopters, so our troop only had two helicopters instead of the authorized thirty. It wouldn't have made much difference even if we had helicopters because I was carried on the troop TO&E roster (Tables of Organization & Equipment) as an infantryman. So much for joining the military to go to school and learn a trade.

It didn't really matter how the troop roster carried us. We were one of many units at Fort Hood with no mission and little equipment. I suspect that we were considered cannon fodder in case of war in Europe. We had rifles and trucks and, in an emergency, could have been sent anywhere. We also were issued heavy winter clothing, so it was pretty obvious that we were not held in reserve for duty in Viet Nam. Our life was endless inspections, make-work details, marching and loafing.

All through 1967, various units from brigade size down to company size would be formed at Fort Hood for deployment to Viet Nam. Every few weeks, several of the men in our troop would either be assigned to one of these new units or get orders to deploy to Viet Nam as individuals. The rest of us considered these guys lucky. We were bored and demoralized. Periodically, we would also receive replacements in our troop, either troops returning from Southeast Asia or new guys just out of training. While the armored units at Fort Hood appeared to lose and gain troops from similar units stationed in Germany, our cavalry troop soldiers had two possible military career options. They were either going to leave Fort Hood to go to Viet Nam, or they were going to spend the rest of their short military careers at Fort Hood, Texas.

One thing we did continually in 1967 was train for riot control. It was a common theme at Fort Hood. Everywhere we looked, we saw troops practicing the slow one-step shuffle with rifles held to the front, bayonets extended—riot control formations. While riots had been a common occurrence in the black districts of scattered cities throughout the country, our troop was always given the impression that we were training for different riots: antiwar demonstrations. Rumor had it that the 2nd Armored Division was being held in reserve to reinforce the primary riot control troops that were to be used in Washington. We were told that, if called, we would either be used as a human fence with bayonets protecting federal buildings or as a slow shuffling fence of bayonets to clear streets and control crowds. Repeatedly, we were taught that human beings feared "cold steel" and that the sight of our bare bayonets was a psychological weapon. Mobs would back up when the line of bayonets advanced.

As I recall, we trained in platoon formations, which would, in actual service, link with other platoons in our troop. If necessary, our troop would link with other troops; our squadron with other battalions. While the training was hot, dusty and monotonous, it was interesting to learn that there was some logic used to control crowds. Classes were given to explain how small units of disciplined troops could use city terrain to control a mob. As long as we held our line, we could split large mobs into smaller, more controllable, leaderless groups by maneuvering sections of the group into alleys or side streets. Avenues of escape were also considered in the plan. Certain streets were left as escape routes, since we were not attempting to trap or kill a mob, but to disperse it. It actually sounded as if it might work, as long as our line held.

To ensure the line did hold, discipline was stressed. We would not have loaded weapons; we each had an M-14 rifle with a bayonet—in other words, a spear. Behind each platoon were four armed men: the platoon leader, a radioman, a rifleman and a NCO with an automatic weapon. If any opposing gunfire was received, armed soldiers behind the bayonet rank would engage it. Soldiers on the line would hold the line and not break into a mob themselves.

While our troop was never activated for riot duty, it was common to meet and talk to guys from other units who had gone to the Detroit riots. According to their stories, the Michigan National Guard had been undisciplined and uncontrollable. They had turned riot control into urban warfare and had been firing the .50-caliber machine guns on their armored personnel carriers (APCs) into any building from which a shot was fired. Several years later, in 1970, when four students were killed at the antiwar demonstration at Kent State University, I was not surprised to learn that a National Guard unit was involved. While people may not have thought much of soldiers during the Viet Nam War years, we soldiers on active duty thought even less of the National Guard.

Sometime in mid-1967, I was promoted to specialist four, the technical equivalent of a corporal. Corporals, by the way, were relatively rare. Artillery batteries had corporals, usually the company armorer was a corporal, and NCOs who had been reduced in rank might be corporals. Nearly all of the troops who were promoted went from private first class to

Spec 4, even in the infantry. The barracks myth was that after ex-corporal Napoleon and ex-corporal Hitler, the military system was trying to minimize delusions of grandeur in corporals by eliminating them.

Even though I had been promoted, I was still at Fort Hood and time seemed to drag. My brother was now in a hospital in Viet Nam recovering from malaria; his letters didn't make Viet Nam sound like fun. On the other hand, he apparently was doing something before being hospitalized. We at Fort Hood were just marking time and accomplishing nothing. Every so often, I would fill out another 1049 (Request for Transfer) to go to Viet Nam, but it seemed as if I was doomed to sit out my entire three-year enlistment in Texas. The days seemed endless; monotonous duties and endless inspections five and a half days every week. When released for the weekend following inspection at noon on Saturday, we spent our free time drinking beer or killing time. We felt like prisoners. I had volunteered, but I used to wonder how draftees kept their sanity. Is it any wonder that men fled to Canada to evade the draft? Who would ever want to throw away two years of their life vegetating at an Army installation? How could the Army force men to live such a nonproductive existence? Our service in Texas was much, much worse than serving in Viet Nam. No matter how bad times would get in Viet Nam, I was always grateful that I wasn't in Texas.

In the fall of 1967, I received orders to report to a new assault helicopter company being formed at Gray Army Airfield. This post was located about eight miles from Fort Hood and was specifically used to house Army Aviation units being trained for deployment to Southeast Asia. Finally, I was getting closer. I packed my gear and caught a bus to the airfield, where I joined a company with less than a dozen soldiers. Every day, however, more troops would arrive, slowly bringing the unit up to strength.

As the company filled its positions, we started getting class after class on Southeast Asia, the subjects ranging from climatic conditions to propaganda. There are only a few things I remember from the training, but I distinctly recall the part about snakes. We were instructed that there are a hundred species of snakes in Southeast Asia; ninety-nine are venomous and will kill you; the other one swallows you whole. Our NCOs said that going off base was as dangerous as being in combat because the VD rate was extremely high and that there was an incurable strain of syphilis. If anyone caught the "black syph," they were to be permanently exiled to an island in the Pacific and officially listed as POW/MIA. Since the Army never lied to us, I suppose that our POW/MIAs are still there. We were also told that most Americans referred to the Vietnamese as "gooks." This term, our NCOs claimed, came from the Korean word for a foreign soldier, which was *megook*. When our troops landed in Korea, natives would point at them and say, "Me Gook." Naturally, if that's what they called themselves, so would we. Another thing we learned was how to spell Viet Nam—it's *two* words, *not* one. We were told that it means Far South, not Farsouth. If we were taught anything else about the Republic of Viet Nam, I don't recall it.

When our company was up to full strength, equipment started being issued that clearly implied we were going to Southeast Asia—lightweight jungle fatigues, canvas jungle boots and M-16 automatic rifles. The clothes and boots didn't mean much to us, but the new rifles fascinated us. Most of us had only used the M-14 rifle, and the M-16 was like a toy compared to the heavy M-14. Much lighter with a black plastic stock instead of a heavy wood stock, the M-16 was also capable of being fired on full automatic. All we had to do was just pull the trigger and *RIPPPP!* There went twenty rounds.

In order to become familiar with our new weapons, we spent a week on the rifle range and were issued unlimited ammunition to fire at any rate of fire we wished at the pop-up targets. Some guys were firing a full magazine on full automatic at every target. Soon, everyone became bored with shooting. Boredom ceased immediately, however, when one of the many cattle that roamed Fort Hood wandered onto the range. Everyone manning the firing positions turned the selector switch on his rifle to full automatic and lines of tracers would converge on the unlucky cow.

Those cows, by the way, were all over Fort Hood. Supposedly, local ranchers, who were registered Democrats, were allowed to graze their cattle on the military base for a dollar per head per year. If a rancher found the carcass of a cow killed by rifle, artillery or tanks, the Army reimbursed the rancher for the cow. In the spring, we would see the ranchers catching calves to brand, and there would be a pile of branding irons and a propane torch in every pickup truck. Every rancher carried branding irons bearing his own brand and all of his neighbors' brands, so that he could mark cattle belonging to anyone. Each calf would be branded with the same brand as that of its mother, who usually stood nearby idly watching. Of course, plenty of calves were missed, as the ranchers didn't venture into active artillery impact areas. During the fall roundup, all cattle caught without brands were "donated" to the Texas Democratic Party and cheap grazing would continue for another year.

After our week on the rifle range, our company pilots were sent to northern Texas to pick up our helicopters. We were expecting thirty, but they returned with only twelve. Normally an assault helicopter company consisted of two lift or transport platoons and one gunship platoon. The lift platoons generally had ten slicks each, which were UH-1D or UH1-H model helicopters used to transport troops or supplies and armed with a machine gun on each side. Since they had no external armament such as rockets and miniguns, when viewed from the front they were clean, or "slick." The gunship platoon generally consisted of eight UH-1B or UH-1C model helicopters that could be armed with one of several possible choices of armament—rockets, flexguns, miniguns, 40mm cannon. A maintenance slick and a command and control (C&C) slick brought a normal assault company's total to thirty. The twelve ships we received were all UH-1Cs, or Charlie model gunships. We learned that our company was going to be a gunship company used for border patrol or as an escort for other helicopters attempting to rescue downed pilots.

Discovering that twelve ships were all we would have was not good news for the enlisted men. Since almost everyone with an MOS of helicopter mechanic wanted to fly as a crew chief, the odds of flying didn't appear good. Instead of the thirty crew chief positions that we had expected, there would be twelve. Most of the guys would be stuck in maintenance. The odds became even worse for those of us who wanted to be crew chiefs when it was decided that anyone going back for a second tour in Viet Nam would be given first choice for the crew chief positions. Two guys chose to do so. Now, we had only ten slots left. Prior to picking the other ten crew chiefs, our CO decided that all potential crew chiefs must have a flight physical. The physical was nothing more than a minor checkup at the base dispensary, and I felt confident of soon being a crew chief. The next day I was stunned to learn I had flunked the physical because I wore glasses.

I was really pissed! No one had ever indicated that my eyeglasses would stop me from flying. I had met instructors in training and guys at Fort Hood who wore glasses and who had flown as door gunners and crew chiefs in Viet Nam. Why couldn't I? No matter who I asked, I got the same story. I could not wear glasses and pass the flight physical to fly in the States. In Viet Nam, where I would be in combat, however, *all* physical requirements were waived. I would later fly with a machine gunner who had his right-hand trigger finger and middle finger shot off. He had no problem passing a flight physical in Viet Nam without those two fingers. If he had lost those fingers as a civilian, he wouldn't have been considered fit to be drafted. Amazing logic.

About the same time I got the bad news about not flying, to my surprise I was promoted to Spec 5 or pay grade E-5, the same as a sergeant. Even though our company had just formed and consisted mainly of privates and PFCs fresh out of training, someone in personnel had authorized the company to fill "X" slots as E-5s. Our CO, kindly but not wisely, promoted every Spec 4 with the minimum service time necessary for promotion. I didn't care about the promotion, but it did mean that I was no longer on the KP roster. That was much more important than a pay raise.

Our company continued to train for tropical warfare in Viet Nam by spending the winter in Texas; cold, windy days and even colder, windier nights. In early January, a rumor started that our company was not going to Viet Nam, but to an Air Force base in Thailand. We would be used to escort Air Force rescue helicopters on their missions into Laos to retrieve downed pilots. In our eyes, serving at an Air Force installation was not being in the military; some guys started buying more civilian clothes. A lot of troops in the company believed this story, but it was difficult to give it much credence in late January 1968. The war in Viet Nam changed dramatically that month and the Tet offensive dominated the news. Heavy fighting was occurring throughout Viet Nam and American units were suffering heavy casualties. The local newspapers were filled with stories of the unexpected enemy offensive. Other articles indicated that all units at Fort Hood were expecting to be alerted soon to send reinforcements to units in Viet Nam. I couldn't understand why anyone would think that a company of gunships would be going to Thailand, given the situation in Viet Nam. As always, people believed what they wanted to believe.

Shortly after Tet, all our helicopters were flown to California, where they would be partially disassembled, loaded onto ships, and then sent to Southeast Asia. At the same time our gunships were flying to California, the rest of the company was loading the smaller items assigned to our company in large, metal Conex containers. Our jeeps, trucks and Conexes were then loaded onto flatbed railcars and made ready for a train ride to the West Coast. About a dozen guys accompanied our vehicles on the train. They would sail the Pacific Ocean, accompanying our helicopters, trucks and gear to our final destination.

As for the rest of us, it was back to the barracks to sit and wait. The general consensus was that we weren't going anywhere for at least a month, since it would take that long for our equipment to cross the Pacific. Most of the troops were disappointed that we hadn't been allowed to sail with our equipment, because every day at sea would count against the 365 days we would have to serve in country. In retrospect, it's hard to determine why we didn't all sail; we sure didn't accomplish anything sitting around Gray Airfield. Generally, we pulled light work details around the airfield in the mornings and were released to do whatever we wanted after the noon company formation. We were told that, if we stayed out of trouble and out of jail, we would continue to be trusted. Since we didn't really know for sure if our destination was Thailand or Viet Nam, the unknown forced us to be good.

After several weeks of boredom and waiting, we knew our equipment must be somewhere in Asia and, therefore, we weren't very surprised when we were told we were no longer allowed to leave base. Periodically, we would be assembled in the company area with our duffel bags and rifles to wait for trucks that never came. Finally, one Saturday morning we assembled again. This time we knew it was real. The company KPs had been pulled out of the mess hall and had grabbed their gear and joined us. The KPs wouldn't have been released for a drill.

We were finally on our way! But we weren't the only ones going someplace. It was early April 1968 and Martin Luther King had been killed the previous day. Riots were again breaking out in cities throughout the United States, and Fort Hood was being drained of men for riot control.

American cities were burning again and a lot of soldiers weren't that interested in putting the fires out. Black troops from other companies in the battalion were coming to our company orderly room to try to go overseas rather than fight American blacks in our cities. As our company waited for our ride to an unknown airport, the rest of our battalion was getting ready to saddle up for duty in Detroit. A lot of men were uncomfortable about the possibility of fighting friends and relatives. I remember thinking about the situation and wondering what I would have done had I been ordered to Detroit. While I didn't have any strong antiwar feelings, I was very disturbed about using American troops against Americans. I have often wondered how many of those men who were sent to Detroit kept right on going into Canada.

As we were sitting on our duffel bags waiting to go overseas, we discussed this matter among ourselves. A majority of our guys seemed to seriously consider Canada a legitimate option for a citizen-soldier who was ordered to fight fellow citizens. In their semicivilian minds, Viet Nam meant war, but Detroit meant murder. We were so green and naïve. By April 1969, we would have marched on Disneyland, if so ordered. In another year, a lot of us were going to have been changed dramatically. Civilian morality would be converted into combat practicality. We were going to learn to function as a team in a combat situation where everyone on the team was important. *We* were what was important, not any damn civilians. Our fellow soldiers were the only ones who could be trusted and the only ones who gave a damn.

After a year in Viet Nam, most of us would feel that no matter what we thought about the military in general, we would probably never again be part of a group that trusted and depended on one another so much. Thirty years later, many combat veterans will still tell you that they don't trust civilians; they only trust each other. We knew that at night the guys on guard were awake because we knew how we would fight off sleep when it was us sitting behind the machine gun. We knew that the guys on our flank were going to protect our flank. But in Texas, April 1968, we had no idea what was going to happen to us during the next year. Most of us thought that, except for a tan and some medals, we'd be back in the States in a year, unchanged. God, were we dumb.

After sitting outside our barracks for hours we boarded buses for our trip of fifty miles to an Air Force base near Austin. As we pulled out onto the main highway, we soon noticed that we weren't the only troops leaving Fort Hood. Traveling to Austin, we passed a solid line of two-and-a-half-ton trucks carrying troops to control the riots. Fort Hood must have been empty. While we were headed for Asia, two armored divisions were heading for American cities. Looking back, it seems strange that I have never met anyone who ever mentioned being involved in riot control duty in 1968. Thousands of troops went to the riots and soldiers always talk about previous duty stations. But no one has ever mentioned riot duty. Shame? Guilt?

At Austin we received a surprise. We had been prepared to fly Air Force cargo planes to Asia, but there was a civilian airliner sitting on the runway for us. All of the military planes at the air base were being used to transport troops to the fighting in America. From Austin, we flew to Alaska and then to Japan. In both Alaska and Japan, we were only allowed to stretch our legs by walking around the airport while our plane refueled. In minutes we were back on board and back in the air. After leaving Japan, we had been flying for sixteen hours and no one had yet said where we were actually going: Viet Nam or Thailand. We were bored with reading, card playing, and talking; we just wanted to get to wherever the hell we were going and off the plane. Finally, after several more hours of flying, the pilot announced that we were starting our descent to land and unload at Bien Hoa, Republic of Viet Nam. So much for rumors of duty in Thailand.

Our plane went into the normal descent used by all aircraft landing in a combat zone, dropping out of the sky like a rock to escape any possible antiaircraft fire. I would fly into Viet Nam several times and always landed this way. I was never sure if the pilots landed so quickly to scare new troops or if they really thought there might be enemy ground fire. If they did it to scare us, it worked. Most of us held on to our seats, terrified at the thought of being shot down before we even touched the soil of Viet Nam. I suppose most green troops expected the country to be one big battlefield where no place was safe from the automatic weapons of the enemy guerrilla soldiers. In April of 1968, however, there were probably more bullets in the air above rioting American cities than over Bien Hoa. We gave an involuntary sigh of relief as the tires hit the runway and our plane coasted to a stop. After taxiing over to a small hangar, we took our rifles from the overhead baggage compartments and departed the plane, walking down the steps and onto the surface of another world.

As we exited our plane, we shuffled into the invisible wall of heat and humidity of the tropics. The heat and humidity didn't impress us, however: most of us had trained in the southern states and knew what hot weather was like. We realized that this heat wasn't that bad. Sure, it was hot, but so were Georgia and Texas. I think we were disappointed with the weather; we were expecting worse. Where was the 120-degree weather? Where was the monsoon rain? Everything looked dry and dirty, especially the troops lined up to ride our plane back to the States.

Earlier in the war, the military had been much more formal and had required all troops returning to the States to travel in Class A dress uniforms. As the war increased its ferocity, the rules had changed. The façade of a mere police action had been dropped and there was no longer any attempt made to disguise our soldiers as mere advisers. People were being sent home straight from the shooting, and those now waiting to leave seemed to be wearing their cleanest dirty clothes. While the majority had probably been in support units, a decent percentage wore Combat Infantryman Badges indicating that the man wearing the badge had been out in the field carrying a rifle and had faced enemy fire. No matter where they had been or what they had been doing, they seemed to be of one genetic stock: lean, average height, mustached with drawn, hard faces. We didn't look anything like them. They looked like old men; we looked like kids. Most of their faces were thin and their eyes gleamed; most of us still had chubby, baby faces and our eyes were dull, dead civilian eyes. They were tanned brown, while we were bleached white. Eventually, we would become them, but they would never be us again. Those who served in support areas with little or no combat experience might adjust into civilians eventually, but those who were blooded in combat were changed forever.

I know I'm not the only Viet Nam veteran who thirty years later still watches tree lines for bunkers, people or movement. Driving along any road, we still scan the hedges and shrubbery and every now and then catch the flick of a deer's ear and smile to ourselves. If it had been the movement of a man, we would have had him. We constantly watch for movement; thinking of old landing zones, hearing the sound of machine guns.

Our NCOs kept us moving toward a large empty hangar and we soon parted company with those lucky bastards who had survived their year "in country" and were now headed home. God, how we all envied them, even those of us who wanted to be here. Deep down a lot of us thought that maybe we had made a BIG mistake. Perhaps running to Canada would have been the smart thing to do, but it was too late now. We were worried and scared, but more out of fear of the unknown than fear of the enemy. We didn't know what to expect and I don't think any of us felt very confident being in a company of green troops. The majority of us didn't feel our training at Fort Hood had prepared us for combat and silently followed our NCOs. We had no idea what we were doing and wondered if we were going to be sent straight into battle. There were no smiling faces in our crowd of green troops.

As we milled around, mute and dazed, some of our troops who had traveled to Viet Nam by ship with our heavy equipment walked into the hangar. After we were assembled into platoons, they informed us that we would be joining our equipment waiting for us at the 1st Infantry Division base at Di-An (pronounced *Ze-On*), fifteen or so kilometers away. They had brought several thousand full magazines of ammunition for us and we were told to each grab five magazines of ammunition and to load our rifles and the two ammo pouches on our combat harnesses. After becoming an armed company of soldiers, everyone climbed onto nearby trucks for the ride to our new home, a short trip through populated areas where it seemed every building had been decorated with bullet holes. We were seeing the damage from the recent Tet offensive. Not knowing better, we assumed that shooting buildings with automatic weapons must be part of daily life in this neck of the woods. There was no joking or idle talk as our trucks carried us through the urban battleground still being reclaimed by civilian survivors of the Tet offensive. We were lost in our own thoughts as we tried to take in the unreal scenery—tropical vegetation mixed with suburban destruction—along the road. Many of us half expected to be engaged by enemy soldiers at any moment, while others appeared to be dazed by the sudden realization that they were in Viet Nam. The rumors of duty in Thailand were still in their minds. But they were starting to recognize this duty assignment might be for life.

Arriving at Di-An, we found a typical Army base camp: a small city of dirty tents slowly assimilating the color of the surrounding soil. Our trucks drove along the dusty streets of the small compound, then stopped between the two vacant fields that were to become our home. One field contained parked helicopters; some of our company tents were already erected in the other field. The troops from our company who had come by sea had arrived several days previously and had put up their own squad tents. As always in the Army, the NCOs soon had the company off the trucks and broken down into details to put up the rest of our tents. Before dark, all tents were up, the field kitchen was functioning, and the company headquarters was open for business. For the next few days we filled thousands of sandbags. After we received a welcome of incoming mortar rounds, we gladly filled thousands more. We soon had four-foot-high sandbag walls around every tent and felt pretty secure. We had no idea that our sandbags were worthless against 122mm rockets.

A few days after our arrival at Di-An, we met our first Vietnamese. Several old men had been hired to help fill sandbags and every tent was assigned a female "hooch maid" to wash clothes and shine boots. Each of us was charged four dollars a month to pay them, doing our part to destroy the Vietnamese economy since a hooch maid would make as much as a captain in the South Vietnamese army. Common sense should have dictated that we be paid the equivalent of our Vietnamese counterparts while we were stationed in their country; instead, we helped to ruin their economy with our "high" wages and extravagant ways.

Truthfully, we were not impressed with these small, skinny people. We were like giants. Even the smallest man in our company was taller than any of our male laborers. How could tiny, poor folks, such as these, even think of standing up to well-fed, healthy, rich Americans? We didn't know, or maybe only forgot, that small people with determination and automatic weapons can stand up to anyone. Appearances are deceiving. Of course, being normal Americans, we did very little to learn their language, and expected them to learn ours.

We didn't spend much time together, anyway. While they worked around our tents, we would be somewhere else, usually at work on the helicopters parked along our flight line where no Vietnamese were allowed. Since we were a late arrival to the Di-An base camp, our flight line was located where no one else wanted to be—next to the Graves Registration Company of the 1st Infantry Division. Graves Registration is what the military calls a morgue.

The 1st Infantry Division is called "The Big Red One," because of the unit patch—the number one, colored red on a field of green. There was a saying in the division, "If you're going to be one, be a Big Red One!" Of course, the unofficial motto of the men in the Graves Registration unit was, "If you're going to be one, be a big dead one!" Several times each day, we would be working on our helicopters or filling sandbags when a slick would land on the helipad next door in a cloud of dust. Every landing caused us to involuntarily stop whatever we were doing and turn our heads toward the helipad. As the slick settled down with its rotor blades still turning (no one ever shut down at this helipad), the pallid gray men next door would slowly stroll across the road carrying stretchers. None of our neighbors ever ran to greet their customers. Why should they? There was no hurry. We would watch quietly as the limp bodies of eighteen-year-old boys were placed on stretchers and then carried across the road to disappear into the neighbors' workshop. There was a war going on around us, but we were totally oblivious. Each arrival of a slick made us stop and think, however.

We really didn't have much work to do. Most of our ships were not at Di-An. In order to have our flight crews gain some combat experience, most of our helicopters and crews were assigned temporarily to other helicopter companies as an extra gunship. Soon, some started to return home with bullet holes in their fuselage and rotor blades. Not all the bullet holes were from the enemy: some of the crews shot up their own ship because of target fixation. People would become so focused on a target they ignored everything else. A gunner would move his machine gun with a running man and not realize that the gun barrel now pointed inside his ship or at the rotor blades. Pilots occasionally flew their ships into the blast of their own rockets in their obsession to hit a target.

After several combat flights, some of our crews realized that the VC were actually using live ammunition and were trying to kill them. Recognizing that they were not out on a field problem in Texas, several enlisted crewmembers became very interested in transferring into maintenance. As expected, the guys who had strutted around back in Texas wearing their cool flight jackets and sunglasses were quitting first. The quiet introverts in the flight platoon just kept on doing their jobs. While it might seem difficult to believe, no one was ever forced into flying as a helicopter crewmember. Even though some units had barely enough crewmembers to fly the minimum number of helicopters needed each day, if someone didn't want to fly, then he didn't have to fly. Maintenance was never overstaffed because some people didn't want to fly, however. It always seemed that every unit was short of the minimum number of people needed to get everything done. In order to function as a company, someone had to haul water, transport food and supplies, hump ammunition, put rockets together and so forth.

Supplying the company with water alone was a chore no one thought about, but we couldn't just turn on a faucet to get water. Someone had to take a tank truck to the compound water distribution point, load it up with nonpotable water, bring it back to the company and then distribute it to the overhead water tanks for showers. The same truck would then go for a load of potable water, which was mixed with the remaining nonpotable water in the tank to be delivered to the mess tent and to the individual five-gallon cans sitting next to each tent to supply water for washing clothes and morning hygiene. There was no MOS for water boy, so one of the platoons was a man short because we needed water. Other daily chores robbed other platoons of manpower. In addition to the troops tied up doing company chores, some troops were hurt or sick, on emergency leave or R&R, or transferred and not replaced yet. It always seemed that there were just enough troops to keep a company functioning, but barely.

Since some people had quit flying, my hopes were high that I might soon get a slot as a crew chief. It didn't matter here that I had flunked my flight physical in the States. This was the land of opportunity, and any warm body passed the Army's physical requirements to fly in a combat zone. I felt confident I would eventually get a ship, as either a crew chief or a gunner. Gunner seemed to be the easier of the two jobs since the gunner only had to maintain the armament on the gunship while the crew chief was responsible for maintaining the entire helicopter. Whenever someone quit flying, I would quickly volunteer to take his place, but now I was being told that I couldn't be a gunner because of my rank. Gunners were only Spec 4 positions and I was a Spec 5, so I volunteered for a demotion. But even that didn't work. I was going to have to wait for a crew chief position to open and stay in maintenance until one did. I sure wasn't happy. I wanted to see combat firsthand.

After several weeks of relatively light duty at Di-An, we were stunned when told that 20 percent of the company would be reassigned to other units. We had naïvely thought that those of us who came over together would stay together for our yearlong tour of duty in country. Of course, we couldn't stay together. If a company stayed intact for a year and then shipped home, it would have to be replaced by another green company. It was normal practice to break up a green unit as soon as possible, sending some of its troops to other units and replacing them with more experienced troops from those units. This type of personnel exchange was not popular with the troops who were being transferred away from their friends, but it served several purposes. It obviously gave the new company some experienced personnel, but it also allowed both units to get rid of troops who were problems or perceived to be problems. I guess that I was a problem. I was sent to Cu Chi.

Actually, this system of trading problems worked out well

most of the time. A problem soldier in one unit turned out to be a good or even excellent soldier in another unit. Many times the only problem was a personality conflict. Some people just don't get along very well. Just because a man doesn't work well with one person doesn't mean that another person and he would not get along well. Sometimes just changing squads made a difference. Ninety percent of the time, someone else's minus turned into another person's plus.

If I was perceived to be a problem at Di-An, it was because I didn't want to be a helicopter mechanic. I wanted to be sitting behind a machine gun on a helicopter. I had made it very clear to the maintenance sergeant that I wasn't interested in working in maintenance forever. I did the minimum maintenance work possible and aggravated him further by volunteering for guard duty on the compound perimeter so I wouldn't have to work on helicopters on which I had no chance of flying. I believe that if he had given me an opportunity to eventually get on flight status after x months in maintenance, I would have worked my tail off. I was hoping that he would get tired of me and transfer me to another platoon. But I had never expected I would have to leave our company.

I was going to Cu Chi, wherever and whatever that was. Those of us leaving for Cu Chi were informed that it was the main base camp of the 25th Infantry Division and it was situated in a Viet Cong stronghold about twenty miles away on the main invasion route to Saigon. The village of Cu Chi hugged a flank of the base camp, but might as well have been on the moon since we were never allowed to visit our neighbors. The village had been named for a huge Cu Chi tree, one hundred feet high and seven feet in diameter that had stood in the village for more than a hundred years. The French had cut the tree down in 1946 because local Viet Minh guerrillas held their meetings in its cool shade. If they hadn't cut it down, I'm sure we Americans would have. Just because it was there.

Eight of us left for Cu Chi on the morning of May 5, 1968, the start of "the second offensive" or "Mini Tet." Heavy

fighting had erupted throughout the country again. We were
told that Cu Chi was under heavy mortar and rocket fire and
ordered to wear flak jackets and steel pots for our trip. Leaving our friends, we reluctantly climbed onto a truck for a ride
to the shack serving as the Di-An flight terminal. A large
Chinook helicopter was waiting for us. Within a half hour,
we had landed at the 269th Combat Aviation Battalion at Cu
Chi and quickly assigned to the 116th Assault Helicopter
Company. A short truck ride delivered us to our new home.
We were welcomed to the 116th Assault by numerous explosions of incoming 122mm rockets.

Like all green troops, we had no idea what was happening;
we remained standing next to the truck as the rockets impacted throughout the compound. Our driver, much wiser
than us, was out of the truck and running for his life at the
first loud crack of a rocket detonating. Abandoned to our
fate, we just stood next to the truck, not knowing what to do.
After hearing a few explosions of impacting rockets, we followed our driver's example and ran into the bunker next to
the orderly room, where we met our first sergeant. When the
rockets stopped, we officially reported into the company and
the first sergeant assigned all eight of us to the maintenance
platoon. Once again, I tried to talk my way into a flight platoon but he said that no one flew without first spending time
in the maintenance platoon. This unit wanted people to learn
how helicopters functioned and how to fix them before they
flew on them. At least he hadn't said that I would stay in
maintenance forever.

We had thought that we had a lot of sandbags around our
tents at Di-An, but Cu Chi was Sandbag City. At Di-An
we had only had one row of sandbags surrounding our
tents: here sandbags were stacked everywhere. Underground
bunkers were covered with several layers of sandbags. The
bunkers were large enough to hold twenty-five to thirty men
and consisted of a walled hole in the ground with pierced
steel planking (PSP) over the hole to support the sandbagged
roof. These bunkers offered protection from flying shrapnel,
but a direct hit from a rocket would destroy a bunker and its

occupants. But enemy rockets were area weapons and not very accurate; it was rare for a bunker to take a direct hit.

At Di-An, we had been mortared a couple of times and had thought being mortared was being in the war. Mortars were considered only a nuisance at Cu Chi: BIG 122mm rockets were landing on the compound at the rate of over a hundred a day. I don't recall the local VC ever using the small 60mm mortars at Cu Chi; they seemed to have a large supply of 82mm mortars. Several times mortar rounds tore our company hooches apart. Unlike a lot of other compounds where the helicopters were the targets of the nightly mortar rounds, the VC of Cu Chi were after people, not equipment. The mortars got our full attention when they were impacting in our own company area, but if they were hitting several hundred meters away, we had little to worry about. I always wondered why the enemy troops firing the mortars walked the mortar rounds straight down a target line, never veering right or left. If they had turned the mortar tube to the right or left once in a while, they could have caught those of us who were sitting outside of our bunkers, ignoring their work.

Rockets were a different story altogether. They were fired at any time, while mortars came in at night. The VC/NVA frequently launched rockets when we were congregated for morning formation or at mealtime. Mortars were fired using a fixed tube and crew, but the VC and NVA just leaned rockets on rice dikes or bamboo tripods, aimed them in our direction and fired them, using timers. They came in haphazardly and we never knew where one would land. God, they were impressive, though. Noise like the loudest crack of lightning that we had ever heard and throwing white-hot shrapnel through the air that could cut a man in half. Even though rockets were dangerous, about 10 percent of the guys would sit on top of the hooches to watch them explode rather than sit in the bunker and hope one didn't come through the bunker roof. We couldn't run or hide from 122mm rockets. The only guys I knew who were killed by rockets in the 116th were working on a helicopter in broad daylight. A lone rocket came into Cu Chi one morning and landed next to them. In May and June of 1968, rockets were impacting around us so often that flak jackets and steel pots were worn everywhere on the base, but I never heard of these items saving anyone from rocket shrapnel. Most of us considered our protective helmets and flak jackets to be a nuisance and rarely wore them when out of sight of our superiors.

Anyone taking a quick tour of the 116th Assault Helicopter Company would think it was only a transient unit in temporary facilities. The company seemed to be trying to decide whether to stay at Cu Chi or not. The company had wooden squad hooches with galvanized metal sheet roofs, all connected by a maze of wooden sidewalks leading to a mess hall, the various clubs and the company orderly room. But everything appeared makeshift, without permanence. The company flight line somehow managed to look even more temporary: it consisted of scattered sandbag revetments to protect sitting helicopters from mortar fragments in a wet, marshy area ignored by the other helicopter companies. Our motor pool was much too wet and muddy to be called a swamp. The maintenance hangars were tents set on top of steel Conex containers holding piles of uninventoried spare parts. The other helicopter companies had engineered metal and wooden hangars with hard-packed roadways between well-built helicopter revetments. They all looked as if they planned to stay around for a while. The 116th looked as if we planned to abandon camp.

Another feature that the 116th had that we didn't have at Di-An was an underground tactical operations center (TOC) that could operate in a rocket attack. While it was better than the TOC located in a tent back at Di-An, it would have been a death trap if there were a ground attack. A satchel charge thrown in each entrance would have buried the TOC staff alive. The shoddily built wooden mess hall had an ambience that seemed to say, "Eat and get out!" For recreation we could drink cheap whiskey and beer at an Officer's Club, an NCO Club or an Enlisted Men's Club. Drinks were cheap and generally warm. If we weren't on duty in the evening, we could either sit in one of the hot clubs or sit in an equally hot hooch. The hooches were spartan sleeping quarters for sixteen men with just enough room for bunks and lockers. No luxuries, but much better than what the infantry had in the field. Like soldiers everywhere, we soon adapted to our new environment and considered it home.

A few days after arriving in the 116th, the company ran out of beer. Another soldier, Joe Rossi, and I were told to take the company lowboy truck to Long Binh and pick up a load of beer. Reporting to the quagmire that the 116th used for a motor pool, I was told to drive the long truck around the parked vehicles. Making the circle without hitting anything qualified me as a truck driver, and my military driver's license was officially upgraded and signed by the motor pool sergeant.

Since heavy fighting was still occurring throughout the area, we had to join a convoy for security. Going from the motor pool to the convoy staging area gave me a lot of practice in making tight turns pulling a long trailer. One right turn and one left turn. I had somehow made the turns but I was hoping there was a straight highway all the way to Long Binh. There wasn't.

As our convoy left the base camp, I watched the trucks in front of me barely maneuver around a sharp right-hand turn outside the gate. They were all shorter than the long monster behind me. Coming up to the turn, I swerved into the left-hand lane, forcing ARVN vehicles off the road. I needed room. Pulling the steering wheel right, I made a quick turn and somehow dragged the entire trailer around the corner without taking down the nearest building. We were then on a straight road and I put the gas pedal to the floor. Catching up to the convoy, I relaxed a little and tried to see the country through a cloud of billowing dirt.

We had only traveled a few miles when a jeep with two MPs drove alongside, motioning for me to pull over. Turning right, I brought the truck to a stop on the road shoulder as the rest of the convoy passed. After the last truck went by, an MP walked over and asked to see my driver's license. Handing it to him, I wondered why he wanted it.

"Why didn't you stop when you ran over the woman in the village?" he asked.

"What woman?" I stammered.

"You made the turn too tight and your trailer's rear wheels killed a woman," he replied.

Joe, an old soldier who had been in country eleven months, turned red and shouted, "What the fuck are you guys doing? You pulled us out of a convoy for a damn gook? Sever, get this truck back in the convoy!"

Being more afraid of Joe than two MPs, I put the truck in gear and pulled out. We left the MPs standing in a cloud of dust—holding my driver's license. We drove to Long Binh, got our beer, and brought it home. I never heard a word about the woman or my license. Apparently, one more dead civilian was irrelevant.

■■■

For the next few months, I labored in the never-ending, day-after-day, seven-day workweek of a mechanic in a helicopter maintenance platoon. I'll be the first to admit that I wasn't the best or hardest-working mechanic in our company and, for the first month, I did the very minimum required of me. I constantly told my platoon sergeant that I wanted to fly behind a machine gun in one of the flight platoons and he constantly told me that I was stuck in maintenance. As in all maintenance platoons, two or three of the experienced mechanics did 90 percent of the work, while the rest of us slowly learned what we were doing. No matter where a new mechanic had been stationed prior to coming to Viet Nam, he could not possibly know as much as his counterparts in country. There was no other place in the world where helicopters were flown until they were falling apart. Our people in maintenance would do more mechanical repairs in a week than most military mechanics would do in six months. Eventually, the more experienced mechanics in our platoon finished their one-year tours of duty and returned to the United States, forcing the rest of us to learn how to repair helicopters whether we wanted to or not. My platoon sergeant probably knew I would adjust to the job; I eventually became a fairly good maintenance team leader.

Being a team leader meant nothing at all: there were no benefits to the job. We not only didn't get any pay increase for the increased responsibility but we also had to work longer hours. If takeoffs were scheduled for 0600, maintenance team leaders would be out with the flight crews at

0500, continue working with their team through the day, and then finish the evening repairs after the company returned from their mission. Some maintenance days were twenty hours long and we worked seven days a week. We were always short of people. I often wondered how many helicopter mechanics were still sitting back at Fort Hood, bored and killing time.

While I did get used to working on helicopters and had excellent people working with me on our team, I can't say I truly enjoyed the work. We didn't have a hangar like the other helicopter units so we worked on our ships in the mud and rain or under the hot, burning sun. Our only job benefit was that, after we had torn apart a ship for the mandatory inspection following every one hundred hours of flight, we'd put it back together and then be rewarded with a half-hour ride on it. I believe that we were given our ride because of an old Army Air Corps tradition that the person who tore the ship apart and then put it back together flew on it first. As the team leader, I would sit in the right-hand pilot's seat for a test flight while the rest of the team sat on the floor. The test pilot would usually let me fly the ship for a while after he was satisfied with its performance. I had no idea how to fly a helicopter, but several pilots talked me through flying around the base and even landing the ship if conditions were perfect. I suppose that flying the ship was meant as a reward. But I never gave it much thought.

When I joined the 116th, we still had some B-model gunships and D-model "slicks" (troop carriers); we were possibly the last Army unit in Viet Nam to have these relatively old, outdated aircraft. Our company and the Navy were the only units I saw in 1968 that still had gunships with flex-guns—two M-60 machine guns mounted on each side of the ship, which were operated hydraulically to shoot to the side, forward or downward. Since other units were getting the high technology Cobra helicopters, we soon inherited "C" or Charlie-model gunships to replace our B-models, and new H-models to replace the D-models. We also received several miniguns—the rotating electric Gatling guns—to replace the flexguns. The Cobras were the Army's version of a cheap jet fighter because they could fly fast with more firepower than regular gunships. Enlisted men who either flew as crew chiefs or gunners or hoped to do so wanted nothing to do with the Cobras. Most pilots drooled over Cobras, but the Cobras had a crew of two—both officers. Actually, just getting on a gunship seemed a hopeless dream. Our gunship platoon, with the radio call sign "Stingers," consisted of seven or eight B/C-model helicopters along with a totally unauthorized D-model that they had "found" somewhere and armed with a 20mm cannon mounted between the skids. The cannon was "borrowed" from the Navy, and its muzzle blast blew out both chin bubble windows when the gun was first test-fired. The gun platoon never had enough crewmembers to fly even five of their ships, so there wasn't much of a chance for any of us to ever fly as part of the crew on a gunship. Most of us, not having any comprehension of what our gun platoon actually did every day, hoped to fly with them eventually.

The 116th had the radio call sign "Hornets," and the two "slick" platoons had the radio call signs "Wasps" and "Yellowjackets." Each slick platoon had nine or ten D- or H-model helicopters that were used to "combat assault" infantry into landing zones (LZ) and to ferry troops and supplies. Each slick platoon was authorized twenty enlisted personnel to fly as either crew chiefs or gunners, so if I was going to fly in our company, the odds were that I would be flying on a slick.

Stingers, Wasps and Yellowjackets went out to the war while the rest of the Hornets stayed behind the barbed-wire perimeter at Cu Chi feeling as if we were in jail, not in a war. We were always busy working on the helicopters, as they were constantly wearing out, breaking down or being shot up, but our war was constant drudgery, not excitement. We had been rocketed and mortared so often that we didn't even find incoming rounds exciting unless, of course, they were impacting around us. A rocket would impact with the crack of a lightning bolt and no one would even pause from what they were doing unless it hit nearby. It took multiple rockets to make us run for the bunkers. We ran for the bunkers a lot in May and June of 1968.

In June, our flight platoons had a bad day we always referred to as "The day in the pineapple." I was in maintenance and not out in the field so I have no idea what actually occurred. In the NCO Club, I heard so many different versions of the story about that day that I wondered if anyone knew what had actually happened. The generic story was that our slicks had carried loads of infantry into a field of pineapples surrounded by a perimeter of low shrubs. As customary on an assault, our gunships had pounded the perimeter with rockets in order to kill any enemy troops that might be hiding to ambush our slicks as they landed. Prior to the gunships' arrival, however, an enemy unit had been crossing the field and the NVA soldiers, surprised by the approaching helicopters, had dropped down in between the rows of pineapples to hide. They huddled close to the pineapple plants, concealing themselves rather than taking the chance of being seen. All of the enemy soldiers were lying between the rows of pineapples when the slicks landed right on top of them. As our infantry jumped out of the helicopters, they were greeted by blasts from AK-47s as the enemy infantry rose out of the pineapple rows in front of them. A lot of men and a lot of helicopters stayed in the pineapple field.

The ships that could still fly returned to Cu Chi, where quick combat repairs were made with the famous "hundred-mile-an-hour tape." Whenever the infantry needed helicopters in a hurry, bullet holes and maintenance problems were fixed with duct tape. Our ships flew all day until the infantry in the pineapple had secured a firm defensive position and all wounded had been evacuated. Every ship that could possibly fly from the company was out supporting the fight in the pineapple that day. All I know of the fight for certain is that the 116th created a new record by having all of its aircraft down with combat damage that night. For months afterward, I would cringe anytime I heard someone in the club start a story by saying, "Remember the pineapple?" It was frustrating to realize that I was doomed to spend the war as a mechanic fixing helicopters that others rode into battle.

The fight in the pineapple was part of history, but it hadn't affected those of us in the maintenance platoon. Except for more unscheduled work. When I think back on my days in the maintenance platoon, what I remember most is working in the pouring monsoon rain in darkness as black as the anthracite coal of my homeland. Life in the maintenance platoon was work followed by more work.

Even in the maintenance platoon, something would occasionally happen to get our adrenaline flowing. On one occasion a mistake almost destroyed our platoon. Every evening an Army fixed-wing aircraft, known as a Mohawk, would fly into Cu Chi only several meters above the runway. It's interesting to note that we needed these aircraft to fly aerial photography missions, but the VC didn't. Several times our infantry had found aerial photographs of our base camp that were a mosaic of pictures stolen from the PX photography booth by Vietnamese employees. The pilot of the Mohawk would jettison film containers of aerial photographs along the runway for a military intelligence unit based adjacent to our flight line. This plane dropped off film every day late in the afternoon as we walked back to the company area for supper. One evening, however, the Mohawk came roaring toward us and jettisoned his fuel tanks instead of the film. Time stood still as the fuel tanks seemed to float lazily down toward us, taking hours and hours to reach the earth. We were like deer caught in the headlights of a car. We stood in our tracks knowing that we were going to be instantly consumed by flames when the tanks exploded. No one moved. I guess the tanks must have been empty auxiliary tanks. When they hit the ground, there was no fireball, just millions of pieces of shrapnel flying everywhere. By some small miracle, no one was even scratched, though the shrapnel whistled through the air around and between us. The 116th AHC had almost lost most of the maintenance platoon.

On another evening during the heavy rains of the monsoon in June, several of us were trying to find a hydraulic leak on a helicopter. Our maintenance pilot had started the ship and was keeping it running so that the hydraulic fluid was pressurized in the various hoses and tubing. We had removed all of the various inspection panels in order to check the hydraulic fittings and lines for the source of the leak when the explosions of impacting 82mm mortars startled us. They were hitting on the end of our flight line and were being walked toward us rapidly. A mortar round impacted nearby. Instantly I went blind and could feel warm liquid streaming down my face and chest. I automatically wiped my eyes with my shirtsleeve and could see through a red haze that the hand that had touched my face was dripping bright red blood. My heart almost stopped and I immediately thought that a mortar fragment must have hit me in the face and the pain hadn't registered yet. Looking at my partners, I couldn't believe that they were laughing at me. They found the expression on my face hilarious. When they pointed at a hydraulic line, I realized what had happened. The mortar hadn't hit me; the hydraulic line in front of my face had burst and covered me with red hydraulic fluid.

Besides working on our helicopters, the mechanics periodically served as guards on the base perimeter at night. Most of us enjoyed the chance to carry a loaded weapon instead of a wrench. Each night our company had to provide guards in four bunkers on the camp perimeter at the eastern edge of the main runway facing miles of scrub jungle where our neighbors, the Viet Cong, lived. Each bunker had two smaller fighting positions on each side and was separated from the next bunker by a hundred meters of open ground. Several meters in front of each bunker stood a two-meter-high section of cyclone fence, which was called an RPG screen, its purpose being to detonate any rocket-propelled grenades shot at the bunker. In front of the RPG screen, three Claymore mines were set, facing outward to spray hundreds of ball bearings toward the enemy if someone in the bunker closed the electrical firing switches. Three soldiers manned each bunker and, if the battalion officer of the day and the sergeant of the guard were from our company, they generally

picked one of our bunkers as their command post for the
night. I had to spend many a night on the bunker line. For
some odd reason, someone of much greater intelligence than
I had decided that Spec 5s weren't real NCOs, so they could
pull regular guard duty; but then again, since Spec 5s were
NCOs, they could also pull duty as sergeant of the guard. It
was hard to argue with that logic.

Evenings on the bunker line were relaxing compared to a
normal evening of working on helicopters or hanging around
the hot noisy clubs. Out on the bunker line, we'd set out
the Claymores, check the barbed wire to our front, and test-
fire our machine gun and grenade launcher on the big white
egrets that spent the twilight minutes of every evening in
the trees on the other side of our barbed wire. Then we would
sit around and talk, waiting for the sun to set. Since the guard
duty roster included troops from every platoon, guard duty
was where we got to know other people in the company.
Twelve hours at night on the bunker line gave us the chance
to meet other people—and there wasn't much to do except
talk.

A favorite topic of our discussions was the general inade-
quacy of our first line of protection, the bunker line. Every
soldier is a general at heart, and no matter what our rank, we
knew exactly how things should be done as long as we didn't
actually have to do them. Unlike other large base camps,
there were no artificial lights on the perimeter. Grass and
weeds grew waist high in the barbed wire, preventing clear
fields of fire in front of the bunkers. Rumor had it that the
area to our front was honeycombed with tunnels where companies of VC spent the day. (After the war, these rumors were
found to be true.) While our bunkers were well built, most
guards considered them to be death traps. After twilight
faded into darkness, most guys sat on top of the bunker or at
one of the flanking fighting positions. Most of us thought the
VC had positions in our barbed wire from which RPGs could
be fired into the bunkers. It was generally believed that our
perimeter guards were sacrificial lambs placed on the bunker

line as an alarm system, not as a defense expected to hold the line.

Whoever the officer was who was responsible for ensuring the security of Cu Chi, he sure had a lot of confidence. Out on the perimeter we knew the line wouldn't hold against a determined attack. There were too many gaps, too few men trying to cover too much area. Surprisingly, very few attempts were actually made to infiltrate our lines. I do recall one night when I was sergeant of the guard and our officer spotted a man moving through the grass in front of our position. We watched him through our starlight scope, but couldn't get permission to shoot, because there was an infantry platoon out on ambush several hundred meters to our front. The higher-ups back at battalion HQ wouldn't even let us throw a grenade. We watched this man for about an hour, then he disappeared. At daylight, we found no sign of him.

Out on the bunker line everyone soon learned why soldiers wore long-sleeve shirts in the heat of Viet Nam. The Air Force and Navy allowed their personnel to wear short-sleeve shirts, which seemed to make sense in the hot tropical climate, but they didn't have to guard their perimeters. When the sun went down and the mosquitoes came out, we were grateful to be wearing long-sleeve shirts. You can always roll your sleeves up if it gets hot, but you can't roll them down if they aren't there. No matter how much mosquito repellent we rubbed over our exposed flesh, there were always some mosquitoes willing to ignore the repellent for a taste of blood. The mosquitoes rarely bothered some troops, and I was one of those lucky ones. No matter where I was in country, I was rarely bitten.

Rainy nights in the monsoon season were the worst times to have guard duty because the heavy rain usually forced us to stay inside the relatively dry bunker. It would be damp, humid, pitch black and full of mosquitoes. The bunker floor was covered with wooden pallets so we wouldn't have to lie in the mud, but rats and mice scurried through the pallets during the night. These little critters were prey for the local snakes, which would often come into the bunkers hunting rodents. More than once, I sat behind a machine gun in the dark, peering out the firing port with half-closed eyes, when a snake would materialize in front of the gun barrel, flow like a liquid muscle into the bunker and drop onto the bunker floor in front of my feet. I sure wasn't going to grab it with my bare hands: it might be a krait or cobra. By the time I thought about shooting, it would already be inside. Once inside, it would slither under the pallet boards where we couldn't see it. No lights, including flashlights, were allowed in the bunker. When a snake decided to visit, we sat in the dark, moving as little as possible, until the sergeant of the guard showed up with his flashlight or the sun came up. Usually we waited until daylight; very few sergeants would use their flashlights. Those were very long nights.

As soon as it was daylight, we'd pull up the pallets. But we never found a snake; then we'd wonder if the snake had only been imagined. They were real, and were either hiding between the sandbagged walls or had left through one of the side entrances in the darkness. We once tore a bunker apart to replace the rotted sandbag walls and found three cobras living in the spaces within the wall beneath the firing port.

After we had pulled guard several times, most of us tended to go from overcautious to overconfident. New troops thought we were going to be attacked at any minute, while older troops seemed almost too relaxed and cocky. Even after watching gunships pour machine-gun fire on unknown targets several hundred meters outside the perimeter, some troops seemed to believe that there were no VC within miles of the compound. I always knew that there were men with rifles on the other side of the wire and attempted to stay alert. I suppose that some men fell asleep on guard duty, but I never saw anyone do it.

If we learned anything in the Army, guard duty taught us why people throughout history have worshiped the sun. After spending a wet, humid, mosquito-filled night trying to see someone coming to kill us, the first sign of light gave everyone a mental high. Not only had we made it through the night, but even in the monsoon season, the morning rain seemed somehow warmer and the soft glow of the overcast sky helped to warm our tired, dirty carcasses. Those of us who had stayed awake in high school English classes remembered the words of Tennyson's Vivien, "This old sun-worship, boy, will rise again, / And beat the cross to earth . . ." We knew what she meant, and agreed with her. At daybreak we were always the most vulnerable, but the VC never took advantage of us then.

The night guards would be relieved at 0700 by the day guard, who was usually one of the company's walking wounded. The night guards would then return to the company area to clean their weapons, take a shower if water was available and have a short nap before returning to their normal work assignment at 1000. During daylight hours, there would only be one guard on every third or fourth bunker and, if the enemy had been more daring, they could have probably inflicted more damage with a quick daylight attack than they ever achieved with their nighttime attacks. Several snipers could have easily taken out the daytime guards and opened a hole in the perimeter that a regiment could have poured through. Once in the perimeter they could have raised havoc within the compound. Granted, they would have sustained heavy casualties, but they were losing men around Cu Chi every day. Maybe they weren't as suicidal as we thought they were. On the other hand, perhaps they didn't realize how vulnerable the compound was during the day, when everyone was engaged in their normal day-to-day functions.

I suppose we all were shocked to find walking wounded on guard duty. Most of us falsely assumed that if we were wounded we were out of the war. One didn't escape the war that easily. It really made us wonder about the whole system, however, because we all knew boys back home who had received draft deferments for relatively minor physical defects. A boy couldn't be drafted if missing a finger, for example, but get that finger shot off in Viet Nam and he was just fine for further combat. Eighteen- and nineteen-year-old wounded boys sat on our bunkers while Vietnamese boys couldn't be drafted until they were twenty-one. American boys who had taken machine-gun bullets and survived were patched up in Japan and returned to their units because they could sit on top of a bunker all day as a target. There was one boy in our company who had been shot in the leg and returned from the hospital in Japan to spend his days sitting on top of a bunker with his leg in a cast propped up on sandbags. He was one guard who wasn't going to run away.

Guard duty on the perimeter was probably a confidence builder for those of us who eventually went to work trying to knock out enemy bunkers. I always imagined that the enemy felt just as insecure in their bunkers as we did in ours. We knew damn well what would happen to us if someone threw a grenade in our bunker. Bunkers were not impregnable. Their bunkers were probably constructed similar to ours— with exits and limited visibility. No one in a bunker could see everything outside the bunker by looking through the low fan-shaped firing port, and the exits were just a place to hit with explosives. We learned that bunkers had fighting positions on their flanks and not to get preoccupied with a bunker and get shot by its flank protection. We were learning important things doing routine duties. I was never afraid of VC bunkers as much as I was afraid to be in one of ours. I always knew we could take their bunkers just as I knew that they could take ours.

The more I pulled guard duty on the perimeter, the more I realized that we were just serving time. We might be armed, but we were still in jail. Barbed wire fences surrounded us. Outside the wire were armed men who would shoot us. We wore identical uniforms that were purposely meant to be completely different from the typical clothing worn by those on the free side of the fence. Our days and nights were structured so that we followed a routine determined by others. It was possible to spend an entire year behind the wire of a base camp and never see any other aspect of the country. If, in fact, we were winning the war and winning the hearts and minds of the population, why was the local village still unsafe for American troops in daylight hours? If the local population were our allies, why were we not allowed any contact with them? Something didn't seem right.

The only contact that most of us had with Vietnamese was with the hooch maids and the mess hall employees. There was a boy of ten who worked at our mess hall and who was shunned by his fellow employees. He was one of the few Vietnamese allowed to stay on our compound at night because his life was worthless off base. Apparently, he had turned in some local VC to an American patrol and now had to stay on base for his own safety. If the other employees shunned him for helping our side, it wasn't hard to figure out which side they were on.

Generally, we had contact with our Vietnamese employees only at lunchtime. They came into the company area after most of us had left for our jobs on the flight line and they had already gone home by the time we returned for supper. While most of our hooch maids were older women with teeth stained black from their habit of chewing betel nuts, the hooch maid where I lived was a teenage girl named Mai. She and I became friends. I soon realized that she had developed a real crush on me. She would always hang around after lunch and, if I lay down on my cot for a quick nap, she would lie down next to me and nap, too. I always thought of her as a little sister. I wasn't looking for a romantic relationship or a sexual encounter. My priority was to get out of maintenance and into a combat position on a flight crew; I hadn't come to Viet Nam for romance.

During lunch we would make a quick trip to the base PX, since it was closed in the evenings. I would usually try to get something for Mai—cigarettes or soap that she could barter in town. In return, she added a bit of femininity and softness to my spartan barracks life. I suppose that I should have attempted to learn more of the language from Mai, but like most Americans, I wasn't interested in learning another language. Besides, the hooch maids were more interested in learning English from us. They knew that proficiency in English was a sure method to advance in their world of contract labor.

For the entire summer of '68, I was stuck in the maintenance platoon. I constantly pestered my platoon sergeant to let me transfer into one of the flight platoons and his answer was always no. As summer turned into fall, I was losing hope of ever getting into a flight platoon. I had already made up my mind that, if necessary, I would extend my one-year tour by six months to get into a flight platoon to see the war. There was a glimmer of hope in October when Wilsher, a friend who had served in Texas with me, somehow talked his way into our gunship platoon. If Wilsher could get out of maintenance and into guns, the least that I could do was to get into a slick platoon. Every day I asked my platoon sergeant about flying, and every day he said, "No!"

I have to admit that even though I constantly bothered my platoon sergeant about transferring into a flight platoon, I was finding my job in maintenance to be interesting. Helicopters have many more moving parts than other aircraft and the more parts move, the more things break. The vibrations of normal flight literally tore them apart also, so there was constant repair work to be done. I found out that once I had learned my job, I enjoyed keeping busy. I also learned that the more I worked on the flight line, the less the company NCOs bothered me. I suppose it is the same no matter where you work. Most people leave busy people alone, since they realize if they bother the busy man they might be asked to help him.

In late October, I received an R&R to go to Taipei, the capital of Nationalist China. I would get out of the country for five whole days, but more important, it was five days away from our helicopters. On the day that I was to go on R&R, I walked up to our orderly room where our company clerk handed me my paperwork and told me to find my way to Camp Alpha, the R&R processing center at Tan Son Nhut. I had eight hours to get to Camp Alpha to catch my flight and had no idea where it was or how to get there. I was advised to catch a helicopter ride to Tan Son Nhut at the Cu Chi air traffic control tower and, once there, to ask directions to Camp Alpha. After grabbing a borrowed suitcase full of bor rowed civilian clothing from the other guys in my hooch, I trotted down the runway toward the air traffic control tower. Any Air Force fixed-wing aircraft or Army helicopter that landed at our compound was expected to pick up troops waiting at the base of the control tower and give them a ride to the aircraft's next destination. There were no scheduled flights and no need for a ticket counter. Anyone wanting a flight just reported to the small office at the tower base and he would be put on a manifest for a particular destination. Sooner or later, an aircraft would land that would be headed in the general direction of wherever he was going.

Usually there was constant air traffic at our airfield but it was a slow day and I sat for hours in the shade of the control tower waiting for a ride. Keeping me company, but kneeling in the hot sun instead of sitting with me in the shade, was a group of fifteen VC prisoners, wrists tied behind their backs and sandbags over their heads as blindfolds. As I sat there watching and waiting, a helicopter landed a few meters away from the group of VC suspects. Several of the passengers jumped off the ship and walked over to the prisoners. They randomly picked four of the prisoners and led them over to the helicopter, where each little blindfolded, trussed Vietnamese man was grabbed by two Americans, picked up and thrown into the open cargo bay of the helicopter. After loading the prisoners on board, our soldiers climbed back onto the ship, which then took off and flew a low circle around the base.

I sat in the shade, idly watching the ship fly around the base, wondering why it was coming back to land so soon after leaving. The helicopter pilot brought the ship back to the exact spot from which it had taken off, then slowly hovered back toward me. It stayed about two meters above the ground as it gradually moved in my direction, until it came to a hover over a large pothole full of rainwater. An officer stood up in the cargo compartment, grabbed a trussed, sandbagged prisoner and threw him out the door into the puddle. He alternated throwing prisoners out of the right and left doors until the ship was empty. The crew chief then jumped off the ship, pulled the four VC out of the mud and moved them back over to sit with the rest of the prisoners.

A few minutes later, a truckload of MPs arrived to pick up the prisoners. Two MPs quickly loaded all of the VC onto the truck. As the truck drove away, I thought about the incident that I had just witnessed. There were a lot of stories of VC prisoners being thrown from helicopters, but the stories always had the episode occur high in the air. I had never heard of it being done at low level, but if someone were going to throw me out of a helicopter, I would want to be thrown into a mud puddle at low level. I could only imagine what went through the mind of a blindfolded, trussed man as he was picked up and tossed out of the door of a moving helicopter only to land in the warm, soft mud a split second later. Good way to give a man a heart attack, I guess.

Eventually an Army helicopter headed for all points south landed and picked up the transients sitting around the control tower and dropped a few of us off at the sprawling air base at Tan Son Nhut. Walking into the Operations Office at Hotel Three, I asked some Air Force enlisted men how to find Camp Alpha and was told to sit outside and to get on the first bus that stopped. Bus! There were buses? This couldn't be the same country that Cu Chi was in. Walking outside of the shack, I sat down in the sand. Shortly afterward an Air Force bus pulled up to a stop. In a few minutes it had deposited me outside the prisonlike compound of Camp Alpha and I was on my way out of the war for five days.

When I reported in at Camp Alpha, the sergeant at the compound gate looked at my orders, then bitched and moaned that I was supposed to have reported twenty-four hours before the flight, not one hour. While he might be mad, both he and I knew that I had to be put on the flight manifest. After he let me into the compound, I had just enough time to buy some additional civilian clothing and some shoes at the PX before it closed for the day. Quickly changing into civilian clothes, I turned in my fatigues and boots to the Camp Alpha laundry, where the laundry staff was smart enough to demand payment in advance. They knew most troops would be coming back from R&R broke. I exchanged my Military Payment Certificates (MPC) for real greenback dollars, then joined the flight to Taipei, a crowd of lean, short-haired, tan young men dressed in civilian clothes. We didn't look like civilians, though. We looked as if we were still in uniform; our brand-new civilian clothing with sharp creases from packaging made it obvious that each garment was on a body for the first time. Buses arrived to take us to a civilian plane and we were soon on our way over the South China Sea heading to Taiwan.

After landing at the Taipei airport, we were bused to the R&R Center and given the standard local orientation on the Orient. The R&R Center cadre droned on and on while we fidgeted in our seats. Finally set free for five days, everyone hurried outside to grab one of the numerous taxis, like vultures awaiting their prey, parked nearby. Their drivers would take the passengers to the "approved" hotels; we had to pay our room bill in advance prior to being released from the R&R Center. We were in a hurry to get away from the Center and to get to our hotels as quickly as possible—the remaining hours before midnight counted as a full day of R&R.

Squeezing into a taxi with three other guys, I quickly gave the driver the name of my hotel and naïvely trusted him to take me there. The driver was more interested in trying to collect commissions from bars and drove around the city, attempting to talk us into stopping for drinks at each bar we passed. Eventually, he realized that we were serious about getting rooms for the night first and he remembered how to drive directly to our different hotels. I was his last passenger and, as I paid my fare, he offered to wait until I was ready to go out for the night. Since I only planned to find my room and throw my gear in it before hitting the streets, I figured that I might as well go with him. Telling him to wait, I went to the front desk and was given the keys to a small room situated near the entrance to the hotel restaurant and about twenty feet from the front desk. While it would probably be noisy because of its location, I didn't care. The Army had taught me that I could sleep anywhere. Opening the door of my room, I threw my suitcase on the bed, then returned to my driver. After leaving the hotel, I received another tour of Taipei while my driver tried to convince me to visit every local bar and girl that he knew.

I didn't really want to meet his friends because of the warnings given to us at the R&R Center regarding the high VD rate among street girls. We had been advised that if (read: when) we wanted female companionship it was advisable to frequent only the government-licensed bars because the girls working there were given two medical inspections each week. We started visiting licensed bars and, even though I was a typical sex-starved young man fresh from the war, I didn't pick a girl at the first bar. I was curious as to what was available in the marketplace. After visiting four or five bars, I tired of just looking and picked a slim young black-haired beauty. After buying her (and the driver) a drink, I asked her if she would be interested in spending some time with me.

Nodding yes, she grabbed my hand and led me over to the bar, where the bartender surprised me by filling out a contract in triplicate. I was asked for fifteen dollars and, after I paid him, we all signed the contract. Each of us kept one copy. When I showed the contract to my driver, he explained that it stated I had purchased the girl's time for twenty-four hours and that if I was unhappy with her during that time I could return her and a refund would be given prorated on the time used.

"Are you serious?" I asked incredulously.

"Well, they won't really give you your money back," he replied. "They make you take different girl for rest of time."

Arriving back at the hotel, I paid my driver and made arrangements for him to stop back the next day. My girlfriend and I walked through the lobby past several young Chinese men, who laughed and smiled at the girl and me. We both smiled back at them and walked the short distance to my room. We could still hear them laughing behind us as I shut the door. After locking the door, my girl decided that she wanted a bath before we hopped into bed. I needed a bath a lot more than she did, since I still had several months of Vietnamese dust and dirt embedded in my skin, but being the perfect gentleman, I let her bathe first.

As the tub filled, she slowly undressed until she stood naked in front of me. I started to reach for her but she laughed and quickly hopped into the tub full of hot water. Well, if she was going to taunt me by lolling naked in the tub, she was going to have company. Undressing as fast as possible, I was soon as naked as she, and jumped into the tub with her. There wasn't room in the tub for two bodies and all the hot water, so a torrent of water spilled over the side and out under the door into the hotel lobby. The laughing in the lobby turned to shouting. Fists pounded on our door. The men outside were screaming in Chinese. My girl yelled right back at them. I just grinned.

Paying no attention to the commotion outside the door, we bathed together, then went to bed, ignoring the water on the floor. For some odd reason, after we went out the next day, we returned to the hotel to find that we had been moved to a room on the third floor. We must have made an impression on the hotel staff; whenever we ate in the hotel restaurant or walked through the lobby, the staff would point to us and giggle.

The next few days were spent loafing: visiting clubs at night and visiting her family during the day. Strangely, what I remember most about Taipei is the building where her parents lived. The outside of the building was a gray, drab, unfriendly-looking government type of architecture that said "basic shelter." The apartment building, however, was a real neighborhood. The layout of the building forced the occupants to interact with each other because there was no central stairway or elevator. We would enter the apartment on the first floor, say "hello" to everyone, walk across their living area, and open the door to what appeared to be a closet. This door opened onto the stairs to the apartment on the second floor, a door in the second-floor apartment led to the third-floor apartment, and so on all the way to the top floor. All the way up to her parents' apartment, we would stop to talk to people in each apartment. In the same way we met people living above her parents as they traveled downstairs or upstairs on their errands. Everyone seemed interested to meet an American, and it seemed so nice to see smiling, laughing Oriental faces for a change. Thirty years later, I have no idea what my girlfriend looked like, but I can still picture the old Chinese gentleman who lived on the third floor. A farmer at heart, he was raising fifty ducklings in his apartment in a pen that he had made by wrapping chicken wire around the legs of his bed.

Visiting Taipei was interesting and fun, but five days isn't very long and it was soon time for me to be heading home. We left the hotel and went to visit her parents so I could say good-bye. Once again, I was told their story—where they had lived on the mainland and how someday they would also be going home. I found it intriguing that they were convinced that someday they would be returning to mainland China. They had taught their daughter to memorize everything possible about the ancestral village. Even though she had never been there, she could talk about the old village for hours and planned on going back home with her parents. Taiwan was not their home. While I'm sure her parents never made it back, I hope she did.

We left her parents and returned to the hotel to find a party starting for all the soldiers who were on R&R. Each soldier was given a bottle of wine, and a banquet had been set out for us. All of the hotel employees joined us at our tables, and even though we had no idea what we were saying in our separate languages, we had a great time together. While our stay at the hotel had been pleasant, we had never expected to be treated as special guests. As soldiers in an unpopular war, we knew that we wouldn't have been treated this well in our homeland. Some of the guys were moved to tears by the honest outpouring of friendship and the concern shown to us. After finishing our meal, my girlfriend and I thanked our hosts for their hospitality, shook hands with our fellow guests, then walked upstairs to my room. I moped around the room for a while. Not having much to pack, I figured that I might as well go back to the R&R Center. I didn't feel like going back to Cu Chi, but I would. I told my girlfriend she might as well go home, but she insisted on going to the Center with me. As our taxi pulled into the parking lot at the R&R Center, she asked if I would run into the PX and get her a carton of cigarettes. I told her that I was broke, but she replied that she was buying them and handed me the money. Walking into the PX, I was mildly disappointed that she had accompanied me to the Center only so she could get some American cigarettes to sell on the black market. I bought her the cigarettes and took them outside to the taxi, but when I gave them to her, I was surprised to have her hand them right back to me. She knew that I was broke and had bought me the cigarettes as a going-away present. It was another very nice gesture and I really appreciated it.

I don't know if all the troops on R&R were treated as kindly as I had been, but there were a lot of sad faces boarding our plane. We knew some of the guys on this plane were only going back to Viet Nam to die. We were returning for the start of the annual dry-season offensive, when troops on both sides were more mobile and more aggressive. Heavy fighting would be waiting for us. The future didn't appear very bright.

The flight back home was uneventful. We landed and walked from the air-conditioned plane into the stench of the third world. In five short days everyone had forgotten the scent of Viet Nam, and the seminauseating odors of a relatively clean Air Force base made our nostrils flare. What did our home base camps smell like? After putting on my clean fatigues from the laundry, I could smell faint sweat and urine odors. What had they been washed in? Water buffalo piss? But perhaps the clothing only smelled from me, an odor that I had just been used to smelling and had never noticed. Well, I wouldn't be clean for long.

Instead of walking to Hotel Three to catch a helicopter flight, I went to the Eighth Aerial Port to get a ride back to Cu Chi on an Air Force C-130. I had never been on one, but several people had told me they were fun to fly on because of their noise and their severe rate of climb and descent. I was put on a manifest for a flight to Cu Chi and was told to join the crowd sprawled over the terminal floors—sleeping, talking and killing time as they waited for a flight. I sat down with a large group of ARVN paratroopers waiting for a ride to I Corps and listened for hours to their tales of leave in Saigon. Most of the ARVN who spoke broken English were "rice paddy daddies" from little villages out in the bush. Saigon was another planet to them and they had to tell me about its wonders, including their first visit to an indoor movie theater. Some had met local girls and, of course, they made me listen to their tales of conquest. They could die now: they had been to heaven.

As I sat with the paratroopers, an American lieutenant walked by and caught my eye. I realized I had been in basic with him. We greeted each other and I couldn't believe how he had changed. In basic, he had been a draftee just doing enough to get by, but he had turned into a walking recruiting poster. He appeared to be in top physical shape and was literally dressed to kill—grenades hung everywhere on his battle harness. He walked with that confident strut of someone who knows how to do his work, carrying a full rucksack and an M-16 carbine. While I hadn't wanted to go to OCS because I might miss the war, he had gone there to prolong his stay in the States. While in OCS, however, he found his calling and realized he enjoyed the military. Now that he was in combat, he felt he had the best job in the world. He was a platoon leader in an infantry company and loved every day. His flight was called before we had much time to talk, but we traded addresses and promised to keep in touch. Two weeks later I happened to glance at the back page of a *Stars and Stripes* newspaper and read his name on the KIA list.

IV

I had been back from Taipei two days when our maintenance sergeant walked over to me as I was getting ready to track the rotor blades on a gunship. Both of the blade tips had been marked with different colored grease pencils and once Cecil Johnson, our test pilot, had the ship running, I would lean a tracking flag ever so slightly into the blades. The flag was a four-meter-high, F-shaped metal pole with a nylon strap covered with masking tape attached vertically between the two horizontal bars of the F. The purpose of my work was to have both blades just barely kiss the flag, leaving a mark on the masking tape. If both colors overlapped on the masking tape, we were confident that both blades traveled the same course in their circular path. Any slight difference in the marks of the two colors indicated that, unless I adjusted the rotor blades, we could expect vibrations in the aircraft. Even though every helicopter company in country had a ship named *Good Vibrations,* our goal was to keep vibrations to a minimum. Seeing the sergeant approach me, I guessed he was curious as to how the blades were tracking. He caught me by surprise when he said, "Hey! You still want to fly?"

"Yeah!" I answered, wondering what he was up to.

"Well, the Yellowjackets need a crew chief. Go see their platoon sergeant and you can start flying on slicks," he replied.

Wow! After all this time, I was going to be a participant in the war. I would get a chance to shoot back. Being on the receiving end of rockets and mortars didn't count as warfare. I handed the tracking flag to one of my team and ran to the company area looking for the Yellowjacket platoon sergeant. After finding him at our TOC bunker, I explained that my platoon sergeant had released me to join his flight platoon. He welcomed me to the platoon, then promptly took me to the supply room to get my flight gear. The supply sergeant issued me a battered old flight helmet, "chicken plate" (chest armor) and gloves. I wondered why I would need gloves. I didn't expect my hands to get cold in Viet Nam. Later, I learned the gloves were to protect my hands from fire if I was in a ship that crashed and burned. While the supply room had whole sets of Nomex fire-retardant flight uniforms available to protect our bodies from the flames of a crash, only a few in the company would wear them. Almost everyone wore jungle fatigues because our friends in the infantry wore them and because no one seriously believed that anything would save our carcasses in a burning helicopter. A Huey went from ignition to fireball in nine seconds.

After I got my flight gear, my new sergeant told me I would have to wait a week or so until a few short-timers went home before I could move into the platoon hooch, but I was getting my own ship immediately. I was told the tail number of the UH-1H helicopter that was now mine and informed my ship was out in the field on a mission. When it returned in the evening, I was to do a postflight inspection and fill out the logbook. I would be flying the next morning when the ship was scheduled to fly "ash and trash" missions, which were resupply missions we flew to scattered compounds throughout III Corps. He told me to stay in the company area while I waited for my ship to return to Cu Chi. I went back to my hooch, wondering if I was doing the right thing. I had become used to my job in maintenance and I knew I was going to miss the work and, most of all, the guys who worked with me. I sat around talking to Mai until she had to leave our base camp with the other civilian workers, but I never told her I was going to be moving into a flight platoon hooch. After she had left for the village, I took a walk down the flight line to try to find the revetment where my ship would park. I was anxious to see which slick was going to be mine and I was hoping it might come back early. When my ship returned from its flight that evening, I helped the crew perform their postflight inspection and checked it out to see what kind of shape it was in. It was just a typical slick, stripped bare for combat—no frills such as passenger seats, seat belts for passengers, pilot doors or cargo doors. Except for the number painted on the tail boom, my ship didn't appear much different from any of the other twenty slicks in the company.

That evening I met my new platoon sergeant in the NCO Club. He told me the time of the next day's flight and where I would be going. He didn't offer any advice other than to tell me to pay attention and to learn by watching the experienced gunner on the ship. I went to sleep not knowing what to expect the next day. But I looked forward to flying over the wire on the perimeter and entering the war. The following morning, I was at my ship ready to go an hour before anyone else showed up. The gunner arrived first, appearing out of the darkness carrying our two machine guns. He quickly attached the guns to the mounts on each side of the ship, one gun for him and one for me, then crawled into the ship and went to sleep. The aircraft commander (AC) and pilot strolled over and did a quick preflight inspection. Within minutes we were lifting off. No one told me where we were going or what we were doing. I supposed it was just another day to the pilots and gunner but, since it was my first day, I was expecting a day of excitement. At a minimum, I would see the country and experience more of the war. We spent most of the day flying men and supplies to Special Forces camps and Military Assistance Command Viet Nam (MACV) compounds. Later that day, I realized I had no idea where we had been. While we did get to see a lot of the countryside, I was disappointed. It didn't seem like we were part of a war; we were more like an airborne delivery truck.

The mission on the second day was closer to what I expected my job to be. The previous day's company mission had all the slicks in the company operating alone, carrying men and material for whichever unit they were assigned to that day. But on my second day, my ship was part of a group of ten slicks flying together and operating as an assault company. Our ten slicks would be carrying infantry into landing zones (LZs) as our company gunships covered us. We left Cu Chi in the dark and at first light were landing in an abandoned rice paddy to pick up our first load of infantry. Our skids had hardly settled to the ground when the pilot started yelling at me to point my machine gun down at the ground, not at our infantry. I assumed that I was supposed to be covering the brush behind them and was anticipating having to fight our way out of the pickup zone (PZ). No one had given me any instructions about standard operating procedure. I supposed I was going to learn how to do things by doing them. We spent the day inserting infantry into scattered landing zones, and all of the LZs were cold. No enemy fire was received and apparently none was expected; we weren't allowed to shoot suppressive machine-gun fire into the tree lines on any of our approaches and departures.

My third day's mission was inserting troops from the 199th Light Infantry Brigade into jungle clearings miles from any sign of any human activity. There were no roads, villages or houses in view. I had no idea where we were and guessed it didn't matter. I supposed that someone higher up had picked our landing zones based on information that made each site a likely area of enemy activity. On this day, all of the clearings picked as landing zones were expected to be hot LZs, meaning we could expect enemy opposition at each landing. Approaching our first LZ, I wasn't sure what to expect. Would NVA machine guns and RPG fire greet us? How would I react? There was nothing that I could do now except to wait and see what happened. As I glanced around our ship, I noticed how the infantrymen on board looked tense. They also had been briefed that the LZ was expected to be hot and no one wanted to be on an exploding helicopter. Coming in fast, our flight of ten slicks was told to open up with our machine guns on the LZ perimeter. I fired two shots and my gun jammed. As I frantically tried to get it working, the troops sitting on my side of the ship peppered the tree line with

M-16 fire. Suddenly, the tree line in front of me was torn apart by explosions and I almost jumped out of my seat. The explosions were the impacting rockets and 40mm grenades being fired by the Stinger gunships covering our flanks. This was my first sight of a gunship in action. I hadn't expected to see them at treetop level, protecting the flight of slicks. I had always thought that the gunships stayed high above the LZ, shooting rockets into the trees while the slicks touched down.

I had no time to watch the gunships do their work. I needed to get my machine gun working but had no idea what to do. Trying to get my gun operating while rockets exploded in the trees, I glanced up to see another helicopter fly past us. Out of nowhere, our company smokeship had appeared in front of me. It flew between the slicks and the tree line, spewing a thick trail of white smoke to hide us from anyone in the trees. While Smokey looked impressive, flying on the smokeship was a dangerous job. The smokeship, flying low and slow as it laid out its smoke screen in a horseshoe around an LZ, drew considerable automatic weapons fire. Smokey's job was to conceal the infantry as they dismounted and to act as an easy target. I had heard our guys talk about Smokey in our clubs; they claimed that Smokey was shot down at least once a month. I had never heard anyone express a desire to fly on the smokeship.

Smokey and the gunships had gone roaring by us and I still couldn't get my machine gun working. The aircraft commander was shouting at me to get some bullets into the tree line while the infantry on board were bracing themselves to dismount. God, I was green. My hands were all thumbs. Fiddling with the gun, I didn't know what to do. Maybe I was green and dumb but, on the other hand, no one taught me anything about the machine gun, the radios or flight procedures. It was, "Here's your gear, there's your helicopter, go."

The skids never even touched the ground of the LZ. Our load of infantry jumped while we were slowing down, drifting forward to land into the grass. When the LZ was expected to be hot, the troops were out when they judged that they were low and slow enough to un-ass the ship without breaking a leg. It always struck me as odd that the military would spend weeks of training teaching troops how to parachute out of aircraft, but let them learn the hard way how to jump out of moving helicopters three or four meters high. No one wasted time waiting for the ship to land. A helicopter was vulnerable as it landed and no one wanted to be on it if RPGs started flying out of the tree line. As soon as the last man jumped, the gunner and I yelled, "Clean!"

The AC instantly lifted off, following the ships taking off in front of us. We had probably spent five or six seconds in the landing zone. We were airborne again, all machine guns on the ten slicks chewing up the jungle foliage except for mine. I was still trying to clear the jam. On our way to pick up more troops, the gunner and pilots made it clear that I was a dumb ass and had better get my shit together before I screwed up in a hot LZ. Fortunately, the few times I fired my machine gun the rest of the day, it worked fine. I was still clueless about what to do if the gun jammed and, just as important, I was clueless as to why it was functioning. I was going to have to learn how to use the machine gun.

After shutting down at Cu Chi that evening, the pilots did their quick postflight inspection and left. The gunner had already wandered off to clean the machine guns, so I was left alone at the revetment. I finished my maintenance inspection, filled out the logbook, and then turned in my daily log pages to our tech inspectors. The logbook pages, by the way, were where the crew chief was noted as the "CE" or "crew, enlisted," and that is why some pilots called their crew chief "Charlie Echo." Once the tech inspectors collected everyone's logbook pages for the day, they would then assign a maintenance team leader to start repairs of complex damages or problems that couldn't be fixed by the crew chiefs. A few evenings prior, I had been the one who had been doing the repair work. I didn't miss it at all.

Rather than head to the mess hall for supper after leaving my slick, I realized I had better get some instructions regarding the M-60 machine gun. I needed to learn what I was supposed to do with the gun if I planned on keeping my job as a crew chief. While we had M-60s on the bunker line, except for our evening "mad minute," when we would test-fire our weapons, I'd never really used one. I had no idea what I was supposed to do with it if it malfunctioned or jammed. We had never had a jam or malfunction during a "mad minute" and I suppose I thought I just pulled the trigger and the gun fired until I ran out of ammunition. That's what they did in the movies.

Walking toward the gunship revetments, I went looking for my old friend Garcia, the armorer for our gun platoon. I knew Garcia would help me out. Garcia and I had come over from Texas together and, as the gun platoon armorer, he knew how to use a machine gun and how to keep it functioning. Noticing some activity near a gunship, I walked over and found Garcia and the Stinger platoon sergeant, Johnny Holman, replacing the rocket pods on a gunship. Not wanting too many people to know about my stupidity, I was planning to wait until Johnny left before asking Garcia for help. We were just engaged in idle conversation when Garcia asked, "Why are you flying with the slicks? You should have asked to join the Stingers and fly guns."

His question caught me off guard. I didn't know what to say while the platoon sergeant was standing next to us. I had really never considered I would have a chance to be on our gunships. I had just assumed I'd have to spend months on the slicks prior to even thinking about guns. I stammered, "I didn't think that I could fly guns without spending time on the slicks first."

"Bullshit," said Sergeant Holman. "Slicks are for kids. Let me ask some of the other platoon sergeants about you. Garcia and Wilsher say you're okay, and if I think the guys in the Stingers will have you, you'll be a Stinger."

Several hours later, Garcia came over to the maintenance hooch where I was still living. I hadn't moved my gear over to the Yellowjackets hooch yet. "Hey, grab your gear and get it over to the Stinger hooch. Now!" he said.

"What's the rush?" I asked. I wasn't flying the next day and could move over then.

"Hey, if the Stingers ask you to join them, you do it right now. They'll take it as an insult if you make them wait. You want them to ask someone else?" Garcia replied.

"What about the Yellowjackets?" I asked. "Don't I have to tell their platoon sergeant where I'm going?"

"Fuck them," Garcia shot back. "The first sergeant already has you transferred to guns, let's go."

Since I didn't own anything, moving was easy. I carried my clothes, boots, M-16 and bedding fifty meters to the Stinger hooch and settled into my new home. I would learn that I had walked fifty meters into another world. Joining the gun platoon was unbelievable. I had always wanted to fly on a gunship (that's where the action was), but I had given up hope. I considered myself lucky just to fly on the slicks.

Knowing two of the guys in the platoon made my transition into the guns easier. Garcia and Wilsher were both Stingers and both had served with me at Fort Hood. They welcomed me to the platoon and made the necessary introductions, then a few of the guys picked me up, carried me out of the hooch and threw me into the closest stormwater ditch full of stagnant water, urine and ten thousand varieties of tropical diseases. After climbing out of the evil-smelling, murky water, I was given beer after beer while we sat outside the hooch letting my foul clothing dry on my carcass. I listened to their stories and advice while saying as little as possible. I was a little intimidated by the guys in the platoon; several sounded as if they had as much time on gunships as I had in the Army. Their time, however, was spent on combat assault missions, not stateside garrison duty or delivering supplies. To quote one gunner, "I've been in more firefights than you've been in grocery stores."

The Stingers were notorious in the clubs for their stories about daily fights with local VC and infiltrating NVA. And after having worked on some of their bullet-ridden helicopters, I knew there must be some truth to the stories. As the new guy, I kept my mouth shut and listened. I wanted to stay with these guys and knew that they had thrown people out of the platoon if they didn't fit in or pull their weight. I was determined I wasn't going to blow my chance to fly with the elite of our company.

Some soldiers in the company believed everyone in the gun platoon had a death wish, but I looked at them as real adventurers. Looking back years later, however, I realize that most of the other guys in the company never wanted to fly guns. There were no monetary incentives to be on the gun crews; slick crews received the same flight pay, as did half of the maintenance crews. The excitement of combat and facing the enemy every day was what the Stingers loved. The gun crews were a different breed of people; I've always been proud to be one of them.

Soon after I settled into a hooch just a little dumpier than the one I'd left, our platoon sergeant came in and announced who would be flying the next day and gave the rest of us our assignments. There weren't many guys in the platoon who wouldn't be flying. I hadn't realized that the Stingers were normally not at full strength, and with guard duty and other company tasks, there were usually just enough guys to put a crew chief and gunner on three or four ships with only a couple of guys left over. I wouldn't be flying my first day with the Stingers; I was told to spend the day with Roger Backes. His ship was being released from maintenance and I was told to work with him. We would replace its armament system and then Roger would be my mentor for a couple of days. He would fly as crew chief and break me in as his gunner. I couldn't help but wonder why the slick platoon hadn't done this with me. I was also told that if things worked out, I would probably get my own gunship when Roger returned to the States.

The next morning, those of us not flying that day made morning formation and police call of the company area. Afterward, I was walking along, laughing and joking with Garcia and Wilsher, when one of the Stinger gunners walking alongside of me said, "You'd better laugh now, 'cause you ain't going to think things are so damn funny after you've been out in the field with us." His sarcastic statement shocked me. *What the hell did he mean?* I wondered. During my brief time in the company, I had met most of the Stingers in the club and had always considered them to be laid back, ready to laugh at anything. I would come to learn that most of the guys were only putting up a front; only they knew what they really thought. I must admit I didn't do much laughing out in the field.

V

We went to the maintenance area and waited until our maintenance test pilot, Cecil Johnson, flew Roger's ship on a post-inspection test flight. Having just come from the maintenance platoon, I knew we might as well get comfortable waiting, because we couldn't do anything until Cecil was satisfied with the performance of the ship. He would check out the systems on the ground and then fly outside of the perimeter wire to check out its performance in flight. If he didn't like the way a ship handled after being torn apart and put back together, it would not leave maintenance. Cecil returned from his test flight, parking the ship at the maintenance tent. He didn't like the way it flew. It was mid-morning by the time some minor adjustments were done, the ship had passed the test flight and Cecil set it down next to a gunship revetment. The ship was all ours; we had the rest of the day to get it ready for combat. Doing the heavy work first, Roger and I helped Garcia mount the rocket pods and sight them in. The rockets were sighted in to hit a target Garcia had painted on the side of the 3/4 Cavalry's maintenance hangar, and were not expected to be anywhere near where the aircraft commander's rocket sight would indicate they would hit. None of the Stinger aircraft commanders or pilots used the expensive sights in the helicopters, for which Uncle Sam had paid thousands of dollars. Sights were for amateurs. Each pilot drew his own crosshair with a grease pencil on the windshield. After the first rockets went out, he adjusted his fire or drew a new crosshair. Since our 2.75-inch rockets weren't all that accurate, the grease pencil sight worked fine.

Garcia was short, so the rockets were sighted in to hit high, based on his grease pencil crosshair; that way they should be right on for the taller pilots. It was surprising how accurate most of our ACs were when using their grease pencil sights. Once a ship was running and waiting for morning takeoff, our AC would fidget in his seat until he found his normal sitting position used when diving into a gun run. He would then straighten out his arm to mark the X on the windshield with his pencil. Nine times out of ten, the first rockets hit the target. It was a skill they learned with practice: when the pilot in the right seat was allowed to try his luck, there were usually numerous X's on the windshield before he hit the target.

Finishing with the armament, we took a break for lunch and went to the "gook store." Every compound in Viet Nam seemed to have a PX (post exchange), which sold Western products, and nearby a "gook store" that sold Vietnamese souvenirs and junk that only Americans, both military and civilian, would buy. The PX sold material things—one went to the gook store to purchase what was needed for your soul. Wooden carvings of a hand with the middle finger sticking straight up. Embroidered shirts and jackets bearing childish quotations on their backs. Baseball hats that looked like baseball hats and not the ugly Army issue "fatigue hat" that was supposed to be a baseball hat but made the wearer feel like the village idiot. Cigarette lighters that didn't work very well, but had cool engravings on them. Military patches and insignia, such as flight wings that upon closer inspection were actually the outstretched legs of a girl lying on her back. We went to the gook store to buy Stinger patches to show the world that I was now in the best gun platoon in the Army. Since I was now a Stinger, I was expected to flaunt it, so the seamstress at the gook store had to be visited. Every one of my four fatigue shirts needed to have our bright red platoon patch of a hornet carrying rockets sewn on the left pocket. In addition, I needed a bright red Stinger shirt with our emblem on the pocket. The shirt was to be worn at company parties, and anytime the platoon went en masse to one of the infrequent shows put on at the NCO Club or the EM

Club. Stingers sat together and attempted to be the loudest
and drunkest group at any function. It was my understanding
that our officers were actually worse than we enlisted men.
Since they were paid more, they could afford to be drunker
and louder.

The red shirt wasn't bought only to wear at parties, however; platoon tradition expected one to flout death and the
enemy by wearing the red shirt into combat on his last day in
Viet Nam. Depending on individual unit policy, most flight
crews were allowed to quit flying two weeks before going
home to the States. In our platoon, while we might quit early,
it was still expected that we would go out on our last day
wearing no chest armor but only a bright red shirt to draw
enemy fire. The VC and NVA deserved one last chance.

We returned to the Stinger hooch with my purchases and
found Mai, sitting on the wooden sidewalk, waiting for me.
Seeing me approach, she broke into tears, crying and shouting at me, "Why you go Stingers? They number ten. Kill
mamasan and babysan! VC kill you for sure; VC say they kill
all Stingers." She grabbed my arm and pleaded with me to
come back with her to the maintenance hooch. Shaking her
off, I explained that I wasn't going to be killing women and
children and that no VC would get me. I knew that gunship
crews were not exactly popular among the Vietnamese, and I
could only imagine what stories Mai had heard in Cu Chi village regarding our actions in the field.

But there was no way to comfort Mai and she went away
crying and sobbing. While I was not going to quit the gun
platoon for her, whenever I didn't fly, I would try to stop in
the maintenance hooch to talk. Eventually, she started visiting the Stinger hooch and learned we weren't as bad as our
reputation. Whenever I went to the PX, I bought her items,
such as cigarettes or soap, that she could barter in the village.
Of course, if I bought these items for Mai, I also had to buy
them for the Stinger hooch maid too. It was the way things
were done. More often than not, I would pick my clean
clothes off my bunk in the evening and the scent of Mai's
perfume would drift from the shirt collars. I suppose she put

the perfume on the collars to remind me that she was still looking after me.

I would have liked to sit and talk with Mai, but Roger and Garcia were anxious to get back to the flight line to get Roger's gunship ready for combat. All the time Mai was crying, they were waving for me to come with them. As we strolled over to the flight line, I could tell they were wondering why Mai was making such a commotion, but neither of them asked any questions. While they may have thought that we had a sexual relationship, nothing like that was happening between us. We were friends. Perhaps Mai was trying to save my soul—as well as my life.

Returning to the gunship, we loaded the seats, ammunition, smoke, fragmentation and white phosphorus grenades, as well as assorted odds and ends. After loading nineteen rockets into the tubes on each side, the ship was ready. Backes then gave me a half-day of instructions on what my job entailed while flying on the gunships.

Like any job, there was a lot more to it than met the eye. For example, there were five different communication systems. We listened to our own crew, of course. We could listen to the other guns and also the C&C (command and control) helicopter, which carried our commanding officer along with the commanding officer of the infantry unit we were working with on that particular day. There was also the option of listening to the infantry network and Armed Forces Viet Nam (AFVN) for civilian music. We could listen to some or all of the above. I would learn to listen to three at a time, occasionally all of them, but mostly just two. At first, it would be maddening trying to figure out who was talking and what was going on, but I learned to pick up what was important and filter out the rest. Roger also saved me from potential embarrassment and harassment by warning me to never, ever, use military language from World War II movies. Only new guys ever said "Roger" or "Wilco." And everyone who heard their radio transmission mocked them. "Talk like the nineteen-year-old kid that you are," he advised. I was also told to always use "meters" when describing distances, since using "yards" or "football fields" was the mark of an amateur. Basically, he was telling me things that would fool our pilots into thinking I knew what I was doing. As in all jobs, knowing the jargon of the work denotes competence. Roger went out of his way to help a new kid (twenty-one years old) avoid potential embarrassment from the old guys (most were nineteen) at work.

Roger took a pair of machine guns out of a little shed sitting next to the revetment. He first showed me the flanged feed adapter used on gunship machine guns. We didn't put C-ration cans on the sides like slick crews. The feed adapters were readily available from supply but I never saw anyone except gunship crews use them—they made a big difference. He showed me how to tear the machine guns apart and then made me put them back together. He had me take off the barrel and practice loading and firing whole cartridges out of the receiver without looking at the gun. I learned I shouldn't get in the habit of looking at the gun when clearing a jam. If it jammed when I was firing at something, I had to keep my eye on that something. I was not to let a man disappear into the vegetation while clearing a gun. I had to keep my eye on him, clear the gun using my fingers as eyes, and get right back on target. But Roger warned, "Be ready for this to happen: The gun is really jammed bad and someone is firing at you. Ignore him. Clear the gun, don't freeze, there's nowhere to hide, get your gun working, and then get him." He showed me how to quickly clear the gun, if jammed, and why it probably had jammed. I'd never considered what to do if the gun wouldn't stop firing, a situation known as "a runaway gun." Roger told me to grab the ammo belt with my left hand and twist the belt. He showed me how to liberally douse the feed tray with gobs of LSA (Lubrication, Small Arms) and explained why not to lubricate either the buffer or the gas piston. I also learned that I should always keep my machine-gun combination tool on the ammo can where I could reach it. Unlike a lot of units, we didn't safety-wire the gas piston retaining nut on our gun barrels and would need the combination tool to tighten the nut periodically.

Continuing my lesson, he explained that almost all gunships in country fly circular clockwise patterns with the right side of the ship down and, since the gunner sits at the right door, he would do most of the shooting. Stingers, of course, were different. Our aircraft commander sat on the left, so the ship flew left side down doing counterclockwise circles. As a consequence, on our ships the crew chief did most of the shooting at individual targets. The crew chiefs of the Stingers considered themselves the best. They deserved the privilege of doing most of the shooting. While it was okay to let the gunners fly at the left door once in a while, no one made a habit of it. The crew chief had the responsibility of keeping the gunship in the air, and flying left door down was his only reward.

I was told to pay attention to how I held the gun. Our machine guns had short butt plates from flexguns instead of infantry stocks and the gun was held tight against the outside of a shoulder. "Watch where you let the brass fly," Roger advised me. Machine guns ejected seven hundred pieces of hot empty brass cartridge cases per minute from the right side of the gun. Crew chiefs shot from the right shoulder and kept their guns cocked slightly to the right so that the hot brass wouldn't be sprayed toward the front of the ship and down the shirt collars of the pilots. Gunners, on the other hand, normally shot lefty in order to be able to quickly pivot backward, shooting behind the ship as it passed the enemy. An advantage of having door gunners on helicopters was their ability to protect the rear of the ship in combat. In order to reach out and place bullets under our tail boom, the right door gunner had to shoot from his left shoulder. Roger advised me to cant my machine gun slightly or a lot of hot brass would be ejected down the neck of my shirt when I flew as his gunner. Like every new gunner, I learned how true this was by putting hot brass down my shirt when I was shooting from the right seat. The brass felt white-hot when it landed and started burning the base of the throat. I would involuntarily shift my body, which caused the hot brass to drop lower, where my chest armor would pin it against my flesh. It always hurt, but I ignored the pain and kept firing my gun. It didn't take many lessons before I learned how to fire a machine gun from my left shoulder.

I was warned not to kick the empty brass and the links from the belted ammunition out the door. He advised me to let it pile up on the floor until the ship landed. Kicking out the brass while flying was dangerous; it could fly back into the tail rotor blade and ruin it. Moreover, if we were flying over the tops of the slicks, the brass dropped from a gunship could hit and damage their rotor blades as well.

He strongly stressed that I pay attention to what I was shooting at and not get "target fixation." I had to be ready to stop shooting instantly. I must always watch the rotor blades; if the pilot turns and dips the blades, they can swing into my line of fire. Slicks and Marine Corps helicopter gunships had machine guns on mounts with stops to determine how high, low, forward or backward their guns would shoot. Their crews couldn't shoot their ships to pieces, but we held our guns in our laps and fired freehand. We could and probably would shoot our own helicopter blades and possibly the helicopter itself. It was possible to shoot yourself down! When I was shooting at someone who was shooting back at me, if the blades came down, I was to stop firing immediately. "Let him shoot, yell for the pilot to lift the blades, but don't shoot your own rotor blades; take the fire," Roger calmly said. Now that was hard to imagine doing, but I would find that I was always more afraid of the pilots' anger for shooting my rotor blades than of enemy gunfire. I always released the trigger and let the enemy shoot whenever the blades dipped into my line of fire.

After warning me not to shoot our blades, he then said, "Don't shoot the rockets. The AC will say, 'Coming hot,' before he fires any rockets. You have to pay attention to what is happening and not shoot the rockets as they leave the tubes."

While the rockets weren't armed until they did several spins and traveled a fixed distance, they still might blow up if hit with a machine-gun bullet. Once the rocket had left the tube, I could start firing, but I had to watch what I was shooting at. I was not to get carried away with trying to hit the same target that the rocket was going toward, because machine-gun bullets travel fast enough to catch the rocket. If a bullet hits the rocket motor while it is in flight, the rocket will start flying corkscrew patterns and be liable to hit anywhere except the target. Roger also advised me to keep my helmet visor down while the rockets were being fired. The igniter caps on the end of the rockets were blown back toward the gunners as the rockets left the tubes. While they generally didn't hit us in the face, they might. All of the crew chiefs and gunners had scars on their legs from being hit by the igniter caps; so would I.

Each crew chief and gunner kept a minigun can of ammo on the floor between his legs to hold belted 7.62 machine-gun rounds. When I was assigned my own ship, I would paint my ammo can bright red to draw fire. It sat in the open doorway, a bright red target for the guns of the NVA, but enemy bullets never hit it. While a minigun ammo can normally was packed with fifteen hundred rounds, once we removed the cardboard partitions between the stacked belts, two thousand rounds would fit in the can. Along the outside edges of the ammo can, three or four extra machine-gun barrels would be hung, ready for instant replacement if a gun jammed or slowed down its rate of fire. When we were airborne, machine guns were held on our laps, safety off and ready to fire at all times. When approaching any base or refueling point, as soon as the ship reached the outside perimeter line of barbed wire, the barrel was removed and hung on the ammo can. Anytime a machine gun in our platoon had a barrel attached, it was going to fire if the trigger was touched. No one ever used the safety; we didn't want to fumble for the safety if we had to shoot fast. While removing the barrel, I was to shake it to feel the piston move. If it moved slowly, there was carbon built up on it and another barrel should be used or the piston cleaned.

Contrary to popular belief, machine-gun barrels didn't melt down from excess use and barrels didn't get too hot to function—at least not when they were being cooled by the constant airflow of a helicopter in flight. But heavy, constant use would build up excessive carbon on the gas piston, which slowed the internal mechanisms that drove the bolt back after firing, chambering and firing the next round. This slowing of the system caused the gun to jam. Since we would fire thousands of rounds of ammunition in a day, the gunship crews probably knew how to keep their machine guns functioning better than any other troops in the Army. Barrels that had their pistons gummed up with carbon were taken apart at the first opportunity. The piston was removed, thrown in the dirt, ground into the soil with a foot until it was as bright as polished silver. It was then replaced into the barrel and the barrel was good as new. Our flight gloves saved our hands from being seared on hot barrels when we decided to change barrels in the middle of a firefight. Each ship carried an asbestos glove to wear when changing hot barrels, but I never saw anyone use one. After I burned my hands several times, melting my gloves into my skin while changing hot barrels, I learned where to grab the barrel.

Most of our extra machine-gun barrels had their bipod removed by the gunners. Usually each ship had two extra barrels with an attached bipod to be used if we were shot down and the machine guns had to be fired from a prone position. The barrel with the bipod was considered to be there only for emergencies and was not to be used unless absolutely necessary. Some gunners also removed the flash suppressors on the end of the barrel, but once anyone has fired a machine gun without a flash suppressor, he quickly realizes why they are on automatic weapons. They aren't used to suppress your flash so the enemy can't see your muzzle blast, as most people think; they allow you to fire and still see. When firing an automatic weapon without a flash suppressor, there is a constant flash about a meter in diameter several meters out from the end of the gun. It's very impressive, but difficult to see through; moreover, it makes you feel extremely vulnerable. Of course, we all knew that the original M-16 rifles that we used had the three-prong flash suppressor for a different reason: to break the wires on C-ration cartons. Without them the infantry would starve to death.

Each gunship carried several cases of the various types of hand grenades available. Smoke grenades were the most numerous and were used for marking targets or landing zones. As the lead gunship would guide the slicks into the LZ, a thousand meters from the touchdown point the AC would say "trail smoke." The crew chief and gunner would each pull the ring on a smoke grenade, let the spoon/handle fly and hold the top of the smoke grenade by their fingertips. The colored smoke billowing out behind the lead gunship made it appear that it was part of a civilian air show, not a combat assault. On the AC's command the grenades were dropped to mark where the lead slick of the ten-ship flight was to land. Since smoke grenades might bounce and roll for quite a distance after being thrown, the crew chief and gunner made sure that two different colors were thrown, usually red and yellow. The smoke from green and purple grenades seemed to dissipate in the slightest breeze. The C&C ship flying overhead would radio which color was the landing point. "Trailing smoke" was another reason to wear gloves, as the billowing smoke grenade became extremely hot and it was a point of pride never to drop a grenade until ordered to do so. I would feel my fingertips melting away and clench my teeth from the pain, but like everyone else in the platoon, I never dropped the grenade until the AC shouted, "Mark!" Of course, while "trailing smoke" with one hand, we were expected to be firing our machine guns with the other hand, so we had to have the gun braced on our legs and not let the gun get away from us. Quick short bursts of fire would allow us to control the gun.

The other grenades on board each ship were used in some fashion against people. Concussion grenades, which threw no shrapnel, were used on swimmers. Fragmentation grenades, which, when exploded, threw thousands of small pieces of metal outward, were used on just about any target. White phosphorus grenades, encased in a lime-green porcelain shell, were used to sink wooden sampans, to start brush fires and on people. Once phosphorus landed on flesh, it used the oxygen from a body to continue burning. I often wondered what would happen if an enemy bullet hit a WP grenade. Would the porcelain shell then rupture, filling the ship with burning phosphorus? I didn't like or trust WP grenades and, usually, after using those on board, I would conveniently forget to replace them until a pilot would remind me to put some on the ship. CS and CN grenades were both types of tear gas and we didn't like to use either one of them; they were notorious for having bad fuses. Both types would occasionally detonate instantly after releasing the spoon, gassing the thrower instead of the target. The smoke, concussion and tear gas grenades could be tossed out the door, since there usually wasn't any need for pinpoint accuracy. When throwing fragmentation or WP grenades, though, we were generally trying to hit a specific target—a bunker firing port, an individual fighting position, or a floating sampan.

"It's a lot easier hitting small targets if the AC watches the target through the chin bubble at his feet and gives the command to drop the grenade," Roger explained. "Leaning out the door to the left while moving forward makes it difficult to be accurate when you throw the grenade. Some guys are naturally good at hitting their mark with a grenade, but not many. If you're not hitting what you're aiming at, ask the AC to line you up on target and ask him to give the command to throw." He was right. I would learn that I would usually be closer to the target when the AC lined up the target in his chin bubble and then called the throw.

Besides our machine guns and grenades, most crews generally carried spare weapons: M-16 rifles, captured AK-47 assault rifles, M-79 grenade launchers or shotguns. While these weapons might be used once in a while on a mission, they were generally kept on the ship for the pilot and AC to use if the ship went down. The officers carried .38-caliber pistols, but no one wanted to depend on a pistol if other weapons were available. If you were shot down near the Cambodian border, the more firepower available the better. It might be a long walk home.

Roger explained that, as a crew chief, I would have to learn each type of armament system carried by the gunships used by the platoon. While most of the gunships had an assigned crew chief, each crew chief was expected to fly on any ship in the platoon. There would be many times when the normal crew chief wasn't available and another would take his place. It was imperative, therefore, that all the crews have a working knowledge of each type of armament system.

The majority of the Stinger gunships had a rocket pod on each side, each holding nineteen rockets. These rockets were about five feet long, 2.75 inches in diameter, and consisted of a motor pushing a screw-on ten-pound high explosive (HE) warhead. We also used seventeen-pound HE warheads; and sometimes ten- or seventeen-pound variable-timed (VT) warheads, which gave an airburst of shrapnel above the heads of troops in the open. Also available but not used much in our area were fléchette rounds that exploded several meters above the ground in an airburst. As with other rockets, arming of the warhead occurred after a certain amount of thrust and spinning action had occurred after firing. While HE rounds exploded on impact, when using fléchettes the AC would fire from an estimated distance to his target so that the rocket motor would burn out near the target, causing detonation of the warhead. The warhead contained approximately twenty-five thousand nails with little stamped fins that were packed in red dye. When the round detonated, the red dye scattered in the air, allowing the pilot to see where the fléchette round had hit. It was rumored that the dye also acted as an anticoagulant so that bleeding from nail wounds wouldn't stop. Another type of rocket available was the white phosphorus round, which sprayed hot, burning phosphorus over an area. Our platoon leader, Nine Six, would normally determine the type of rockets to be carried on each ship. If we were going to work open or brushy areas, one pod might contain white phosphorus while the other pod held fléchettes: WP to get them running and fléchettes to nail them in their tracks. If heavy bunkers or timber fortifications were expected, the entire load might be seventeen-pound high explosives.

The majority of the time, all rocket pods were loaded with ten-pound HE warheads. The best thing about using rockets was the ease of rearming. On the nineteen-round pods, the rockets were just slid fin end first down the tube until a spring-loaded pin snapped into a groove on the motor and held the rocket against the electrical contact. The smaller seven-round tubes were loaded from the rear of the pod by moving each electrical contact out of the way and pushing the rocket forward until a spring-loaded pin caught the groove. With either system, every now and then a rocket would vibrate loose from its pin and start inching forward out of the tube as we were flying. Whoever was sitting nearest to it would loosen his seat belt and climb out of the flying ship to kick the rocket back against its retaining pin. When I watched men loading rockets, I had always noticed that, while they did it fast, they seemed to handle the rockets carefully. I had thought that they were careful because of the possibility of the rocket exploding, but found out that they didn't want to drop a rocket, because the fall would affect the motor propellant charge. Dropped rockets probably wouldn't fly straight and weren't to be used because a wide-flying rocket might hit our ground troops. While everyone treated rockets with care, no one was afraid of them. Many guys smashed the fléchette warheads with hammers to get the nails for souvenirs. I always wondered who had been the first guy brave enough to determine it could be done.

While most of our ships had the nineteen-round pods, there were some gunships in Viet Nam with twenty-four-round pods, but they weren't common. These ships were called "Hogs," because they put their nose almost into the dirt and plowed forward on each takeoff, struggling to become airborne. Other gunships used flexguns, miniguns or 40mm cannon and could only carry the additional weight of seven-round rocket pods on each side. The ships carrying the nineteen-round rocket pods were set up to fire a pair of rockets whenever the pilot pushed his button, while the ships with the smaller pods fired a single rocket at a time. When I joined the platoon, we had one ship with a 40mm cannon on its nose and were in the process of having another ship outfitted with miniguns at the insistence of our company commander. Prior to my joining the platoon, they had several ships with twin M-60 machine guns—or flexguns, as they were called—on each side, but we no longer used them. The flexguns had disappeared. Since none of the gunners liked or wanted to take care of either the 40mm cannons or miniguns, most ships just had rockets.

Art Silacci was the crew chief of the 40mm ship, and he spent more time working on his 40mm armament system than on the rest of the helicopter. We probably wouldn't have had a 40mm ship, commonly known as a "Frog," if he hadn't been willing to spend so much time maintaining the 40mm cannon. I would eventually fly as his gunner several times in order to learn the armament system so I could replace him if needed. The 40mm cannon hung in a round pod on the nose of the gunship, and ammunition was held in a sheet metal container sitting left of center behind the AC. As the gun was fired by the AC, a motor pulled the heavy, linked rounds out of the container and through a flexible chute that went through the control panel between the pilots and out to the gun. The only problem with the system was that the ammunition motor didn't seem to have enough power to do its job. The crew chief would have to turn slightly sideways, while still firing his machine gun, and use his right foot to push the rounds forward into the chute. I had to do it a few times and thought it had to be the most awkward position ever used in combat. I never would have guessed that someone fed a weapon system its ammunition by using his right foot held chest high while sitting with his torso turned to the left. Especially at the same time as he was firing a hand-held machine gun from the open doorway of a moving helicopter.

As Roger continued my lessons, one of our ships was in the process of being rigged with twin miniguns mounted above small rocket pods. We walked over to talk to Garcia and to look at its armament system. Garcia had previously told me that I would probably be assigned as crew chief on this ship since most of the platoon didn't like miniguns—in other words, the new guy gets whatever no one else wants. These rotating, six-barreled, electric-powered Gatling guns were complicated, jammed incessantly and were a lot more work for the crew chief and gunner.

A minigun was mounted on each side of the helicopter above the rocket tubes, close enough to the crew chief or gunner so that they could lean on the barrels with their outboard hand if they wished. Of course, this also meant that when the guns were firing, at two thousand or four thousand rounds per minute, the crewmember sitting next to them experienced an instant excruciating headache. The two guns were supposed to be fired by the pilot in the right seat using an expensive sighting system. When the pilot turned the sight to the right, for example, the right gun turned to the right, while the left gun stopped at a predetermined point so that it wouldn't continue firing, eating away the front of the gunship along with both pilots. Shooting straight ahead, sideways or pointing downward, each gun would fire two thousand rounds per minute, but when a gun jammed or met its stop on a sideward turn, the opposite gun automatically doubled its rate of fire. This was the way the system operated in other gunship platoons.

In our platoon, the expensive sighting system stayed locked in place on the ceiling. Just as they did for firing rockets, Stinger pilots used a crosshair drawn on the windshield with a grease pencil and the guns stayed pointed forward. I'm not sure, but I think that our pilots did this so they had the fun of using aerial maneuvers to fire at a target with the stream of red tracers. They couldn't care less about targets to the sides; the crew chief and gunner would control the left and right sides with their machine guns.

While two thousand to four thousand rounds a minute might seem as if a target would be drenched with bullets, a gunship could not carry enough ammunition for such a sustained rate of fire. The guns fired a three-second burst, then stopped until the AC pushed the firing button again. He didn't pull the trigger on his cyclic stick as in movies, because the trigger operated the radio, not the armament. These short lapses between pushing the firing button conserved enough ammunition so that our ammunition supply would last more than a couple of minutes: only nine thousand rounds were held in the four trays sitting on the floor. Depending on the situation in the field, on any given day, these trays might have to be reloaded every hour or two. The crew chief and gunner had to learn to reload quickly, but efficiently. The belts of ammunition had to be coiled correctly, as the belted ammunition was ripped from the trays so fast that the slightest kink in a belt could break it. If the belt broke, there went half of the armament system. So the crew had to load the ammunition trays with care.

A lot of information was being fed to me that afternoon and I was trying to remember everything. I wasn't feeling very confident, but Roger assured me that it would all start meshing together. I just had to pay attention to what was going on. He kept stressing "pay attention."

"You ever watch the gunships working out at night near the bunker line? Did you notice how they dive down from five hundred meters, tracers flowing down to the enemy until the gunship pulls out of its gun run at two hundred meters?" he asked.

"Sure," I answered. "All the guys on guard duty watch them."

"Well, those gunships aren't Stingers. They're guns from the 25th Aviation Battalion and they don't fly low. We're the only gunship platoon in Viet Nam that is down low and slow, looking for trouble. We're so low that once when my ship was out of rockets, my AC shredded a bamboo thicket with the rotor blades to flush out some VC shooting our infantry. I shot two VC within the circle of our blades."

"I thought all gunships stayed high," I said.

"We're going to be right above our infantry. Don't shoot them."

He had brought up an item that was a constant fear among our crews—that during a firefight, an American might be hit by mistake. I really hadn't given any thought to this possibility. I guess I assumed that we fired at known enemy positions well out in front of our infantry. But the enemy had learned how vulnerable they were to massive American firepower and had adopted a tactic known as "grab their belt." In other words, let our soldiers walk up as close as possible before shooting. The closer our infantry were to the enemy positions when the fight was initiated, the less likely that heavy artillery or jet strikes could be used. Our pilots worried about possible friendly casualties when firing rockets in close support of the infantry and the machine gunners constantly watched where the infantry was located. Many of us had friends or relatives in infantry units and no one wanted to be responsible for American casualties. We prided ourselves on being out in the field as equal partners with the infantry. To shoot an American, even by accident, was unthinkable.

Next we went over the instrument panel, and Roger explained that the crew chief sat on the left in order to be able to see all the instruments. While the pilot was supposed to be monitoring the gauges, it didn't hurt for the crew chief to keep an eye on them. The pilot would frequently be busy listening to the artillery radio net and plotting our flight path to ensure that we didn't fly through the same airspace being used for artillery rounds. All crewmembers were expected to watch for other aircraft at all times, especially those the pilots might not be able to see; for example, those below and behind us. No one likes a midair collision. We went over flight procedures, combat procedures, landing/takeoff procedures, refueling procedures (always done *hot,* i.e. aircraft running), emergency procedures. I was really impressed with Roger and I still appreciate how willing he was to explain and to show me everything I would need to know about my job. If I did things right in the field, it was because of him. If I screwed up in the field, it was because of me. Using him as a model, I would try to make things easier for new guys by passing on his knowledge.

* * *

My orientation was done and the ship was ready for the next day. Since I would be flying as a gunner, he instructed me to get my flight gear and two machine guns and put everything in his helicopter that evening. Garcia would wake us in the morning. As gunner, I was to go immediately to the mess hall and fill our water container with ice. This ice, made from superchlorinated water, would melt during the day and provide water for our four-man crew: AC, pilot, crew chief and gunner. Roger would grab four C-ration meals and then help me carry our water container to the ship. There was nothing more to learn that afternoon, but I was going to get an education that I would never forget. Soon I was going to learn more about myself than about warfare.

That evening I wore a shirt with the Stinger patch sewn on a pocket for the first time in the NCO Club. I felt self-conscious, knowing I had not proved myself to be a platoon member yet. As the new guy in the platoon, I had to buy drinks for everyone at the bar, which made me feel even more self-conscious. I couldn't relax and enjoy myself at the club; I was still thinking about my training session with Roger. I had not realized there was more to the job than just sitting in a doorway with a machine gun. My mind was still blurry from all the information that Roger had crammed into me during the afternoon and I wondered if I could remember all of his advice. One thing I knew, however, was that they would have to throw me out of the platoon to get rid of me; there was no way that I would leave voluntarily. I had waited too long for this chance.

The club was open for only a few hours each evening, so we had a few drinks and then headed back to the hooch. Opening the door, I was surprised to see that most of our platoon were already sleeping. I would soon learn how tiring a day hunting the enemy could be. After the single lightbulb illuminating our dreary hooch was turned off, I lay awake on my bunk half the night—thinking and wondering about the next day. Tomorrow was going to be the real thing. The next morning I wouldn't be flying supplies or airlifting troops in and out of LZs; I would be out on a gunship hunting men—

armed men. Every young soldier wonders how he will react in combat and, naturally, I viewed the next day with mixed feelings. We all knew that some people froze or broke under the pressure of armed combat. What if, after all my talking about getting into action, I found out I couldn't take it? Was I being foolish or crazy? There were thousands of guys back in the States terrified of the draft because they might be sent to Viet Nam. There were thousands of men in infantry units in country that would give anything to have a job behind the wire at Cu Chi. I'd read somewhere that, in every war, the men in the front want to get back to the rear and the men in the rear want to get up to the front. I knew that I wanted to experience combat, but I don't think I had fully considered what being in combat meant. Starting tomorrow, real bullets would be coming at me. I had to wonder why I was doing this when I didn't have to. I wasn't doing it for glory, patriotism or excitement. Just to prove something to myself. I had always wanted to be a soldier, and if I was a soldier, I wanted to be a soldier in combat. Something drove me to find out if I measured up to standards, to determine what I was made of, to see if I could function under fire. I wanted to learn if I could control myself when my life was in danger. I believe that I honestly thought that I could go into combat, face the enemy and be better for the experience. I had no idea how it would affect me emotionally and mentally. Maybe I should have been thinking about the reasons why so many guys quit flying.

VI

I tossed and turned all night. Shortly after I fell asleep, Garcia shook my leg and shined his flashlight in my face. It was time to get up and see the war. I hurriedly dressed while the rest of the crews puttered and calmly got ready for another day of work. As the new guy, I wanted to imitate the veterans and act nonchalant, but I was terrified of being late. I wanted everything to go smoothly my first day. I rushed to the mess hall to get our ice and walked to the flight line without breakfast. Roger stayed at the mess hall and ate breakfast, then wandered down the flight line with plenty of time to spare before takeoff. Our pilots showed up, did their preflight inspections and then briefed us on our missions—where we were going and what to expect. My first day of flying in the gun platoon would be spent working with a battalion of the 25th Infantry Division south of Dau Tieng, looking for North Vietnamese regulars hidden in the Ho Bo Woods.

Taking a quick look around the flight line, I noticed the only activity was at the three gunships and at our command and control (C&C) helicopter. "Where is everybody? There's no one at the slicks," I asked as I scanned our flight line. Roger told me that the C&C ship would leave first to pick up the infantry commander, and the guns would leave shortly afterward and would meet the C&C ship in the general area of the LZ at first light. The slicks would probably leave a half-hour after us to pick up their loads of infantry. Depending on the infantry commander's plan for the mission, the slicks would either bring out the infantry for an insertion im-

mediately or hold with the infantry at a staging area until a
suitable LZ was determined. Depending on military intelligence, the whim of the infantry commander or observation
of enemy activity this morning, the LZ picked by the infantry commander the previous day might not be the LZ
used today.

All three gunships had their rotor blades turning and the
pilots were checking radio frequencies and writing them on
the windshields with grease pencils. By the end of the day,
the right windshields of each ship would be covered with
scrawled grease pencil markings. The pilot of a ship was responsible to ensure that the AC didn't fly through artillery
fire and constantly checked the radios to determine where
local artillery fire was being used. Because of the numerous
small fire support bases scattered around the countryside, we
just couldn't assume that we weren't sharing the same part of
the sky with high explosive artillery rounds.

Roger and I slid the side armor on the two pilots' seats forward, closed their doors, then jumped in our seats and fas-
tened our seat belts. We didn't close their doors for them to
be polite; we did it because it was difficult for a pilot to do
it himself without being a contortionist. Our AC quietly
said, "Coming up," and our ship started to slowly lift off the
ground. "Clear on the left," said Roger. "Clear on the right,"
I replied. The overloaded gunship's engine strained to lift us
inches off the ground to shuffle and hop out of the revetment.
Momentarily hesitating after clearing the revetment, we then
slowly moved forward, skimming the ground until our blades
churned the cool early morning air into magic and we were
flying. I was going out to war. I smiled: too naïve to be
frightened.

I would come to love the early morning takeoffs. In the
darkness it was relatively cool, the ship and armament were
ready and the crew confident. The morning was the best time
of day in the gun platoon. We felt so alive. Probably because
we knew that the day might end without us, we tried to appreciate little things such as the coolness and the early morning camaraderie. Later in the day we might feel different:

coming back in for fuel and ammo with the ship shot up and each man thinking, "I'm not going back out." Even the ships exuded confidence in the morning. The morning coolness and quiet made the sound of the turbine engines different. There was a distinct whine of anticipation; the rotor blades turned faster and faster until they bit the cool morning air with a confident sound not heard in the hot afternoon take-offs. The ship responded with more power in the dense morning air and I would swear it bucked with anticipation like an old warhorse. The Army was right when they named helicopter troops Air Cavalry.

Taking off in a loaded gunship was a new experience for me. I'd flown in UH-1Cs before, but not one full of ammunition, high explosives and fuel. The revetments built to protect the gunships from mortars and rockets had a wall of sandbags to the front and another wall to the right, so we bounced to the left and out onto the road between revetments. I hadn't realized that gunships were so overloaded they could hardly get off the ground. We would have to skim the ground, building up airspeed, dip to get translational lift and finally gain altitude. This could only be done in the coolness of the morning when the engines were strongest and the air densest. In the heat of a tropical afternoon, gunships dragged their skids along the runway and used more runway length to take off than light observation planes. Many times the crew chief and gunner trotted down the runway next to a moving gunship, thereby lessening its weight so it could get off the ground. As soon as it was moving forward and inches off the runway, they'd jump in and it would bounce and claw its way off the ground to barely make it over a three-foot-high barbed wire fence at the end of a short runway.

Our three ships fought to get airborne as always, skimming along the runway, slowly gaining altitude until we were high above our bunker line and outside the perimeter wire. Turning left we flew through a darkness unbroken by any light except the soft glow of the instrument lights inside of our ship and the rotating anticollision lights on our companion ships. As the morning light slowly melted away the night,

I could see the low trees and shrubs sticking above old fields covered by the shroud of ground fog. Everything looked the same to me and I had no idea where we were or what to expect. Glancing to my left I saw Roger sitting there relaxed, his feet up on the door frame, appearing unconcerned and bored. I wondered how long it would take for me to look so confident. It wouldn't take long, but I would become apathetic, not confident.

Arriving at our AO (area of operations), our C&C, keeping at a distance so as not to give any sign indicating where the troops would be landing, radioed the direction of the first LZ to our lead gunship. Our three gunships flew in the direction given and confirmed which one of the numerous abandoned rice paddies had been picked for the LZ. Our lead gun then followed a compass heading which would take us to the inbound slicks carrying the infantry into the assault. Artillery rounds were impacting on the LZ as our lead gun turned to escort the ten slicks into the LZ. The slicks were notified they should expect a hot LZ and they were to fly into the landing zone with their door guns firing into the tree lines on both sides of the LZ. My ship stayed to the left of the flight of ten slicks in order to fire rockets into a tree line on their left side when they landed. The other gunship followed the flight and would fire into the right tree line. As the artillery was shut off, the lead gun lost altitude quickly and went into a long power glide as it guided the slicks straight into the LZ. The lead gunship flew with its skids in the grass, its crew chief and gunner trailing smoke from the grenades held in their outboard hands. As they approached the touchdown point, they threw the smoke grenades into the grass and our C&C radioed the lead slick which color marked his landing spot. The ten slicks, trailing a kilometer behind the lead gunship, glided into the LZ, flared slightly and landed quickly. The infantry jumped out, and the slicks took off. They made it look simple.

We had fired only a few pair of rockets into the tree line as we covered the left flank of the assault. But I hadn't been prepared for the noise of the rockets as they left their tubes a meter from my legs. I heard the AC calmly and softly say, "Coming hot." Instantly the blast of the rocket's raspy, coarse roar jolted me, the rocket's igniter cap blowing back and hitting me in the leg. It felt like I'd been shot. Even though Roger had warned me about the caps flying back at us, I wasn't prepared. At the time, I expected I would eventually get accustomed to the rocket's discharge. But I never did. They always surprised me.

As the rockets blasted out of their tubes, I held my fire. Since the slicks were landing on my side of the ship, I couldn't shoot downward so I didn't have to be concerned about shooting a rocket. I had fired several hundred rounds over the rocket tubes into the trees and brush on the right side of the LZ, not seeing any particular target, just hosing down the vegetative cover and hoping to keep the enemy's heads down while our infantry landed. My machine gun functioned perfectly, no jams or misfires. At least my first assault with the gun platoon had gone smoothly. The LZ was not hot; no enemy fire had greeted the insertion. Nothing to this job.

Well, now what? I wondered. The slicks had headed for a nearby fire support base to await orders to either return to pick up these troops or to bring in reinforcements. Their next orders would be determined by what was encountered by the first troops now on the ground. We on the third gun flew to Dau Tieng to rearm and refuel. When we returned, the second gun would head for Dau Tieng and so on. Third gun generally carried the most inexperienced pilots. Sending it back first to refuel and rearm kept an experienced crew out in the AO to act as lead gun. Though I didn't realize it at the time, I later learned that the shape of the LZ and the terrain surrounding it determined the configuration that the slicks flew into the LZ. They didn't just fly in a straight line, landing behind each other. The slick pilots were capable of using one of many types of formations that the pilots prided themselves on being able to fly while still keeping each ship within the distance of the length of a half rotor disk from the rotor disk of the ship ahead of them. The slicks had to land in a tight formation so that the infantry landed at its maximum fighting force. We never saw squads of infantry standing out alone in an LZ because their slick landed outside of the flight formation. Our slicks put them all down together, every time. They didn't just dump their troops and fly out of the LZ haphazardly, either. Their departure had also been preplanned to minimize the danger of flying low and slow over possible enemy positions. Of course, sometimes there were no good choices, but that was part of their job. And, of course, enemy gunfire sometimes stopped slick crews from ever flying out of the LZ, but that, too, was part of their job.

After my ship returned from refueling, we flew our low circles above the heads of the ground troops while I sat gazing out of the doorway with no idea what we were doing or what was happening. It appeared that the infantry was going to wander through an area of low second-growth jungle that had once been laid bare by the Rome plows of our engineers. They were hoping to find a North Vietnamese base camp. Actually, most of the infantry were probably hoping that they wouldn't find it. Our gunships were ten or fifteen meters above them—flying figure eights or circles—trying to find enemy ambushes, equipment or soldiers that would be flushed out of the bush ahead of our infantry. All I saw was a blur of trees, brush and scattered footpaths.

How was I supposed to find anything? Everything looked the same and everything was gray in the early morning light. Where was our infantry and how could I have lost sight of them? If I did see someone with a weapon, how would I know if he was friend or foe? I was not doing a very good job of covering the infantry. But I was new and I would learn.

The other gunship on station radioed that they had found a 122mm rocket set up to be launched. Where? I was looking and looking and saw nothing. Finally, I saw people. And there was the rocket. It was our infantry that I saw; several men carefully checking the rocket for booby traps while their comrades waited patiently on the trail behind them. Obviously, someone had set it up and was ready to launch it, but where were they? The whole North Vietnamese Army could have been down there and I probably wouldn't have seen them. It took time to develop eyes. Eventually, I'd learn to see the hands or parts of faces of people in the bush. A compass reading by the ground troops indicated that the rocket was aimed at a nearby fire support base, so whoever set it up knew what they were doing. After most of the infantry had passed the rocket, a few of the troops at the end of the patrol lingered to destroy it with explosives. Now, certain that there were enemy troops in the area, the infantry moved slowly and cautiously, searching the surrounding shrubs and thickets for the men who had placed the rocket. We couldn't blame them for going slow, as they expected that all the nearby trails were mined or booby-trapped by departing enemy troops.

While the troops on the ground searched the area, the decision was made by the commanders flying above us on our C&C ship to land more troops into another abandoned rice paddy about a kilometer to the southeast of our original LZ. Our slicks were radioed to pick up more infantry and to circle "the Yellow APC" until a gunship came for them. I couldn't imagine what the Yellow APC was. Out in the middle of nowhere, in the nondescript scrub jungle, sat a U.S. Army armored personnel carrier (APC) that had been destroyed by the enemy. No one seemed to know the details of the fight in which it was destroyed, but it was a burned-out hulk that, according to local legend, the VC or NVA had painted yellow. It didn't take much imagination to know the reason for painting it. The VC were telling us, "Think about this, GI. If I can carry yellow paint out here, what else have I carried?" It was a giant warning sign. A bright beacon, it was a recognizable point that our aircraft used as a rendezvous and, for some reason, it seemed to be off limits as a target. I would have expected the APC to be surrounded by bomb craters and pockmarked with dents from machine-gun fire. But the APC just sat there, untouched. Since it was used so often by helicopter units as a rendezvous point, I would have also expected the enemy to place antiaircraft positions nearby, but I never heard of any trouble near "the Yellow APC."

Heading for our rendezvous with the slicks at the Yellow APC, we watched artillery rounds exploding in our new LZ. We had almost made it to the slicks when the C&C called for the guns to return ASAP, and also radioed that one slick with a load of infantry was to drop out of the main flight and accompany the guns. The rest of the slicks were to continue their orbit above the Yellow APC. As the artillery fire ceased, our C&C ship flew over the LZ and found a man staggering around like a drunk. While this could be a trap, it was decided to send one slick into the LZ and have the troops on board capture this man. The gunship crews thought it was a crazy idea; they just wanted to blast him and the LZ. Trying as hard as I could, I didn't even see the man until the slick landed next to him. Several infantrymen jumped out, grabbed him and threw him into the slick. The infantrymen climbed back on board and the slick was immediately in the air, flying the prisoner back to Cu Chi for interrogation.

Since one slick landed unopposed and since there had been a man here, it was decided to land the other nine slicks here also. Where there was one VC, there must be others. Our lead gun returned to the Yellow APC for the slicks while we observed the LZ for any sign of enemy troops. The slicks landed without incident and the troops broke into squad-size units to try to determine where our prisoner had been living. We on the guns divided our time flying overhead cover for both groups of infantry that had been brought into the area. For several hours, the two separated groups of ground troops scoured the terrain of overgrown, abandoned rice paddies and adjacent scrub brush without any results. We flew twenty meters above the infantry in loops and zigzag patterns, looking, looking, looking, and seeing nothing. Maybe gunship duty wasn't going to be what I expected: constant shooting and contact with the enemy. We'd been crisscrossing the same area for quite some time and neither the infantry nor we had found a damn thing. Finding the rocket and the disoriented man must have been flukes. If VC or NVA troops were in the area, surely we would have found them by now.

In my opinion, we were wasting a lot of time and effort looking for an enemy who was probably several kilometers away.

At midday, both groups of infantry were directed to work their way back to their original landing zones to eat lunch and then get ready to be picked up for insertion into different LZs. Number Two gunship would stay with them flying overhead, while Number One and Three guns went to Dau Tieng for refueling and lunch. Our two crews took a half-hour break to eat some C-rations and to stretch our legs a little, then headed back, hoping that the afternoon would be more productive than the morning. I, at least, wanted some action, but the rest of the crew didn't seem to care what type of day we were having. It was just another day at work. Some days are quiet, some aren't.

Returning to our infantry, Number Two gun left for lunch as we prepared for the extraction of the ground troops. They were assembling in small parties to board the slicks for another ride into another landing zone when we were radioed that the mission for the afternoon had changed. Our morning prisoner turned out to be a male nurse who had been slightly shell-shocked by the concussion of artillery rounds hitting our second LZ. He was going to be brought back to where he had been captured so that he could show our infantry the entrance to the underground hospital where he had worked. Our troops at the second LZ would investigate the hospital complex and the troops at the first LZ would stand by as a re-action force, since the hospital was expected to have some type of security force. The NVA nurse was landed at the LZ and guided our ground troops to a thicket concealing a tunnel entrance. Twenty or thirty Americans had walked by it, and we had flown over it numerous times. It looked the same as thousands of other nearby thickets. Everywhere I looked were scattered holes and old fighting positions, any one of which could have led somewhere underground. As the nurse and his escorts disappeared into the tunnel, everyone above ground was alerted to expect the sudden appearance of NVA, who would be flushed from the tunnel complex. Our two gunships on station maneuvered in figure eights and circles, ready to engage anyone scurrying out of a tunnel in a five-hundred-meter radius of the entrance.

As we made our loops in the sky, we periodically came near the tunnel opening. When we passed over their heads, we could see the ground troops had found something in the tunnel; things were being passed up from inside the tunnel and stacked near the entrance. We wondered what was going on underground. There wasn't any fighting occurring in the tunnels, since the troops at the entrance were relaxed and appeared nonchalant. After a half-hour of underground exploration, the men in the tunnel reappeared at the same opening they had entered. One of our slicks soon landed, carrying a squad of engineers with their tools of the trade: high explosives. It had been decided that the tunnel complex was going to be destroyed. The engineers and explosives disappeared into the hole and only the engineers returned. The ground troops and helicopters moved to the side, in case of a secondary explosion, and the traditional cry of "Fire in the hole" came over the radios. Except for a muffled blast followed by smoke pouring out the main tunnel entrance and several nearby holes, it didn't look as if much had happened. If the tunnel and rooms were collapsed, I couldn't tell by looking at the ground surface. The engineers and captured equipment were ferried back to Cu Chi on two slicks, while several of our other slicks brought out field packs and water for the ground troops. They would be staying here searching for an elusive enemy who were hiding under their boots. Our C&C ship and lead gun searched for another LZ for our other troops while the rest of our company helicopters returned to Cu Chi to wait on standby. I would end my first day in the gun platoon without any war stories to tell in the NCO Club.

I would later talk to several of the infantrymen who had entered the hospital complex. They claimed it had been their most eerie experience of the war. None of them had ever seen or heard of a similar complex. After they had crawled down the entrance, they entered a long hallway where they could walk standing almost upright. Candles burned in niches carved in the walls every two meters. Rooms had been excavated to the right and left of the hallway and varied from obvious dispensary rooms to operating rooms and patient quarters. Surgical instruments, covered with fresh blood, lay on the operating table. Blood still dripped from the table into a bucket. In patient rooms, fresh bloody bandages littered the floor and they could smell medication, sweat and urine. It was obvious that people had been in these subterranean rooms minutes before our infantry had entered the complex. Smaller tunnels, without lighting, branched off the main hallway at random intervals and, while a few were tentatively explored, their destinations remained unknown. Because of the scattered AK-47 ammunition dropped in haste on the floor of the tunnel, it was thought that, in addition to patients and hospital staff, a defensive force had also been present. Where was everyone? Also, where were the living quarters for the staff? Every room appeared to serve a medical function, but the staff had to live somewhere and everybody had to eat. Where was the mess hall and food supply? Looking at the ward rooms, they estimated there had been forty or fifty wounded men in the tunnel. Who carried them away? Our guys guessed that counting patients, nurses, doctors, orderlies, cooks and a defensive unit, there had to be at least 125 people minutes ahead of them in the underground maze. None of them was seen either underground or above ground. The captured equipment, books, notebooks and medical supplies gave the officers above ground a sense of accomplishment. Our troops in the tunnel had seen enough. They convinced their officers to destroy the entrance, hallway and medical rooms using high explosives. Not so much to destroy them but to ensure that our troops could get out and not have to search through dark tunnels for over a hundred armed enemy. The whole setup was too damn spooky. Anyone exploring those tunnels would only find death.

My first day on a gunship left me unconfident and demoralized. I hadn't realized how hard it would be to see and track our people on the ground, let alone find the enemy. Everything was a green brushy blur. To make matters worse, the enemy was living underground. Everyone knew about the tunnels, especially around Cu Chi, but I had thought of them as hiding places, not sanctuaries. Local legends stated that the Cu Chi tunnels ran for miles, but it was hard to visualize tunnels under rice paddies, swamps and rivers. Actually, tunnels and underground complexes were not found everywhere, as most terrain was too wet in the monsoon season. However, where conditions were right, with good soils and good elevation, there were miles of them. While I couldn't see into the tunnels, I realized that I would have to learn to be much more observant. It probably wouldn't hurt if I'd learn to monitor the radios as well. I would have known more about the day's activities if I had monitored the infantry radio net more often.

For the next few days, I flew door gunner for Roger and started feeling more comfortable with the routine, even though we hadn't had any contact. We were doing basically the same types of missions as on my first day: flying cover for the infantry, looking for everything, finding nothing. I was then assigned to fly with Art Silacci for two or three days, so I would learn a little about the 40mm armament system on his ship. If Art had guard duty or for some reason couldn't fly, another crew chief would have to replace him and would have to know something about the cannon on the nose of his ship. Since Art would not let anyone else touch his cannon, all we really had to know was how to load it, rearm it and keep ammunition feeding by pushing with the right foot.

Art was one of the quiet, confident types—cool under fire, someone you knew you could depend on. After Roger left our platoon to go home, Art would be the best guy in the platoon. The first day I flew with him, our gunships were no longer working in the scrub jungle habitat, but were flying low over an area of scattered, populated villages and hamlets. Villagers were everywhere, mostly working their fields or puttering around their gardens and living areas. I supposed that the area must be fairly secure since the rice paddies and nearby wooded areas weren't pockmarked from artillery rounds or by bomb craters. We would fly along six or seven meters above the ground, then pop over tree lines or bamboo hedgerows to surprise anyone on the other side. While our helicopters were noisy, this tactic seemed to work. Apparently, it was hard for people on the ground to place where the sound of a low-flying helicopter was actually coming from. When we came up over a tree line, the expressions of the people on the other side left no doubt that they were surprised. Our pilots called this type of work "nerking and gleeping," but I never knew why they did so.

We had been fooling around, looking for VC in this area of hamlets and fields, when Nine Six, our platoon leader, radioed that he had several VC in sight. When he popped up over a tree line, two men in a nearby clearing had immediately thrown their rifles into a hedgerow and were pretending to be civilian farmers hoeing a garden. A third man, without a rifle, had run off carrying a large, flat basket. After calling our C&C ship, permission was granted to kill the two gardeners and to capture the man with the basket. They had been caught with weapons, judged and found guilty. The Second Amendment wasn't acknowledged in Viet Nam. While we waited for permission to kill the two men, one of the farmers left his garden. He had walked through a nearby tree line and was walking as fast as he could toward the village when our first gunship caught him with machine-gun fire. Our ship flew in front of the second farmer, about ten meters above him, and Art fired a short burst of 7.62mm bullets into the man's chest. His white T-shirt turned bright red. Instantly. It was not a little patch of red as in a movie wound, but an instantaneous color change of the whole shirt as the entrance and exit bullet holes drained all of the liquid that his heart could pump. It was a clear visual shock, making me realize that we weren't playing games—this was real. People weren't going to get up and play again in this war game. It was a sobering experience to see a mortal wound inflicted. Perhaps it was because we were so close to the enemy and could see faces. It is not a pleasant experience.

I was amazed he hadn't dropped dead. He didn't even flinch, but just kept on walking. I had never seen a man shot before and I suppose I expected it to be like the movies. People shot by machine guns in the movies are blown backward twenty meters and are dead before their body hits the ground. Not this guy. While we circled around him, Art hit him across the chest with another burst, but he calmly walked out of the garden and over to a well. Reaching the well, he pulled documents from under his bloody shirt and threw them into the well. This guy was impressive. He obviously had something important to protect and, even if he was shot, he was going to make it difficult for anyone to get the documents. Another short burst from Art's gun put this dedicated gentleman down. We had two men down, and one to capture.

Our lead gun spotted the man with the basket crossing a large, open rice paddy with no place to hide. Since he was in the middle of the rice paddy and appeared to be unarmed, our C&C ship radioed our platoon leader to capture the man. Our ship flew tight circles above the man as our lead gun flew underneath us and quickly landed in the paddy next to him. The crew chief and gunner ran over to him, grabbed him and his basket, then put him on their ship. I recall thinking it seemed like such a waste of time to grab an old farmer when the lead gun radioed that the basket held a pistol, several hand grenades and a large amount of Vietnamese money. We were told later that the man was a local VC tax collector and the other two men were his bodyguards. While the lead gun took our prisoner to Cu Chi, our ship headed back to our two kills to wait for an infantry squad from the unit we were working with that day to confirm the kills and to retrieve the weapons out of the hedgerow. As we were waiting for two slicks to bring in some infantry, I received my next lesson.

All new guys on the guns were broken in by having them machine-gun any of the enemy that were shot. I hadn't had this opportunity while flying with Backes for the previous three days, since things had been slow. After talking with people who served in other units, I learned that this was a common practice throughout Viet Nam for gunship crews and for scout crews on light observation helicopters (LOH or "loach"). The theory seemed to be that new people must acclimate themselves to blood and death. Some units literally had new crewmen cut corpses in half with machine-gun fire, but the Stingers were satisfied with several bursts across the carcass. Perhaps the philosophy may have been to ensure joint responsibility. Plenty of men, on both sides, had survived multiple machine-gun wounds, so there was always the possibility that the second shooter did the killing. Whatever the reason, it didn't bother me to fire into blood-soaked bodies, but it did seem like a waste of ammunition. I suppose it was good training.

VII

After several days of Roger and Art teaching me the fine points of basic aerial combat duties of a door gunner, I was ready to be put on the daily flight roster as the crew chief on a gunship with someone else sitting at the right door as the gunner. Now I would be doing most of the shooting at individual targets and throwing hand grenades at bunkers. It hadn't looked difficult watching the other guys do it, but like anything else, watching something being done and doing it yourself are two different things. Roger was going to take some slack time and not fly so often, since he was almost ready to go home. I would be flying as crew chief on his gunship to give him a break, and I learned immediately that flying at the left door position was completely different from flying at the right door. I hadn't realized how much more of the terrain would now be visible to me as I sat in the open doorway positioned on the low side of our normal circular hunting patterns. There was so much more to see and so much more terrain to search. Sitting on the right door side as gunner, I had found it difficult to watch my side of the ship. At the left door position I was finding even more to watch. As the primary shooter, I had to be aware of everything going on around us. For example, if I was told by the AC to put some rounds next to the tall tree in the hedgerow, I better know exactly which hedgerow and which tree he was talking about. Even the shooting wasn't as exciting as I expected. Shooting looked so easy when someone else did it, but trying to keep on a single target was not as easy as it looked, especially when excited. Of course, flying with an experienced gunner didn't make things easier—they had little patience with new crew chiefs. Many a gunner slammed the top of my flight helmet with one of the extra machine-gun barrels after I missed an easy shot. After more experience and shootouts with enemy troops, I learned how to use my weapon effectively, but I never did become better than an average shooter with a machine gun. Roger or Art would nonchalantly fire a five-round burst at an enemy soldier and drop him in his tracks. Not me. People who owned stock in ammunition companies made money when I was doing the shooting.

My first mission as a gunship crew chief was somewhere west of Cu Chi, near the Cambodian border. I recall flying over the burned ruins of a sizable Catholic church near our AO and wondering if it had been destroyed by us, VC, ARVN, or maybe the French. The church looked out of place, sitting by itself along an overgrown weedy canal. There didn't appear to be any population base nearby, no village or town to support such a large church. I suppose the nearest village had also been destroyed, but a large church should have had more evidence nearby of past prosperity. There were no signs of any active farms or hamlets anywhere in the locality. Abandoned, overgrown rice paddies stretched as far as one could see. Shrubbery lined the rice paddy dikes and, at almost every intersection of two dikes, I could see a poorly camouflaged bunker. Some of the bunkers had holes in their roofs from being attacked with high explosives, but most didn't. Who knew which of them sheltered people as we flew over? We were looking for troops infiltrating into Viet Nam from Cambodia, and we could expect to find them resting or hiding in any of the numerous bunkers or tree lines that we flew over. It was like looking for a needle in a haystack.

Scattered randomly throughout the abandoned rice paddies were small elevated areas from which sprouted semi-demolished homes. The entire area appeared to have once been the home of prosperous farming families; the randomly scattered ruins indicated that these homes were originally solid walled, clay tile–roofed buildings. There were none of the homes with straw-thatched roofs and walls commonly seen in most villages. Every ruined home showed signs of heavy damage from explosives and small arms fire. Scanning the terrain, it was easy to see that this area had been the scene of heavy fighting at some time in the past. A quick glance in any direction showed a vacant, unpopulated countryside, scarred by artillery fire and pockmarked with large holes left by detonated Air Force bombs. The bomb craters generally occurred in small groups and were usually near a position that I could visualize someone defending. The craters were not scattered along a long line like a B-52 strike: each group had probably been the result of an individual firefight. Scanning the countryside showed that hundreds of firefights had occurred in this area over the years. It made me think a little: What had all those fights accomplished? Why were we still going out into the same area to fight again? The more experienced troops claimed they could tell how long ago fighting had occurred by noting the color of the water in the bomb craters. The deepest aquamarine color appeared in the freshest craters, while older craters were dirty brown. They claimed the chemicals in the bombs caused the aquamarine color and I suppose they were right. Coming from a coal mining area, I knew that the abandoned coal mining pits back in Pennsylvania were the same aquamarine color because of the low pH and minerals in the water.

We had covered our slicks when they dropped troops into this haunted landscape of bunkers, hedgerows, and ruins. The infantry slowly maneuvered through the overgrown rice paddies, while we flew circles around their line of march. I was looking, looking and looking, but not seeing anything except brush, rice and the ruins of homes. One gunship had left to refuel, and my ship was flying behind our lead gun, constantly searching ahead of the infantry, taking the hedgerows apart with our eyes. For some reason, I happened to look backward and noticed two trees running across the rice paddy. Hitting the floor button to activate my helmet intercom, I shouted, "There's two trees running behind us!"

"Get them!" the AC yelled, while I leaned out to shoot behind us. Empty brass cartridge cases were flying everywhere as I kept my finger tight on the trigger of my machine gun until our aircraft turned slightly right, obscuring my view of the running trees.

"Hold your rate of fire down. You're going to use up all your ammo," the AC advised loudly. Looking at the minigun can between my legs, I saw that I only had about 200 rounds of ammunition left. I had just fired 1,500 rounds of machine-gun ammo at two men and had missed them. The lead gun was in sight of my running trees and starting to roll in on them with rockets. I expected that we would follow with a gun run also, but before we could start our run, our third gunship came back on station from refueling. My AC was told to head for Duc Hoa to refuel and rearm. New on the job, I thought it unfair that we had to leave—it was our ship that had spotted the running enemy troops. We should have been allowed to participate in the kill. I didn't realize that killing men was so common to the rest of the platoon that no one considered missing out on kills anything to be concerned about. There were a lot more where they came from: Cambodia.

When we returned from refueling at Duc Hoa, two bodies with their nipa palm camouflage still attached floated in the shallow shoreline of a nearby river. Instead of hiding or fighting from the brush along the river, both men had attempted to swim away from the two gunships and didn't succeed. While I was still unhappy that we hadn't been in on the kill, I would learn that as long as the platoon got the kill, it didn't matter who did the actual killing. If you didn't get this one, you might get the next. None of them meant anything anyway. As we always said, "Don't mean nothing." Of course, the two guys floating facedown in the river probably wouldn't have agreed. The lesson for the day was that you might as well stand and fight as run away—you're going to die anyway.

Several days later, I participated in a rarity for our company—a night combat assault. These types of missions were probably rare because of the difficulty of performing such an assault without mishaps. Daylight assaults were bad enough; doing one in the dark was asking for trouble. Too many things could go wrong. But this one went smoothly. Heavy artillery fire had prepared the landing zone, and flares dropped continuously from overhead helicopters tried to make the night into day for the landing infantry. But while the flares did light up the rice fields, huge shadows hid the surrounding tree lines and hedgerows. Our platoon was trying to protect the ten slicks unloading their troops, but none of us could see into the dark shadows along the trees and brush. Luckily, the LZ was cold and, as soon as the infantry dispersed, we were sent home to Cu Chi. It had been an eerie experience, flying at treetop level, with flares above us, dark shadows concealing anyone who might be hiding in the tree lines. Everyone was tense, waiting for multiple bursts of AK-47 rifle fire to erupt from the shadows at any moment. Flying several meters higher than the nearby trees and caught in the brightness of the drifting flares, we had to have been great targets. But the enemy wasn't in our LZ.

Going back to Cu Chi was a different matter, however. Several times on our trip home, NVA .51-caliber machine-gun crews floated their distinctive green tracers up into the sky, attempting to bring us down to their level. While I knew that the .51-caliber bullets were only a half-inch in diameter, they appeared the size of large garbage cans as they crawled slowly toward my ship. I never could understand why tracers appeared so different depending on which way they were headed. Firing at someone, the red tracers used in our guns zipped along to the target, but the green enemy tracers seemed to take forever to reach us. I suppose all good things are slow to arrive.

Helicopter crews feared the .51-caliber or 12.7mm machine gun. Legend had it that no one was ever wounded by a fifty-one, only killed. When people were hit, they lost limbs or major organs. Helicopters hit by enemy fifty-ones would fall out of the sky in flames or tumble toward the ground out of control to explode on contact with the earth. These BIG bullets had power behind them and could go through the crew chief and his chest armor, then through the transmission and continue through the gunner and his armor. Helicopters caught in a crossfire of fifty-ones were literally chewed apart. The slow rate of fire from the .51-caliber was similar to a heartbeat, and its solid "thumps" kept cadence with your pulse. Supposedly, the Communists picked the diameter size so that they could fire captured stocks of our .50-caliber ammunition back at us, and we couldn't fire captured enemy .51-caliber ammunition back at them. They did the same thing with their mortars: we used 81mm mortars, they used 82mm mortars. We had to admit that the Commies weren't stupid after all.

The fifty-one machine guns firing at us that night were not engaged by our guns; their locations were just marked on our maps. We forwarded the information to military intelligence. They would send someone out to look for the machine-gun crews. Odds were that these guns and their crews would be hidden underground or kilometers away by the time anyone came after them, but several of the enemy machine-gun crews already had troops after them when we passed above their positions. While we were flying past an ongoing fight between an NVA unit and one of our mechanized infantry units, several lines of green tracers lifted away from the fight and started climbing toward the lights of our ships. They probably thought that we were coming to help the infantry unit, but we couldn't raise our troops on the radio and were therefore unable to help them. This sort of thing happened all the time: tracers came at us but we could do nothing. Just sit and watch the tracers; we couldn't shoot back unless we knew the exact location of our own troops.

After landing at Cu Chi following our night assault, our ships were checked for combat damage, refueled, and rearmed. The crews were then allowed to grab a little sleep prior to the morning mission and the start of another day. The next day consisted of searching jungle pathways and stream banks with tired, burning eyes, seeing nothing of interest, but perhaps missing important signs not obvious to our bloodshot eyes. Coming home that evening, we were flying near

the notorious enemy-controlled village of Trang Bang when
we noticed farmers digging doughnut holes in the fields.
They seemed to be digging holes about three meters in diameter, a meter deep and leaving a column of dirt a meter in diameter in the middle. The crew on my ship had never seen
anything like this and we wondered what they were doing.
We found out the following day that the doughnut holes were
antiaircraft positions for .51-caliber machine guns and that
several helicopters from the 25th Infantry Division had taken
heavy fire from these positions the night after we had seen
them being dug. Perhaps we should have reported these
doughnut holes.

Several days later, we were working nearby with an American infantry unit that was planning to land their troops adjacent to a MACV compound near Trang Bang. Like most
MACV compounds in this area, it appeared to be a small village protected by an earth berm concealing bunkers and
fighting positions behind several rows of barbed wire. Our
C&C ship was unable to make radio contact with the compound and our crew joked about the MACV staff sleeping in
late and letting Vietnamese, who spoke no English, monitor
the radios. C&C decided to proceed with the landing next to
the compound. That should wake them up.

Our lead gun came flying in low, just above the rice paddy
dikes, and marked the LZ with two smoke grenades. The LZ
was an open rice field three hundred meters east of the quiet
MACV compound. Ten slicks quickly touched down behind
the billowing colored smoke to unload their troops and were
immediately surrounded by bullets raising puffs of dust in
the ground all around them. *What the hell is happening?* I
thought. The entire bunker line on the side of the compound
facing our troops had opened fire. Muzzle flashes could be
seen at the firing port of every bunker. We, on the two flanking gunships, immediately flew between the infantry and the
bunker line in order to draw fire away from the ground troops
and our slicks.

"Don't shoot! Don't shoot! They're supposed to be
friendly," yelled our AC. I held my machine gun tight, finger

off the trigger, watching the muzzle flashes of automatic weapons aimed at me. I was disciplined and held my fire. I was still so green I didn't comprehend what all the flashes in the firing ports meant—they were shooting at me. Returning enemy gunfire when told to ignore it would have been the end of my days in the gun platoon. I imagine it is hard for civilians to realize how disciplined our soldiers really were. Young men wouldn't be in our platoon very long if they couldn't lean back, put their feet up on the bulkhead, light a cigarette and calmly stare into automatic weapon fire.

What a screwup! Our slicks had made it out of the landing zone but they were probably riddled with bullet holes. The infantry were lying behind the rice paddy dikes, wondering what was going on and hoping someone on the C&C ship could turn off the bullets coming from the bunkers. Since even the RF/PF wouldn't think of us as an NVA helicopter assault, it was obvious that the VC controlled this compound. We flew by several times and drew heavy fire each pass, but always held our own fire.

My ship left to refuel and, while refueling at Cu Chi, I noticed a bullet hole in our engine. It didn't look too bad and, since we flew into the refueling point with the bullet hole, we figured that we could fly back to the company flight line. Luckily, we made it. We quickly parked my ship, threw our gear into Art's helicopter parked at the next revetment and headed back out with his ship. This was going to be interesting: assaulting one of our own bunker lines. We had almost made it back to Trang Bang when our platoon was diverted to another mission. Apparently, the MACV compound was going to be surrounded by American armored units and gunships weren't needed anymore.

At the time, I found it very frustrating to start a fight, then not finish it. I would never even learn what happened after we left, but I would learn that such occurrences were very common. Gunships were constantly pulled from one firefight to another, and there were many times when we'd wonder what the final result had been on a mission where we'd fight for hours and then be told to leave to help some other group of infantrymen in another fight. Our mobility led us to answer calls for gun support several times a day, and rather than facing the normal, single, quick, hot firefight of the infantry, we could and would see several such actions some days.

I was learning my trade as a crew chief when, to my disappointment, I was told to start flying as the crew chief on our platoon smokeship. "Smokey" was used to fly horseshoe smoke screens around the slicks when they were landing in an LZ. Our smokeship was unusual in that it was a UH-1C gunship outfitted with the standard smokeship oil tank and equipment to pump oil into the hot engine exhaust. While most units didn't use them at all, every other smokeship that I encountered seemed to be a UH-1H slick. I believe that our platoon used the UH-1C for a smokeship instead of using a slick, because once it was airborne, it could maneuver faster and tighter than the UH-1H.

I wasn't thrilled to be flying on Smokey; it was a target, not a hunter/killer. Its purpose was not only to hide the landing slicks and infantry, but to draw fire. I had watched Smokey perform when I was on a slick touching down in an LZ, and my first impression was that it wouldn't last two minutes in a hot LZ. Since Smokey had a reputation for being shot down frequently, my impression was probably right. Actually, the reason no one wanted to be crew chief on Smokey was because the crew chief had to spend most of his time between LZs sitting around waiting. Then at the end of the day, he had to scrub down the helicopter for hours to get rid of the oil and soot covering the tail boom. Whoever flew on Smokey smelled like Smokey. Because of incomplete combustion of oil in the exhaust, lubrication by the oil was causing every rivet on the tail boom to become loose. Loose rivets on a helicopter could be a disaster. While Art's 40mm cannon on his gunship's nose was causing splits in structural pieces all over the front of his aircraft, Smokey seemed to be on the verge of splitting its whole tail boom. You can't fly very far without the tail boom.

I figured I had no choice. It was fly on the smokeship or

nothing. I would pay my dues and put up with Smokey until I could get my own gunship. Garcia had warned me that Smokey was usually used as a test. Screw up on Smokey and you're out of the gun platoon. For several weeks, Smokey was mine, but whatever happened in the past on smokeship runs wasn't happening now. Every LZ was cold. We would go out with the guns in the morning to scout the LZs, do our horseshoe smoke run, then go back and sit with the slicks until it was time to pick up troops again. While the slicks were picking up their passengers, we'd do a quick flyby of the next LZ to determine our flight path to maximize the smoke screen for the slicks as they landed with the infantry. We'd do our job, lay down smoke and shoot into trees and hedgerows, and then go sit at the nearest airfield or fire support base and listen to the radios.

I recall sitting on Smokey one morning as we were shut down at some forgotten fire support base and overhearing a radio transmission from Stinger Nine-Nine, Pat Ronan, to our C&C ship. Pat was asking for permission to kill two men hiding in a bamboo thicket. Nine-Nine was told to mark them with a smoke grenade instead. As we were working in the Trang Bang area, which was notorious for VC and NVA, Pat tried to convince the C&C crew that these two men were probably armed. He wanted to shoot them—not mark them.

"Mark them with smoke," C&C ordered.

Several minutes later, we monitored a radio message full of the roar of machine-gun fire and Pat calmly saying, "Smoke is out. Smoke marks two dead men. Two wounded on board and we are headed for Charlie Charlie."

As Nine-Nine's gunship came in low to throw a smoke grenade on top of the two men, they had both reached for their trusty AK-47s and shot up the ship. Two crewmen were wounded, but not seriously, and the two VC died.

The guns were having all the fun and excitement, while the Smokey crew sat around with the Frog Killers. We called the slick crews Frog Killers to annoy them, insinuating that the only kills they ever got were the frogs beneath their skids in the LZs. We were only kidding, however; none of us wanted their job. While I respected the men in the slick platoons, I wanted to be out with my platoon. Sitting around with the slicks made me feel like a second-class member of the gun platoon. It hadn't been that long ago that I had been hoping to fly on any helicopter, but having already experienced the excitement of flying on the gunships, I wasn't satisfied with Smokey. I wanted to be out with the rest of the platoon: hunting armed men. We did have a minigun mounted in the left door of Smokey for the crew chief to use but it rarely worked. After flying a few days on the smokeship, I thought if I could get the minigun working, maybe my smokeship could spend time out with the gunships instead of sitting with the slicks. Whenever I was back at Cu Chi, I tried to help Garcia get it working. Garcia and several pilots had been trying to make it function properly for quite some time but kept experiencing an electrical problem they couldn't solve. Garcia gave me a variety of wiring harnesses and several electrical circuit boards to test out in the field, but nothing we tried would cure the problem. When the gun fired, we had no idea what we had done right, and when it didn't fire, we had no idea what was wrong. Eventually, the minigun went into storage. More than likely, the gun wouldn't fire during a smoke run because the pump sending oil to the exhaust was drawing too much electrical power. It was probably a simple thing to fix, but there was no one to teach us how to fix such simple problems.

On a mission near the Michelin Rubber Plantation at Dau Tieng, we sat around on Smokey watching our gunships constantly coming in to refuel and rearm. Whatever they were doing, it had to beat sitting and waiting. Late in the afternoon one of the gunships landed with engine trouble and wasn't able to take off, so our crew thought we'd get to join the guns for the rest of the day. No such luck; the mission was almost over and we'd all be going back to Cu Chi soon. The broken-down gunship would be carried back to Cu Chi by a large Chinook helicopter, as Dau Tieng was not considered a safe place for a helicopter to sit overnight. The VC would probably hit it with mortars or recoilless rifle fire; in fact, some of the infantry sitting around our slicks had just been showing us pictures they had recently found in some bunkers near Dau Tieng of female 75mm recoilless rifle teams. Our AC told our fellow platoon members to throw their gear on Smokey and hang around with us for a ride to Cu Chi. "No thanks" was their reply.

They would rather ride in a relatively clean slick than our smelly, oily smokeship. Even our own platoon didn't want to associate with us. Laughing, they headed for the clean slick and the ride home. They never made it. Fifteen minutes after leaving us, the slick fell out of the sky next to an artillery FSB. There were no survivors. Witnesses on the ground saw a black puff of smoke come out of the passenger/cargo area moments before the slick fell to the ground. Black smoke indicated that a hand grenade might have exploded inside. Maybe it was a lucky hit with an RPG. We would never know.

Christmas Day, 1968, would be one of my last flights on Smokey. As a gesture of goodwill, we were told the VC promised to release several captured Americans on Christmas Day. The release site was to be in one of the hundreds of jungle clearings near Tay Ninh. The VC promised to radio the location of the release site some time on Christmas Day and said an American helicopter would have thirty minutes to land and pick up the prisoners. All Christmas Day, there was a slick waiting at Tay Ninh for the radio transmission to pick up the prisoners. But as soon as it had picked up its passengers from the VC, twenty slickloads of troops were going to land into the same clearing. The 116th Assault Helicopter Company and the 187th Assault Helicopter Company lined the Tay Ninh runway along with two companies of infantry. Our crews and the infantry played cards, talked and napped all Christmas Day, waiting to go into a very hot LZ. We expected that the VC would pick a landing zone they could defend and, while we joked about our Christmas present for the VC, we fully expected it to be a bad day for us also. Late in the afternoon, the VC called: the prisoners would not be released. The slicks were told to take the infantry home to their fire support base. The guns and Smokey were told to go home. What a letdown. We were on adrenaline, nervous for action, and then nothing. The prisoners would be released a few days later, after a radio call from the VC gave the Americans listening fifteen minutes to pick them up.

"Well, let's head home," said our AC, as we bitched and moaned about wasting the day sitting on the runway. Leaving Tay Ninh, we flew over to the Cao Dai Temple in the nearby village of Long Hoa. The Cao Dai were a local religion that none of us could figure out. Apparently, they worshiped most gods and had an eclectic mixture of saints, such as Victor Hugo, Joan of Arc, Shakespeare and Sun Yat-sen. It was said that their religion combined Buddhism, Confucianism, Taoism, Hinduism, Christianity and Islam. Since they had their own private army, they must have adopted some Norse gods as well. American soldiers were not allowed anywhere near the temple, probably because we were barbarians and wouldn't have recognized the names of their saints. While it was a Vietnamese temple, I never talked to any Vietnamese who had actually been inside. Out of curiosity, we used to fly next to the temple to try to look inside, but we never got a very good look at it. It really didn't appear to be that different from other local religious buildings. But I don't recall it being decorated with swastikas, like most other local temples.

Shortly after passing the temple, flying slightly above tree-top level and skimming over thatched hooches and gardens, I looked down and saw a North Vietnamese soldier in uniform carrying an AK-47 assault rifle. He was walking out of the back of a destroyed American armored personnel carrier that had been abandoned in the bush. Time seemed to stop. I suppose that we were only over him momentarily and then gone in seconds, but I distinctly remember him looking up at me while his hands went to the AK-47 at his side. Holding on to the machine-gun pistol grip with my right hand, my finger on the trigger, I raised my left hand to wave. His hands stayed on his gun and the gun stayed at his side.

"Merry Christmas, Luke the Gook. I'll see you some other

day," I said to myself as I waved to my enemy. I still believe that if he had raised his AK, I could have cut him down. I never told a soul about seeing him and letting him live. We flew low-level back home and, except for cutting down some palm trees with our rotor blades on the trip back to Cu Chi, our ride home was uneventful. The gunner and I were strongly advised by our AC not to mention the palm trees to anyone.

VIII

The day after Christmas I was assigned to be the permanent crew chief on the gunship that carried the miniguns, tail number 440. Perhaps it was a reward for letting the NVA soldier live on Christmas Day. Like most of our ships, 440 was always referred to by its tail number. A few others were referred to by the name painted on the ship such as *Big Daddy, Here Come da Judge,* or *Good Vibrations.* I always regretted not naming my ship *Naglfar,* the mythical Norse ship that carries the dead into Hell and is constructed of the fingernails of dead men. Getting my own gunship was the best Christmas present I could have received. I would rarely fly again on an oily, smelly smokeship. I finally felt I was a member of the gun platoon.

Dale Gilchrest, a thin, quiet Texan, was assigned to be my permanent gunner because he seemed to be the only person interested in learning how to keep the miniguns functioning. Dale had already served several years in country as a combat engineer and had recently been assigned to the 116th after he extended for another six months' duty in Viet Nam. He had extended, in part to fly as a machine gunner, but also to complete the paperwork necessary to marry his Vietnamese girlfriend. The military frowned on marrying local girls and made it extremely difficult for men to receive permission to do so. The system made it virtually impossible for anyone to complete the necessary paperwork required to get married in the normal one-year tour of duty, so most men who wanted to get married had to extend for an additional six months' duty in country.

Dale kept our machine guns and miniguns functioning while I was responsible for the helicopter. He was one of those quiet, brave soldiers who are a constant inspiration to those around them. I never heard him complain, no matter how bad things were. We soon learned to work together as a team and to depend on each other. Because of the complexity of the minigun system, Dale did not rotate ships like most gunners but was permanently assigned to my ship. He was the reason that our ship performed as a gunship, not me. If the NVA were on the right side of our ship, I never gave them a second thought. When the shooting started, he was the guy I wanted on my right side. I trusted him with my life then and would trust him with it today. We faced a lot of enemy gunfire during our days and a lot of whiskey during our evenings together. While we spent entire days together, we rarely talked. Monitoring the radios didn't allow much chance to talk on the job. After a few days together, we became a good team. Soon we had a fairly good gunship.

It would have been a great gunship if it had had a decent engine. The engine didn't have sufficient power, and our pilots would embarrass me with their complaints about its performance. I felt responsible for my ship's weak engine and used to beg our engine repairmen for another engine. Our maintenance crew was excellent, but they couldn't find anything wrong when they checked the engine. Even though they would not give it a new engine, no matter what they tried they couldn't boost the strength of 440's tired power plant. The standard cures of pouring water into the inlet of the running engine or shoveling walnut shells into the inlet didn't help at all. The engine wasn't dirty, just weak. All gunships were overloaded and had a difficult time getting airborne, but our other guns could hover like an unloaded slick compared to 440. Every time we tried to take off, we dragged our skids, raising clouds of dust, then hopped and bounced for every inch of elevation to reach the magical point of translational lift where a helicopter becomes a real flying machine. If your only experiences with helicopters were watching them on television or riding a slick out of a tight

LZ in triple-canopy jungle then you would be correct in expecting a helicopter to just go straight up into the air and fly away. Not a gunship in 1968. Never happened.

On a typically scorching hot day in the dry season, when all helicopters have a hard time becoming airborne, 440 became trapped in a rice paddy. We had landed in a dry paddy outside of an ARVN base to take a short lunch break. When we tried to leave, we couldn't fly over the four-foot dike around the rice paddy. The dry harvested rice paddy was not long enough for us to build up our speed enough to leap over it. It was damned embarrassing. After burning off fuel and throwing out half of our minigun ammunition to the ARVN troops in order to lower our weight, we finally managed to clear the dike and rejoin our platoon. We had learned a lesson: don't park in short rice paddies with high dikes.

Whatever the shortcomings of our gunship, Dale and I worked together. We were determined to make 440 the best gunship in the best gunship platoon in country. In the morning we would have water and food on board, windows waxed (so the pilots wouldn't have to use the wipers in the rain) and the helicopter ready whenever our pilots arrived. At the end of the day, whoever finished their work first, either on the guns or on the helicopter, helped the other complete his work so that our ship was ready to fly into combat immediately. We never left the flight line unless the ship was ready for the next day. It didn't matter if it was our ship or if we had used another ship that day, it would be ready to go before we left the flight line each night.

As with any gunship in combat, refueling and rearming showed how well a crew functioned. We were damned good. Since we flew three gunships on station, one at a time would break to refuel and rearm. The faster this could be accomplished, the more firepower was available at our work site. For example, if we were in contact with the enemy, the third gun, the first to go back for fuel and ammo, would expend its entire ammunition load before departing, thereby conserving the ammo of the two ships that remained on station. The third gun would depart, and on landing at the nearest refueling point, the skids would barely touch the ground when the gunner and crew chief were out, opening the pilots' doors and sliding their side armor back. Either the crew chief or gunner started refueling, while the other started carrying ammunition for machine guns and miniguns. With the ship running, the rotor blades turning, both pilots jumped out and loaded the rocket tubes. Since the rocket tubes loaded easily, the pilots would then help carry 7.62mm ammo to be loaded into the minigun trays. As soon as the pilots would climb back into their seats, their seat armor would be slid forward and their doors closed, and we'd be dragging skids down the runway and up in the air again. When it had to be done fast because someone in the field needed us, it was amazing how quickly we could rearm and refuel. If things were really hot, we just dumped belts of machine-gun ammunition on the floor and left as soon as the fuel tanks were full. Dale and I could load the machine-gun ammo into the minigun trays while flying to join the action. As soon as our ship started dragging its skids along the runway, the pilot would radio the platoon that our ship was "up" to let our lead gun know we were on our way. Once we came into visual contact with our platoon, Number Two gun headed back and so on. Of course, all three ships rotating back and forth only worked if we were all flyable and not full of bullet holes. If only one or two of the gunships were still flying, we did the best we could.

During my time at Cu Chi, whenever 440 was scheduled to fly, Dale and I were usually both on board. While our pilots changed from day to day, it was rare for one of us to fly without the other. All of the pilots in the platoon flew with us occasionally, but two warrant officers flew with us more than the others: Patrick Ronan as AC and Clifford Wright as pilot. Pat was known as "The Fossil" because of his advanced age, but Cliff Wright was an ancient old man in our company. Pat was twenty-six and Cliff was twenty-eight: most of the other guys were nineteen or twenty. All pilots in the gun platoon flew 440 at one time or another, mainly to use the miniguns, but I remember Pat and Cliff better. I just liked being out in the AO with these two old men. They were both fearless and fun to be with. Probably because both of them had been enlisted men for years prior to becoming officers and pilots, they always treated Dale and me as partners on a gun team. Pat or Cliff generally tried to brief us every morning on the day's mission: where we were going, what we were trying to do, and which way to walk home if shot down. Admittedly little things, but most officers didn't bother to tell the enlisted crew anything about the day's mission. Not that it mattered that much, since after a while, no one cared what the mission was. Every day was just another day at work. It was nice to know, however, which way to start walking if we had to.

November and December of 1968 were relatively quiet in our area of operations, but for those who could read them, the signs were pointing to increased enemy activity. A brigade of the 1st Cavalry Division had recently moved into the area and had based some of their troops at Cu Chi. The cavalrymen all appeared lean and mean and looked like they meant business. Their troops appeared confident and their helicopters were stripped down to basics—no seats or seat belts for passengers, for example. Everything appeared functional for battle, with no frills. They looked like us. None of the shiny, waxed birds coming out of rear base camps near Saigon that were used to taxi VIPs and supplies. Small, lime-green, zinc-chromate patches randomly speckled the fuselage of their ships. The patches covered bullet holes; their helicopters, like ours, were used for the real thing—combat.

Sometime in 1968, a brigade of the 101st Airborne had also moved into the Cu Chi area. Obviously, something big was anticipated. We knew two additional brigades must have been relocated to this area of III Corps for a reason. Possibly, the only reason was to ensure that Tet '69 would not be a repeat of Tet '68 in the Saigon area. The North Vietnamese Army was obviously operating in the area as these two brigades found the trouble they came into III Corps to find, with plenty left over for those of us who were there first.

Late 1968 was the calm before the storm. The year 1969 would bring increased enemy activity with each passing week. New Year's was celebrated at Cu Chi the same as at all Army compounds. At midnight, almost every soldier on the compound grabbed his M-16 rifle and fired a magazine of tracers into the sky. The entire bunker line fired flares to light up the darkness surrounding our camp. The next morning, the Stingers opened up our 1969 ledger by catching three NVA soldiers in an open field and firing the rockets from three gunships at them. As the dust from the rockets cleared, all that was left of the three running men was a lower torso and legs clad in a scorched NVA uniform hanging on a tree limb. It was done to show off, because the ship that I was in was carrying two generals who wanted to observe gunships in action. There was no malice intended. The NVA soldiers would have been just as dead from one rocket, but sixty-six rockets were our New Year's Day fireworks and our way of ignoring the New Year's Day Truce.

The additional two brigades operating within III Corps didn't seem to compress our work areas or lessen our workload. As far as work sites went, '69 was no different from '68: we continued to work all over III Corps and once in a while in IV Corps, the Mekong Delta. Going to the Delta was considered a treat since we would stop and eat at the U.S. Navy compound at Nha Be. While the Army operated on minimum rations, the Navy and Marine Corps were rumored to be supplied with a ration and a half per man per meal. Soldiers entering a Navy mess hall didn't know how to answer when asked, "What do you want to eat?" Since when was there a choice? Steak and eggs for breakfast was a real choice at Nha Be. When we went on a Navy compound, we knew how the South Vietnamese soldiers felt when they visited our compound.

Even though we were stationed at the headquarters compound for the 25th Infantry Division, we were also assigned to work with all of the other infantry units working nearby. We flew all over III Corps and northern IV Corps, working with the 1st Cavalry, the 1st Infantry, 9th Infantry, 11th Armored Cavalry Regiment, 25th Infantry, 82nd Airborne, 101st Airborne, 199th Infantry Brigade, MACV advisers with

Vietnamese soldiers and U.S. Marine advisers with Vietnamese Marines. I supported a lot of infantry operations and
personally liked the 1st Cav., 25th Inf., and 101st Airborne
the best. Most of us didn't like working with either the 82nd
Airborne because they claimed all kills as their own, or the
Marines because it broke our hearts to watch them waste the
lives of their own people.

Working north of Bien Hoa, I watched Art Silacci shoot a
Viet Cong guerrilla who had jumped up along a hedgerow
with a weapon in his hands. Art fired a short burst and the
man fell forward into the rice paddy. Only in the movies does
small arms fire throw someone backward when it contacts
human flesh. When someone is hit by a bullet, his knees usually buckle immediately, then the body collapses. As always,
even though we could see the dead man sprawled in the dirt,
we wouldn't be credited with a kill unless our infantry confirmed it. The platoon of 82nd Airborne troops that walked
up to confirm the kill sprayed the body with M-16 rounds
and claimed the kill. Since the 82nd was being used as a defensive brigade for Tan Son Nhut Airport, they didn't have
much contact with enemy troops. They consistently claimed
our kills, perhaps to make their brigade look better. Since our
platoon had faced the man when he had been alive and
armed, we weren't happy when other troops claimed him
when he was dead. We got over it.

As for the Marines, we flew some missions supporting
U.S. Marine advisers with Vietnamese Marines, and if all
U.S. Marine forces worked like they did, I'd never want to be
in the Marine Corps. One hot afternoon we were called away
from our assigned mission and told to fly nearby to support a
Marine unit in contact. We found a Vietnamese Marine platoon pinned down behind a dike in a harvested rice paddy,
taking heavy automatic weapons fire from several bunkers
and fighting positions dug into a hedgerow a hundred meters
in front of them. We were flying circles above them and there
were several fire support bases nearby for artillery support.
Rather than use gunships or artillery to knock out the bunkers,
the American Marine advisers radioed us to stand by while

their troops attempted to take the bunkers. As a Marine squad ran toward the bunkers, still carrying their full field packs, the NVA dropped them in their tracks. They attempted the same foolish maneuver several times: after losing twelve men killed in action, they decided to let us hit the bunkers. We took out the bunkers and fighting positions in a few minutes and then were released without even a "thank you" from the Marines. Flying back to our original work site, I silently wondered why the Vietnamese Marines needed Western advisers to tell them to run straight into machine guns. They sure were lucky to have Americans telling them what to do. I was disgusted with what I had just seen and wondered what my officers thought of this little firefight. A dumb ass Spec 5, I knew that I could have outflanked those fighting positions if I had been on the ground. It was bad enough not to use either the available gunships flying overhead or the nearby artillery on the bunkers, but to make the troops run across open rice paddies into machine-gun fire while carrying full packs was murder. I was told later they didn't even need their packs that day, since they were only out for an afternoon walk and would be returning to their compound in the evening. If that was the way the Marine Corps fought, they would need more than a few good men to replace their losses.

Maybe the 82nd Airborne was worse than the Marines. Because the Marines never told us to kill their own troops. One morning we were working with a company of 82nd troops who were searching a local village, and as we looped east of the village, we spotted four men hiding in the brush of a nearby woodlot. While the men were armed, we were flying low enough to see they were obviously Americans. They appeared to be a sniper team, since one man had a scope on his bolt-action rifle. Radioing our C&C ship, our AC notified them of our find and the battalion commander from the 82nd replied, "Kill them all, we don't send out four-man sniper teams. They're NVA." We looked at each other, stunned by the order. We were flying our normal left-side-down orbit ten meters above those men, so it was my job to shoot them. Our AC, Scott Hesse, quickly told me to just shoot the bushes around them to get their attention. As bullets started to tear the trees and brush apart, all four men jumped up holding their weapons sideways above their heads. Flying ten meters above them, it was easy to see they were scared and they were obviously Americans. Hesse radioed the C&C ship that we had four Americans under us and again we were told, "Kill them, they can't be Americans." Ignoring the order, Hesse put our skids into the branches above their heads and flew a tight circle while I waved to the four men, motioning for them to head toward the open rice fields. Upon reaching the rice paddy, they *chieu hoi*ed (surrendered) and stood in the open field with their hands and weapons raised above their heads until the battalion commander high overhead in the C&C ship conceded that they were, indeed, Americans. One of our slicks flew into the field, picked them up, and took them back to the 82nd base camp. We wondered if they knew how close they came to dying. Supposedly, Hesse and our platoon leader were severely chewed out later for not following orders from the battalion commander, but if we (I) had shot them, I doubt if a colonel would have been the person in trouble. The four-man sniper team was hidden to intercept any VC returning to the village after the company sweep. Apparently no one told the colonel they were working in his area of operations. As for me, I like to think that I wouldn't have shot them even if Hesse hadn't told me to shoot the bushes. But who knows? I usually followed orders.

Since the 1st Cavalry had their own helicopters, we didn't work with them very often. Reflecting on our few missions with them, however, I recall their confidence and coolness under fire. Late one day we were notified to leave the unit we were supporting and rush to the aid of a nearby cavalry company in contact with the enemy. Flying as fast as possible, we soon found the unit pinned down by heavy automatic weapons fire coming from the intersection of two tree lines that met at the junction of a small canal and a river. The cavalrymen had been conducting a sweep of a vast area of overgrown abandoned rice paddies when a few nervous NVA soldiers started shooting at them while they were still several hundred meters from the tree lines. Since their position had been compromised by a few undisciplined troops, the rest of the NVA, dug into fighting positions flanking the canal and river, joined the fight.

There was nothing unusual about our role in the fight. We shot at enemy positions and they shot at us. What sticks in my mind, however, are the radio transmissions with our ground troops as they traded automatic weapons fire with the NVA. Everyone on the radios was so damn calm and cool. There was no excitement or fear in the radio calls, just the clear, confident words of men who knew what they were doing and were good at their job. As darkness approached, we covered several of our slicks as they flew past the infantry, throwing out requested supplies: water, ammunition and mosquito repellent. There was too much hostile fire for the slicks to land and the infantry had no wounded to evacuate, so all the supplies were simply tossed from the open doorways of the moving slicks. As infantrymen crawled out into the fields to retrieve their supplies, their commander advised us to expend our entire ordnance on the enemy positions and go home. Our platoon leader was on the radio immediately, offering to stay with them all night if necessary, but the ground troop commander just politely said, "No, you guys have done plenty. Thanks for the help. Go on home, we're fine down here." Those guys were in for a long night in the rice. But that's what they did for a living.

The other cavalry unit that we occasionally supported was the 11th Armored Cavalry Regiment, who littered III Corps with their destroyed APCs and tanks, not because they were a hard luck unit but because of their aggressiveness. They had a reputation for finding the enemy and never quitting. The Vietnamese were horrified at their lack of respect for the dead and thought them barbarians because of their habit of putting human skulls over the front blackout lights on their armored vehicles. One morning I watched one of their companies stop outside of Cu Chi and decorate their vehicles with skulls before they drove through the village and into our base camp, where they parked next to the PX to go shopping. They were just showing off, and I suppose their trophies made the impression they wanted. I never heard anyone say a bad word about the 11th ACR; they deserved to flaunt their trophies.

While we worked with everyone, most of our missions in early 1969 were in conjunction with search-and-destroy missions run by either elements of the 101st Airborne or of the 25th Infantry Division. Some days nothing happened; on other days, we jumped from one firefight to another. We would just be finishing with one fight when the radio would relay a call for gunships at another fight. Days just blended together and small unit actions blurred together. Some I can't seem to recall, others I can't forget.

Interested in my work, I learned fast. The more I went out, the better I became. I suppose that I was never better than average at my job, but I learned enough to feel comfortable with my trade. It didn't take very long before I knew my job, but even after months of flying around III Corps, I couldn't really say I had learned our work area. We rarely worked the same area for two consecutive days; every day there was a new set of scenery hiding the enemy soldiers we were hunting. We worked quite a bit around the populated areas of III Corps hunting for the VC and NVA, but spent the majority of our time searching the unpopulated war-torn countryside. Most of the provinces in our area of operations lost their rural populations, as the continuous fighting between the two sides in this civil war chased the farmers and occupants of small villages away from their fields and homes. Even if the government figures were correct that only 1 percent of the population was truly dedicated to the opposition, that 1 percent could cause a lot of military action. In a province of a hundred thousand people, the government might expect there to be a thousand armed guerrilla fighters. Using the typical ratio needed to combat guerrillas, the antiguerrilla forces would then be expected to be somewhere between ten and fifteen thousand men. Eleven to sixteen thousand armed troops continually patrolling and skirmishing through the rural countryside could inflict a lot of damage on civilian bodies and property. In reality, the guerrilla forces were probably much more than 1 percent of the total province population and therefore would be even more likely to produce skirmishes with the ARVN/U.S. forces in the area. Every little firefight in or near a hamlet or village usually resulted in civilian casualties. While the guerrillas might provoke a fight with small arms fire, the fight usually progressed to where our forces used maximum firepower. The neutral civilians caught in the middle of these fights would abandon their homes and add to the masses of refugees clogging the cities. In some areas we forcibly removed the civilians, so that the guerrillas could not disappear into their midst. For whatever reasons, there were hundreds of abandoned hamlets and villages scattered around the areas where we went to work each morning.

We spent day after day searching the numerous abandoned villages and hamlets that may have been prosperous, but were now free-fire zones. Flying over the ruins of homes and the overgrown gardens and fields, I wondered how the region appeared before it became a battleground. My impression was our area of operations must have been lush fertile farming provinces, providing a comfortable living for the inhabitants. Most ruined homes had once worn red tile roofs; their painted shutters now hung loosely on the sides of empty window frames. People with pride in their homes once lived in these desolate, bullet-ridden hulks of masonry. Not all that long ago, people lived and worked in these small hamlets. Fighting with the French did not damage these structures; the scars of warfare were usually relatively fresh. American troops had recently fought in these ruined villages—and so would I. While these destroyed homes might look deserted, there were enemy troops and support operations actively operating around most of the sites. Not all the gardens were overgrown; some were well tended. Paths between ruined villages showed signs of heavy foot traffic. We knew, without a doubt, people still lived in these areas. And we knew they were armed.

The enemy had other places to hide. There was a vast scrub jungle in our area of operations that held tunnel complexes, bunkers and camouflaged hooches. VC and NVA troops seemed to be scattered everywhere and we could expect to come across small groups of enemy troops no matter where we worked. Squad-sized enemy units seemed to be able to set up temporary living quarters nearly anyplace they chose. It was extremely rare for us to engage any of the enemy carrying rucksacks. Enemy soldiers patrolling without their packs were a sure sign the troops were living nearby. In the populated areas, the civilians were hiding and supporting the guerrillas. In the contested areas, tunnel complexes, abandoned homes and scattered temporary structures housed both guerrillas and regular NVA troops.

Our missions were different depending on the terrain, the local population base and the degree of control by either VC or ARVN. In a free-fire zone, anyone we saw was considered to be enemy. In contested areas, we might engage only men in uniform or with military haircuts. Generally, if not taking fire, we tried to stop people from moving away from the infantry by shooting in front of them, then motioning them to stop until the infantry could reach them. On a typical mission in a populated area, we would be firing machine-gun bursts in front of military-age men, who were leaving a village ahead of our infantry. Usually none of these men would be carrying weapons, but they were all suspected VC. Moving along at eighty knots, we came up behind an individual, then pointing the machine gun ahead of the man, the crew chief would walk a line of bullets in the dirt, right up to the man's feet. Not as easy as it sounds. I used to get paranoid that I was going to hit someone by mistake, because I damn well knew I wasn't a very good shot with a machine gun. Most of the men or women I shot at did stop and wait for our infantry to capture them for interrogation.

One boy wouldn't stop, however, and in all my time in Viet Nam, he is the only person I wanted to kill. For some reason,

I distinctly remember my incident with a teenage boy occurred on a Saturday evening. Our slicks had just landed troops next to a village and, when the troops started walking toward the houses, every local citizen vacated the village from the opposite end. We interpreted their leaving as a very bad sign. Their departure indicated enemy troops were in the village and the villagers were attempting to get out before they were caught in the crossfire of the upcoming fight. That's what we thought at the time, anyway. More likely, they were leaving en masse to screen guerrillas escaping in their midst. The dry rice paddies were full of people: men, women and children. They were abandoning their home village and all their possessions: escaping on foot, bicycles or oxcarts. Trying to pick out potential guerrillas in the crowd, we saw an adult male giving documents to a teenage boy on a bicycle. The boy put the documents down his shirt and pedaled as fast as he could through the crowd. All three of our gunships were busy trying to stop individuals who looked suspicious. My AC, Hesse, had a choice, either stop the adult or stop the boy.

My ship went after the boy. Our helicopter would swoop right in front of him and I'd fire a short burst in front of him, then motion for him to stop. As bullets kicked up dust in front of him, he would jump off his bicycle. As soon as we flew past him he'd be on the bicycle again, pedaling for the next village. He had no intention of standing in the rice paddy waiting for our infantry to catch him. Our C&C would not let us kill him, even though we had seen him take the documents. This kid was VC and he was getting away. We chased this boy for several kilometers across bare, dry, dusty rice paddies, trying to stop him, but he was betting that we wouldn't shoot him. Hesse flew our ship so low and so slow that he could have cut the boy in half with the rotor blades if he had wanted to. Every time I'd fire another burst in front of the boy, he'd stop and sneer at me, then he'd be back on his bike as we circled past. Eventually, he reached the tree line, entered another village, and we had to let him go. I still wonder what was in those documents; the map to NVA headquarters? I still think the kid deserved to be shot, and I know I should have shot him and then apologized for misjudging when to stop walking bullets up to his flip-flops. I'm fairly certain that one of our ships shot the adult who gave him the documents, but not sure. There were too many people running and there was too much confusion to be certain what happened while my ship chased the boy, but bodies were lying in the dirt waiting for the infantry to confirm kills when we joined our other ships.

Incidents such as the one with the boy showed us the resolve and determination of the opposition, and made us wonder if we were on the right side. Story after story could be told about the courage of the local VC. More stories could be told about the lack of courage of the South Vietnamese government troops. Something didn't seem right. As the saying went, the South Vietnamese flag spoke for the people fighting the war—if they're not red, they're yellow. ARVN units had a reputation for breaking off a fight before much shooting had occurred. The VC units would stand and fight until death against anything we would throw at them.

Somewhere I have a few pictures of one of our many insignificant fights against bunkers built too strong for our rockets to knock out. It was one of those fights where bullets were flying everywhere, but no one was getting hit. Our infantry couldn't maneuver close enough to knock out the bunkers with grenades, and our rockets were only blowing the camouflage from the bunkers without harming the occupants. Since neither the infantry nor we were accomplishing much, the C&C asked for assistance from the Air Force. Both the infantry and we pulled back to let the fast movers try their luck. An Air Force forward air controller in a small "bird dog" fixed-wing plane came on station and marked the target area with a white phosphorus rocket. As the white puffs of smoke from the rocket drifted up through the shrubs, two Phantom jets rolled in, dropping napalm followed by several 750-pound bombs. Knowing that our helicopters and infantry had both pulled back for a reason, the VC came out of their bunkers and shot at the jets as they dove down on them. Their tactic worked, as they distracted the jet pilots with their tracers and both jets dropped their ordnance too late. While making impressive explosions in the woods, the bombs didn't accomplish anything. The jet pilots made another run without hitting anything again, then left for Bien Hoa to rearm. We went back to work trying to chew apart the bunkers with our rockets. Finally, after we had knocked the camouflage from the bunkers and possibly stunned the occupants, one of the 25th Infantry soldiers crawled next to the bunkers' right flank and killed four VC by tossing hand grenades into the firing ports of the enemy positions.

God! How can I write that? It sounds so damn simple. Just toss a few grenades into the firing port. So easy to say, but who has to do it? Me? You? The soldiers in the bunker have automatic weapons and are not going to let anyone nonchalantly crawl up to their bunker and throw a grenade into it. I saw many brave young American soldiers knock out bunkers and always wondered where they got the courage to crawl into the muzzle blast of an enemy machine gun. It's so easy to think that any one of us could have done the same thing, but that's not true. I never saw infantrymen pushing and shoving each other to be first in line to take a bunker, but sooner or later in a firefight, it always seemed that one man left his squad and crawled forward toward the gunfire and certain death. When an infantryman started crawling on his belly toward a bunker, someone was definitely going to die: sometimes their people, sometimes ours.

Another time, we were called to help an infantry squad from the 101st taking fire from a bunker that had been built under a destroyed American tank. The infantry had been following a trail though the scrub north of Cu Chi when the trail ended at a large bomb crater. Straight across the wide-open crater was a large burned-out American tank leaning over the lip of the crater. Under the tank, the firing port of the bunker viewed the open bomb crater and the trail on the other side. Talk about a secure bunker roof, a whole tank. Our rockets weren't going to be much help unless one went right into the firing port of the bunker.

This squad had an ex-NVA soldier assigned to them as a scout or guide. Depending on the unit that they were assigned to, these men who had switched sides were usually referred to as either a "Kit Carson Scout" or a "Kansas City Star." Some guys bluntly called them what they were—traitors. The KCS kept trying to talk the occupants of the bunker into surrendering and the VC would reply with machine-gun fire. Someone higher up wanted prisoners, so most of the morning was spent letting the KCS try to talk his old buddies into surrendering. We were working at another nearby firefight and would come over every now and then to fire a couple of rockets at the bunker to attempt to disable the occupants with the concussion of the rocket blast. On my ship we had talked about the VC soldiers in the bunker and none of us thought that there was the slightest chance that they would surrender. Hard-core VC fought to the end and, just as we predicted, these men had no intention of giving up. Eventually an infantryman crawled up on their right flank and killed the two men in the bunker with a hand grenade. These guys were hard-core VC, not the type of soldiers that would *chieu hoi*.

To surrender or *chieu hoi* (literally, open arms) didn't necessarily mean that one was going to be taken prisoner, anyway. It depended on the situation: sixteen armed NVA came out of the woods near Trang Bang one Sunday morning with their arms raised. Someone radioed in, "We have a bunch of NVA *chieu hoi*s." The answer came back, "No *chieu hoi*s today, they should have *chieu hoi*ed yesterday." Sixteen men died that Sunday morning. *Xin loi, chieu hoi*s.

On another occasion, we went to help out an infantry unit that had two men dead, killed by a single VC guerrilla who was shooting from a spider hole (a hole with camouflage cover, but with no solid roof) on the edge of a tree line. Our infantry had been crossing a dry field of rice stubble, walking single file toward the trees, when the man inside of the spider hole popped up and quickly sprayed the point and slack man with his AK-47. The rest of the patrol crouched behind dikes while the lone young man continued to pop up and spray AK rounds toward them. Rather than have his men try to assault or flank the spider hole, the ground troop commander, hearing the noise of our rotor blades nearby, called for us to come over and shoot straight down into the spider hole. While my AC was talking to the infantry lieutenant about the situation, I was loading a 12-gauge shotgun with No. 4 buckshot. Spider holes were perfect targets for low-level shotgun work. Coming over him at treetop level, I would just point the shotgun straight down at him and that would be it. Of course, he would hear our helicopter coming over him and would be scrunched down in his hole, waiting to point his AK upward and catch me before I could fire, but I wasn't concerned about him. We had done this plenty of times before, and knowing that he was waiting for us made the task more interesting.

The VC must have realized what we were going to do, because he jumped from his hole and *chieu hoi*ed. Disappointed that I wasn't going to be able to use the shotgun against his AK in a man-to-man fight, I watched two of our soldiers walk over to the *chieu hoi*. While one man checked the VC for hidden weapons, the other soldier picked up the AK-47. Suddenly the soldier who had picked up the weapon threw it on the ground, then reached behind his back and took his entrenching tool (collapsible shovel) out of its sheath. He walked up to the VC, grabbed him by the hair, and hit him in the face with the entrenching tool. Letting him fall to the ground, he then shot the VC and walked away. *What the hell is happening?* I thought. I didn't realize what had occurred. The VC had broken a basic rule of combat and was punished accordingly. If you are going to surrender, you better have some ammunition left. This VC had none. He had just killed two young men and then expected their friends to accept his surrender because he ran out of ammunition. This was one reason why most of our troops kept several extra rounds of ammo in the elastic band on their helmets. It may seem harsh, but rules are rules.

IX

Working closely with our infantry was always interesting and we learned by watching them. After wearing baggy jungle pants with large cargo pockets on the sides of the legs for months, I finally learned the purpose of the pockets. I never could understand why anyone would walk around with anything in these pockets, because when we put things in them, the load was uncomfortable while walking. The cargo pockets were where the infantry put their empty rifle magazines after they had fired the rounds from a full magazine. It would be too awkward to try to put an empty magazine back into the bandoliers across their chests in the middle of a fight. They couldn't empty a magazine and throw it to the side, because then they would have no magazines to reload when resupplied with ammunition in ten-round stripper clips. The pockets were on the pants to hold items temporarily, not to carry them.

Another thing we learned from the infantry of both sides was the amazing strength and stamina of men. It was not unusual to see men shot by machine-gun fire keep functioning though severely wounded. Of course, adrenaline probably kept them going. Many times we would be engaged in small firefights that would end abruptly as the enemy disappeared into the brush. Our infantry would find blood trails leading into the jungle and would cautiously trail the armed, wounded men. Occasionally dogs were brought in to trail the wounded; usually the dogs faltered and gave out while the men kept trudging. Dogs didn't have the stamina to work like men in the heat of the tropics. I saw many a dog lifted out by a slick because it couldn't keep up with a patrol. Dogs were good for only a few hours in the heat of the dry season before the infantry walked them into the ground. A lot of infantrymen said they didn't need the dogs to smell the enemy anyway. They had learned how to recognize the faint, distinct odor of men in the jungle themselves; there was too much smell of humans around the villages and hamlets for the dogs to be useful there.

Working with our infantry let us see some smiling faces for a change; they always seemed to appreciate us being nearby. During those times that we worked near contested villages and hamlets, most civilians seemed to regard us with hatred, contempt or indifference. There weren't many smiling faces greeting us at work. Our whole area of operations seemed to be VC controlled or VC sympathizers. Outside a large artillery firebase north of Cu Chi, there was a tall, bare tree, which would magically sprout a large VC flag from time to time. Trang Bang and Go Dau Hau were so obviously VC controlled that, while ARVN troops lolled around the markets and American convoys thundered up the road, huge VC banners were being strung across the highway. We once flew north to Go Dau Hau, our skids lightly hitting the tops of palm trees along the road, turned around and quickly headed south to find VC flags and banners waving along the road from the same palm trees we had passed only minutes before. There is a famous picture of a naked girl who was burned by napalm at Trang Bang in 1972. If Kim Phuc lived in Trang Bang, her family was more than likely VC and not the innocent villagers they were made out to be by the news media. Given the mistrust, indifference or outright hostility between Americans and Vietnamese civilians in our area, it's surprising that a hundred My Lais didn't occur. Maybe some did.

I remember one morning, leaving Cu Chi, slowly becoming airborne as we dragged our skids along the runway. As we fought gravity and climbed to altitude, I looked out to the right and saw thirty-two American bodies lying in the dirt next to the helipad for the 12th Evacuation Hospital. It may

not seem like many, but thirty-two bodies laid out in a row
are quite a few. We were going out where they had just been.
It was not a good morale booster. For all that we knew, some
of us might soon be lying next to them. Plastic body bags
were supposedly used in Viet Nam; I never saw one. These
thirty-two men were prepared the same as all the other
American dead I saw. A green towel or their green shirt was
wrapped around their face so their friends wouldn't recognize the body. ARVN dead didn't get any face covering, and
enemy dead were usually completely stripped so that enemy
guerrillas couldn't retrieve their uniforms or clothing.

These thirty-two men had died at twilight the previous
evening. At first light their bodies had been brought into Cu
Chi after the medevacs had brought back the wounded from
their position outside of a small village north of Cu Chi. The
doctors and surgeons of the 12th Evac were walking through
the rows of wounded, still doing their triage as we took off.
We knew that only the wounded that had a chance of surviving would make it into the hospital. Those being moved to
the side or next to their dead friends were wounded so badly
that surgical time would not be wasted on them unless there
were no other patients needing treatment. Some of them
would probably soon join the dead lying in the early morning
light next to the helipad. It gave us a lot to think about on our
flight out. There was no joking on this flight.

We didn't have very far to fly: only several miles northwest
of Cu Chi where we would search for stragglers from the
overnight fight. Apparently, an infantry company had set up
a temporary company base camp near a small village so pa-
trols could search for the elusive VC and NVA. Bunkers and
fighting positions had been built and several rows of barbed
wire were placed around the compound during the previous
day. The temporary camp was finished, supper eaten and
most troops were loafing at sunset when a large number of
Vietnamese civilians appeared along a section of the barbed
wire fence.

Now what's this? thought most of the troops. While it wasn't
unusual for small groups of civilians to approach com-

pounds to barter or beg, apparently a hundred or more villagers were massed at a section of the perimeter. Curious boys in their late teens, most of the troops strolled over and stood around the perimeter wire to see what was happening. After a large crowd of Americans had gathered, numerous AK-47s started firing from the crowd of civilians straight into the mass of unarmed soldiers. NVA soldiers had forced— or enticed—the villagers to act as a screen at twilight, hoping that the Americans would be curious and present easy targets. They did.

The automatic weapons fire had wounded or killed numerous troops on the first volley. I imagine that there must have been mass confusion in the American compound. Darkness had fallen and the villagers screamed or yelled along with our wounded, while the American forces fired back from fighting positions. I don't know what happened during the night, but artillery impact craters were everywhere outside the perimeter of the compound. I assumed that gunships from the 25th Aviation Battalion had also been supporting our troops during the night and now it was our turn.

Arriving at the battle site, we couldn't see much because of the smoke from fires in the village, so we had to fly to the side, staying out of the way of the artillery rounds still slamming into the village. I don't recall us firing even after the artillery shut down. I believe we were there for moral support for the survivors of the infantry company rather than to do anything. Mechanized infantry units were lining up to sweep what was left of the village and bulldozers were being trucked in from an engineering unit. I wondered why the bulldozers were needed, but we were called out to support another unit before I could find out. Later in the day, as we returned to Cu Chi to refuel and rearm, I could see the bulldozers turning the village into a big, flat, open field. By late afternoon, no one would ever have guessed that a village had once been located there. I had never seen a village bulldozed before, and I thought of stories I had heard about Lidice, Czechoslovakia, and wondered what was happening here. Where were the villagers? Who knows?

A few days later, shortly after we had left Cu Chi in the early morning darkness, my ship was diverted from the rest of the platoon to do a quick aerial reconnaissance near this same company field position. During the night their perimeter had been probed by enemy troops and our troops wanted us to do a quick recon at daybreak around their perimeter. Our troops had obviously hit some of the attackers because there were trails beaten down in the rice where bodies had been dragged toward the nearest woodlot. Forward of a two-man listening post a hundred meters outside of the wire on the northeast side of the company position, there was a trail of human entrails that led to the upper torso of an enemy soldier abandoned in the rice. He had taken the full blast of a Claymore mine detonated by the men in the listening post. His lower extremities were now molecules blowing through the rice stalks from the wind of our rotor blades. So much for legs of steel, toughened by the long march down the Ho Chi Minh Trail. As we flew away to join the rest of our platoon, we noticed that in several of the nearby villages most of the people were busy making ladders; we reported the ladders to the infantry. Another assault on the company was being planned. The ladders would be carried by the attacking NVA, who would place them on the barbed wire so that the weight of several soldiers on the ladder would push the wire down and open a hole through the perimeter. On their exit they would use the ladders as stretchers to carry their dead and wounded.

We rejoined our platoon, only to witness another incident involving a typical villager in another unknown hamlet I suppose we thought was secure. The hamlet appeared to have suffered very little fighting, as the hooches all had roofs and there were no bullet holes in the walls. A platoon of the 25th Infantry Division was walking single file, meandering through the village, while we flew overhead. The hamlet appeared deserted: the only villager in sight was an old woman hoeing her garden next to a stucco house with a red tile roof. As the point man entered the hedgerow surrounding her garden and home, he triggered an explosion. I don't know what he stepped on, but it was powerful. It killed the point man and the three men behind him and tore the legs off of the fifth man in line. These men weren't bunched up, but were spread out like seasoned troops to minimize the effect of a mine or an ambush. It was a perfect example of what kind of war we were fighting. No matter how good you were, someone else's mistake could kill you. The old woman never missed a stroke of her hoeing even though the blast occurred on the other side of her home: she obviously wasn't curious as to what had happened. She knew.

I sat there with my machine gun, stunned at the carnage beneath our skids: four dead in the blink of an eye. A wrong move in a meaningless hedgerow had turned a boring walk in a friendly village into a tragedy for five families. I looked for a target to avenge our dead, but the only thing moving was the old lady. The dead and wounded were evacuated on one of our slicks and the infantry continued their walk through the village, using their feet as mine detectors. No one bothered the old lady. I whispered a prayer that one day she would forget where she had buried a mine near her home and step on it.

Land mines and booby traps took a heavy toll on our troops, but they weren't everywhere. We were working in an agricultural society and the local people had to be able to function. There were a lot of NVA coming in from across the border and they had to be able to travel without VC mines blowing them apart. In many areas, if we were flying low enough, we could spot the triangular tin sign in bushes or near trails that indicated mines were planted nearby. Not all areas had such signs, but they weren't unusual. Even if we saw the signs, however, our people still managed to step on the mines.

We were working near Bao Tri one morning and it was what we expected: like every mission there—nothing. While we didn't work there very often, whenever our operations sergeant posted the next day's mission as Bao Tri, crew-members started thinking of excuses to get out of the mission. Guys who would fight to get on a ship headed to the

Iron Triangle would talk other people into taking their place on a trip to Bao Tri. As a crew chief, I had to go wherever my ship was going, so if Bao Tri was the focal point of the day, that's where I had to go, like it or not.

On that bright, hot morning we were idly flying low circles around an infantry platoon, wasting time, looking for an invisible enemy in an area so quiet and peaceful the local homes had roofs and walls without bullet holes. Since there was no chance of a fight, we left two gunships to loaf at Duc Hoa while my ship wasted blade time covering our infantry on another tedious patrol searching the area around the peaceful hamlet. It was another endless walk in the sun for the infantry, who apparently were taking advantage of an easy day to build some confidence in their new people. The point man was a lanky string bean of a kid who shuffled his feet through the dust, stiffly leading his platoon along a trail parallel to a small area of shrubs bordering hundreds of acres of wide-open harvested rice fields. Flying past him on one of our many circles, I looked down at him—a few meters under our skids—and wondered if this kid had any idea what he was supposed to be looking for. He spent more time watching the open fields than the brush and held his weapon by the carrying handle. I could tell he was new to his job and wondered if he knew his platoon was using him as a mine detector.

If the platoon had expected trouble, a more experienced soldier would have walked the point, rifle ready, slowly taking the brush apart with his eyes before he took a step. This point man walked with the indifferent shuffle of a civilian out for a stroll. I guessed he was new in country and had not yet had the chance to watch a real point man do his dangerous work. Like everyone else he would have to learn things the hard way. The majority of our gunners had been infantrymen and had told me most small units didn't care what happened to new people. They considered them expendable, "walking dead." The old-timers watched out for each other. Most didn't bother making friends with the newly arrived until they had survived a few fights.

Looping ahead of the infantry, we flew over a small trail leading into the shrubs. I noticed a couple of small rusty metal triangles hanging low from a few branches, indicating the trail was mined. I pointed them out to our AC, who relayed a warning to the ground commander.

We had come around on our circle above the infantry at the same time the point man approached the intersection of his path and the booby-trapped trail. I was about ten meters above him when he hesitated at the intersection. As we flew by, I watched his face and instantly knew that he was going to turn left onto the trail despite our warning. I put my thumbs and forefingers together into a triangle, the international military symbol for a mine, as he momentarily glanced up at me. I shook my head sideways but I don't think he knew what I meant.

Passing swiftly overhead, I glanced behind the ship and watched him take a step onto the trail and disappear into an instantaneous magical cloud of black smoke. He had detonated a booby trap—probably a hand grenade. Staggering backward, he dropped his rifle and tried to stay upright on rubber legs. Two boys behind him threw themselves into the dirt, their rifle barrels pointed toward the brush along the trail. A few of the other guys ran up to the disoriented point man staggering in the dry rice paddy and grabbed him by the arms. He was standing upright, surrounded by half a dozen men, when the call came over the radio, "Our point set off a mine, but he's okay—just shook up a little."

I leaned back in my seat watching them, thinking how lucky this kid was and wondering if he had learned something from his close call, when he suddenly collapsed. A few minutes later one of our slicks landed to pick up his body. We went back to patrolling Bao Tri again. Nothing ever happened there.

The infantry had to go forward, even if the trails were marked as being mined. An infantry lieutenant once told me he could cut his platoon's casualties in half if he could only get them some rest or let them quit patrolling earlier in the day. Walking in the sun or rain all day, then spending half the night awake on guard duty, made his men tired and careless. God, I was tired all the time and my eyes would burn and blur from watching tree lines and shrubs. How could anyone expect the infantry to function without enough sleep? How could a tired soldier, eyes barely open, see trip wires in the vegetation?

Not all mines were set for the infantry. Working the Ho Bo Woods with an armored unit one day, the lead tank set off a buried Air Force bomb rigged as an antitank mine, and I swear the entire tank came off the ground several feet. It was pretty impressive, but I doubt if the tank crew knew what happened. Generally, when a tank or APC hit a mine, it ripped off a track and sometimes killed the driver. I had never heard of a mine lifting a tracked vehicle into the air, but I saw it happen.

Besides mines, booby traps, bullets and mortars from the enemy, we were also killing and maiming ourselves. Every now and then, a young scared infantryman would accidentally fire his weapon while he was riding in one of our slicks, killing a pilot. In the excitement of landing in a hot LZ, infantrymen would occasionally jump out the left door of a slick, turn left and run straight into the tail rotor, which pissed off our maintenance teams: the soldiers' steel helmets would ruin the blades. Our gunship crews were absolutely paranoid about shooting American troops. We never wanted to be accused of harming our infantry and always made sure that we knew the exact positions of all Americans before we started firing our weapons. If there was any doubt whatsoever, we didn't fire. Our rockets were not very accurate, but at least we could see the target and put our ordnance on the enemy, not our infantry. Our artillery, however, occasionally had their first rounds land near or on the infantry. I'll be the first to admit that artillery does a fantastic job and is better on targets than gunships, but the first rounds are critical. In flat rice paddies, with no discernible terrain features, I could understand how the forward observers could make a fatal error and call in the first marking round too close to their own position.

Once, while working the area near Trang Bang, we received a call for help from an infantry platoon in contact. When we flew over to the firefight, we found an American platoon stretched out behind a rice dike. Bullets raised little puffs of dust in the dike as several men fired at our troops from concealed positions in a low hedgerow a hundred meters to their front. Piece of cake. We'd take out these guys in a couple of minutes and go back to our other mission. As our gunships were lining up to come in on the left flank of the enemy, our C&C ship flew over to see what we were doing and called us off. The infantry commander on the C&C had decided artillery would be used to knock out the enemy positions. He advised the ground commander to have his artillery forward observer take out these positions. We were told to move to the east and stand by. *Well, let's see what they can do,* I thought. We had a ringside seat and, while I'd seen artillery work plenty of times before, I'd never seen such an obvious target. Usually artillery rained down on an area, attempting to kill and maim everything in the impact zone. In this location, we had several armed people in a line of shrubs with open rice paddies behind them, in front of them and on their right. We were on their left, so they weren't going anywhere. Listening to the infantry radio net, I heard that the first round was on its way, so I leaned back in my seat and watched to see what would happen. I guessed he was going to try to impress everyone by putting the first round right on target. With the audience he had watching him do his work on such an obvious target, I felt there would be no shots made to bracket the target. He would go for a direct hit. The explosion couldn't have been better—except it was in the midst of our troops, not the enemy.

"Cease fire, cease fire!" the infantry commander instantly screamed over the infantry radio net. What a mess. Four dead Americans. He should have fired over the enemy, then adjusted his fire toward his position. But maybe that's what he thought he was doing—placing a round some distance behind the enemy position.

Rolling in low, we quickly silenced the automatic weapons

fire in front of our troops. We then circled while waiting for
one of our slicks to land and pick up the dead. "Get that FO
on the slick with the dead," radioed the C&C. "Pick up his
gear at the fire support base and get him back to Cu Chi
before somebody shoots him," ordered the infantry commander. The ground troops were told to confirm our kills,
then call it a day, and walk back to their landing zone for extraction. We continued on with our daily work, supporting
other infantry and hunting men, wondering what we were
doing and what we were accomplishing. Four kills for the
Stingers; four kills for the artillery; something just not right
about this score.

Our war was made up of a lot of little firefights: a couple
VC here, a few NVA there. Our goal was to stumble across
the path of an NVA unit on the move or to catch a small
enemy unit by surprise in an encampment. Even though we
constantly searched for the enemy camps, it was always a
complete surprise to find one.

Working the scrub brush of a free-fire zone one morning, an infantry platoon on patrol saw us flying nearby in
support of another platoon from their company and radioed,
"Stingers, we're about a thousand meters to your east and our
point man has some movement to his front. Can you put in
some rockets for us?"

"No sweat, be right there," Nine Six replied.

Heading east, we soon found the platoon strung out along
an overgrown road. Looking along the road, we could see
that the point man had stopped where the road crossed the
head of a long narrow gully leading to the Saigon River. The
point man had caught a quick glimpse of movement on a
path through the bamboo thicket at the head of the ravine and
the infantry lieutenant wanted us to work over the area before his troops walked into it. The long depression ran only
several hundred meters before it ended at the river and hardly
seemed to be a worthwhile target for us. From our viewpoint,
flying low circles above the thickets in the ravine, it appeared
it would be a waste of both time and ammunition. But we
never said "no" to the infantry. They were the ones who had

to walk down that ravine, not us. If a couple of rockets made them feel more comfortable, we would gladly tear up the vegetation for them.

I'm not sure why, but for some reason two of our ships had their rocket pods loaded with fléchette rockets instead of high explosive rounds. Great weapons for people in the open, but not worth much against bunkers.

The infantry pulled back down the road, and once they were out of our field of fire, we made a gun run, firing rockets and machine guns down the gully. Coming back around for another gun run, we could now see that the fléchettes had torn away most of the leaves on the tree limbs. Peering into the openings in the thick vegetation, it was easy to see camouflaged bamboo huts on the southern slope. Maybe someone really was in this ravine. More rockets were shot into the huts and our miniguns sprayed the entire area. We received absolutely no return fire and saw no sign of enemy movement. Since neither gun run had provoked any return fire, I thought the point man had seen a bird or mongoose and I would have bet a paycheck that no one was living in these huts or hiding in the gully.

My ship headed back to Cu Chi for fuel and, as we were leaving, I could see the infantry slowly and cautiously leave the old road to start searching the ravine. I didn't expect they would find anything. The long narrow depression was probably a landing site for fresh NVA troops from Cambodia who were infiltrating into Viet Nam by using sampans on the nearby river. The huts appeared to be only a resting area, where infiltrating NVA troops might disembark from their sampans, have a quick meal and then disappear into the tunnels of Cu Chi. This resting stop was the type of place that should be marked on a map for the artillery to send a couple random rounds into in the middle of the night when someone might be caught stretching their legs in the gully after a long cramped sampan ride from Cambodia. Just one of many points on a map for "harassment and interdiction" artillery fire to fall out of the sky at any given moment during any given night.

After quickly refueling and rearming, we came back on station, where I was surprised to see seven naked bodies and two fully clothed bodies lying in the short grass near the rim of the gully. The seven men had been stripped of all clothing so that local guerrillas could not use it again, but the two women were left fully clothed. Apparently, the infantry didn't have to fire a shot; all of the inhabitants of these huts had been found dead from the fléchettes and machine-gun fire. The company that we had originally started working with that morning was now in contact, so, leaving this platoon to continue their search of the huts, we flew back to help them. It was another of those side missions that I always wondered about. What was in the huts? Why were these nine people living here? It also made me think about the war in general. These people had to be dedicated, living out in the middle of nowhere with only basic provisions and shelter. Eaten alive by mosquitoes every night and then hunted by us during the day, they continued to hide and live for the day their revolution would wear us down. Our superior weapons and advanced technology were meaningless when used against those who had nothing to lose and everything to gain. How the hell were we going to beat such people? This ravine would probably have new huts and new people living in it within a week after we left. If a South Vietnamese Army unit had been sent out here to live in similar conditions, they would have probably deserted. How could the same people be so dissimilar? All the signs were pointing to a long war; this enemy was not going away.

Several weeks later we were working near this area again, and after refueling at Cu Chi late one afternoon, my ship was flying back to join the rest of our platoon, who were engaged in a small firefight. We weren't too far from the location of the gully with the huts when I looked down and saw a naked man taking a bath in an old bomb crater. "Got a man taking a bath," I shouted as I lightly tapped the tip of my boot against my intercom button on the floor.

Keeping the crater in sight, we continued flying, while the AC, Pat Ronan, radioed our C&C for permission to kill the lone man. Permission granted, we quickly turned and flew back to the crater, keeping it on the right side so Dale would get the kill. At first, I was pissed that Pat was keeping the right side of the ship toward the bomb crater. I was the one who had spotted the guy; he should be mine. I realized, however, that as the crew chief I did most of the shooting at individual people, so it was only fair to give Dale a turn to do the shooting.

Since we were alone, and had no one to cover us in case of trouble, we stayed high and flew over the crater at about fifty meters above the ground. Dale's first burst hit the man in the left shoulder and immediately his left side and arm turned bright red with blood. He was hit, but he wasn't dead and he scurried up and out of the bomb crater and ran behind a tall, dead tree standing near the crater. This old dead snag was large enough in diameter to protect two-thirds of his body, but there was always some part exposed. As we flew in circles, he moved around and around the tree, while Dale's bullets tore into the tree and around him. He was obviously hit badly, and I was expecting him to drop from loss of blood, when the *clack, clack, clack* of numerous AK-47s could be heard between the bursts of gunfire from Dale's machine gun. This guy's buddies had been lying in the brush surrounding the crater and were trying to help him. The guy had a lot of friends. While we were taking a lot of fire, from my seat flying left side high on the turns, I couldn't see any muzzle flashes. Most of the shooting was coming from the brush near the crater, which I couldn't see very well from my position at the left door. Dale fired away at the men on his side while I sat there waiting for a bullet to hit me and scanning the brush on my side without finding any obvious targets to engage.

The men in the brush knew their job and Pat quickly radioed our platoon leader, telling him we had taken numerous hits and were going to find a place to land. We broke contact and headed west, while Dale and I leaned far out of the open doorways, turned backward and fired our machine guns at the muzzle flashes winking in the low brush behind us. Placing my tracers into a muzzle flash near the old tree, I could see that the bathing beauty was lying motionless next to the tree. Whether he was dead or alive, I couldn't tell.

We had escaped the enemy fire, but we were in trouble. Both Pat and our pilot seemed concerned about the damage to our ship. The helicopter was losing both oil pressure and fuel, and Pat said the flight controls didn't feel right. He didn't want to chance falling out of the sky on the way to Cu Chi, so he headed for the nearest American artillery fire support base (FSB) to land as quickly as possible. If we couldn't make it to a nearby artillery base, we were going to be in big trouble. Landing in one of the many overgrown rice paddies would have had every VC or NVA for miles around rushing to finish off a wounded gunship. It was an interesting ride. As soon as Pat saw the FSB, he started a quick descent to get us out of the air and on firm land next to the outside strand of barbed wire as quickly as possible. He didn't waste time doing a quick flyby to determine if there were any obstacles in our landing spot, but went straight for the nearest point close to the perimeter wire. As our ship hit the ground and slid to a stop in the high weeds, Dale and I jumped out into the billowing dust. We immediately opened the doors for our pilots and slid back their seat armor so they could get out of the ship as fast as possible. We all knew that our ship had been hit bad and everyone wanted their feet on solid ground and away from our wounded ship before it exploded. Pat shut down 440 and quickly exited the ship. Within seconds of our unscheduled landing, all four of us were standing in the waist-high grass of the old abandoned rice field, watching our rotor blades turn slower and slower until they came to a complete stop. No one was laughing or smiling: we knew we were lucky to be on the ground.

Looking to my left, I saw we would soon have company. Troops from the firebase were walking out of their compound to see why we had paid them a visit. Gunships rarely landed at firebases and we were a novelty. Our crew stood around our ship briefly, wondering what to do. We decided we'd better determine how badly our ship had been hit. I crawled up on the roof to check if the flight controls to the rotor head were hit, since Pat had mentioned that the ship hadn't seemed to be responding normally to his movements of the cyclic stick. I had just started looking for bullet holes when the control tube I grasped pulled loose from my hand. The whole rotor mast and attached flight controls started turning, following the rotor blades' slow rotation. The ship was starting up.

"What the hell are you guys doing?" I yelled at our pilots. Looking to the front of the ship, I was surprised to see both of them standing outside the ship. Who was starting our engine?

"She's on fire!" someone shouted.

Looking to my left, I saw white smoke coming from the side of the ship next to the fuel tank and immediately thought, *This bastard is going to explode.* While I was in midair jumping off the roof of our ship, the pilot, Pete Polak, grabbed our fire extinguisher. I would still swear on a stack of Bibles he emptied it before my feet hit the ground.

Apparently a bullet had started an electrical fire and the burning wires caused a short circuit that was making the ship try to start itself. We were lucky we hadn't gone down in flames. The fire was quickly extinguished and we started stripping our armament and radios from the ship. The troops from the FSB, busy taking pictures of the gunship in their yard, volunteered to take our minigun ammunition and rockets into their encampment. It had been late in the afternoon when we had found the man in the crater and it was now almost twilight. Everyone at the FSB wanted us out of there since we were going to draw enemy fire. The artillerymen carried our ammunition away and advised us we better get ready for mortar rounds impacting around us, as the local community volunteer mortar crew would not pass up such an easy target for very long. The VC living nearby had to have seen us land and were probably running for their hidden caches of mortar rounds.

We weren't planning on staying very long at the FSB. As soon as we had started our descent toward the firebase, Pat

radioed our TOC telling them where we were going to land.
A slick from our company had been immediately dispatched
to retrieve both our gear and us, while a Muleskinner Chinook
had been called to retrieve 440. Within fifteen minutes of
landing, our guns, rocket tubes, radios and carcasses were on
the slick and the Muleskinners were almost ready to pick up
440 and carry her back home. While we didn't consider ourselves to have been shot down, I suppose some people would
have called it that. The VC had only slightly inconvenienced
us, they hadn't stopped us.

Our slick dropped us off at the company maintenance
hangar, where Garcia had a truck waiting for our armament.
We were just loading our gear into the truck when the Muleskinner came in—creating hurricane-force winds—and
dropped 440 into the lap of maintenance. Her wounds would
be taken care of the next day. We left her sitting there, leaking precious body fluids, and walked into the darkness to
clean our machine guns, laughing about almost losing a ship
because of a man taking a bath.

As Dale and I walked along carrying our machine guns, I
glanced over at the hangar and couldn't believe my eyes.
There stood a tall black man who was the best sergeant I had
ever known, SFC Jackson. We had served together in Texas,
where he had been my platoon sergeant for several months.
He was one of those rare men who never questioned the ability or intelligence of anyone. He had the special ability of
somehow quietly letting you think that, no matter what assignment he gave you, he had complete confidence that you
would do it right. No one in our platoon back in Texas had
ever dared give him a reason to doubt his confidence and
trust in us. He saw me running toward him and instantly recognized me. We both yelled at each other and were soon
shaking hands and pounding each other on the back. We
were smiling and laughing, ignoring the nearby people, as
we quickly filled each other in on what we had been doing
since we had last seen each other. When I saw him standing
in our hangar, I had automatically assumed that he was now
assigned to the 116th AHC. Jackson was only visiting, how-

ever, and was assigned to our battalion HQ. Seeing the Stinger patch on my fatigue shirt, he remarked that he wasn't surprised to find me in the best platoon in the battalion. "Where else would I be after having you as a role model?" I answered.

Leaving Jackson in the hangar, I hurried back to our revetment to help Dale clean our guns. Later, as we entered our hooch, the guys in the platoon wanted to know what had happened, where we were flying when we were hit and how badly the ship was damaged. While we could tell them about the shoot-out, I couldn't give them an answer about the condition of my ship. I felt stupid not knowing what was wrong with it, since as the crew chief I was expected to know the status of my ship at all times. I hadn't really checked the ship over for total battle damage because I figured 440 wasn't going anywhere after a fire. I thought I would be able to go over her the next day, but when morning came, I was out flying on a different gunship. By the time we returned in the evening, I learned that 440 had been shot up so badly that it had been sent to a higher-echelon maintenance unit for repairs. That wasn't a good sign, because our maintenance people could do nearly everything. Ships go to higher-echelon maintenance for the same reason people go to hospitals: to die. A few did come back repaired, however, and I secretly hoped that maybe she would come back with a new engine.

No such luck. About a week later, 440 was back again with the same underpowered engine. As all records of the repairs were kept on a separate inspection report and were not entered in her logbook, I never found out the extent of our combat damage. I always meant to walk down the flight line to the other unit and look over their records of the repairs, but I never got around to it. Whatever the damage was, it didn't matter: we had landed safely.

X

One day blended into the next day, as we flew our missions above the infantry. Leave Cu Chi in the dark, come back in the dark, seven days a week most times. Sometimes we flew all day, other days it was fly, sit, fly, sit, sometimes contact, sometimes boredom. We'd search an area and find nothing, come back in another week and get into contact. Troops were obviously infiltrating into our area from Cambodia, as local boys didn't become military-aged men overnight. It takes ten or twelve years to raise a guerrilla from a baby, and the local village populations were not sufficient to keep replenishing the number of troops being killed or captured.

If we did get a break in the field to shut down, we generally did what soldiers have always done: sleep. Usually a break would be taken behind barbed wire at some isolated refueling point, but once in a while, we'd just land in a rice paddy or on a road and block local traffic. I recall once when we landed all three gunships on a road, while our C&C ship scouted out possible landing zones. Local traffic was backed up and one Vietnamese man who was driving one of the three-wheeled bus/trucks, known as a Lambretta, tried to squeeze his vehicle past our parked helicopters and ran into the horizontal stabilizer on the side of my ship's tail boom. He probably did it on purpose to damage the helicopter, and most of our twelve people on site started screaming at him and pushing his vehicle off the road into the dry rice paddy. He was lucky no one shot him.

Shortly after the Lambretta incident, we were sitting on the berm of the road when a young, very pretty Vietnamese girl came out of one of the nearby hooches to hang laundry. Seeing her, the gunners from our other two gunships started yelling obscenities at her. She blushed and started crying, then dropped her laundry and ran back into her home. She obviously knew what they meant without understanding English and she wanted no part of these big, insulting Americans. After several minutes, a skinny, short ARVN soldier came out of the hooch—he was probably her husband. This little unarmed guy came striding across the dry rice paddy to face twelve huge barbarians standing alongside their technological wonder weapons. I was curious to see what he was going to do.

Walking right up to the two gunners who had been yelling at his wife, he stood in front of them and calmly said, "Why you talk number ten to girl? In my heart is full of love for her." What a speech! None of us knew how to answer him. Our two gunners sheepishly apologized for the incident, and both of them really seemed embarrassed. Then the thin little man calmly walked back to his wife, letting us sit in the sun, feeling like the big "Ugly Americans" that we were. That man was an ARVN soldier with courage.

We really didn't have much contact with ordinary Vietnamese, either civilian or military. We had a lot of contact with Viet Cong and North Vietnamese, but we did our talking with bullets. Other than our hooch maids and kitchen help, we did not have the opportunity to meet local people. I always wondered how Gilchrest managed to meet his fiancée, but I suppose they met prior to Tet '68, when soldiers were allowed to go off base and mingle with civilians.

I thought the people in charge made a wrong decision when they limited our access to the civilian population. By restricting troops to the base and not allowing any contact with the Vietnamese, the military was allowing the troops to form a "Fort Apache" complex. We were isolated behind our barbed wire fences in a foreign land and literally surrounded by the enemy. After months behind the wire, most troops started to view all Vietnamese as the enemy. Of course, keeping us penned up lessened the chance of terrorist assassinations off base, but I wonder if we would have lost any more troops overall. Surely we were losing troops to Vietnamese who might not have supported the Viet Cong as much if they had a chance to meet and work with Americans. Granted, we Americans were, on the whole, barbarians. But maybe they could have civilized us a little.

Having no real contact with the population, our troops passed on stories and rumors about the local people until they became local myths. Base camp barbers were found dead after assaulting the bunker line; hooch maids paced off the distance from last night's mortar impacts to better targets for tonight's mortars; boys sold soft drinks along the road with ground glass in the ice, little boys threw hand grenades into parked jeeps, et cetera. Maybe such things had happened at one time somewhere in country, but they didn't happen everywhere or every day. We had no idea what the average peasant thought of us, but it was rare to see anyone waving and smiling as a gunship crew flew several meters above their heads.

We had myths about ourselves also: troops who told their friends that they were fed up and walking home, then left and weren't seen again; the bunker at the Ann-Margret Bridge where sleeping guards would be periodically found dead, with a sign on them reading, "GI sleep, GI die"; a bunker guard shooting his best friend by mistake in the dark; helicopters landing with the whole crew dead. This last story happened at least once, because I saw it.

A light observation helicopter (LOH) scout ship, with over two hundred bullet holes in it, landed on the Cu Chi runway directly in front of our maintenance area. The observer was alive and talking to the control tower as he landed, but died while the rotor blades turned slowly to a stop. His pilot and gunner were already dead as he flew into our base. Another time, while we were out on a mission, a call for help came over our radio frequency. A wounded crew chief from another company was flying a gunship that had been shot to pieces; both pilots and the gunner were dead. He didn't know where he was and was hoping someone could see his ship and give him directions. Our ships gained altitude and scattered, trying to locate him, but eventually the radio calls ceased and we gave up. I never did hear what happened to him, but we guessed that he probably flew west into Cambodia and disappeared.

One of the most common stories was the premonition-of-death story. There were hundreds of them. No matter where I went, every company had its story of this guy in so-and-so platoon or squad who one day decided it was his turn to die. Most stories would have had him distributing his valuables and extra gear to his friends and shortly afterward he would be killed in action. I guess some of these stories are true, but I had to wonder if they were only warnings of suicide. The storyteller usually discounted this possibility by stressing how normal or happy-go-lucky the person was prior to his "premonition."

While not exactly the same thing, I knew men who had previously served as helicopter crew chiefs and gunners and had decided that their luck was running out and that they had better change jobs before an NVA bullet found them. It wasn't unusual to talk to someone with a decoration for valor, working on a maintenance crew or in the motor pool, who would say he knew that he had to quit flying or die. Admittedly, it was more common to find someone who decided to quit flying after his first experience with automatic weapons fire coming at him. It's not like in the movies. The people who quit right away had no one's respect. On the other hand, those who had done their work, day in and day out, month after month, and who had then quit because of their inner feelings, were still considered respectable and maybe wise. That might be. Most of us who continued to go out and face the guns secretly thought that some day we might feel the same way they did. We knew they had come in every night, black and greasy from the carbon and LSA mixture on their faces after firing thousands of rounds from their machine guns; thirsty, because the water in the cooler had been gone for hours; almost deaf from sixteen hours of rotor blades, rockets and guns; tired and feeling a hundred years old. We all knew that tomorrow we would do it all over again. They had done it over and over, just like we were doing it; if they quit because of a premonition, good for them. Maybe we would too. Someday, but not today.

I suppose the only time that I might have been involved with someone close to me having a premonition was one morning spent sitting along a runway waiting to get the word to "saddle up" and work the Cambodian border. We had been briefed by our platoon leader to expect a bad day, as we would be looking for an NVA battalion with suspected anti-aircraft guns supporting them. Our C&C helicopter was out doing high-level flights near the border, trying to determine where a battalion of men was camped under the spreading vegetation of the multiple canopy of treetops making up the tropical rain forest. Meanwhile, we sat in the hot sun and waited. It seemed as if everyone was running on adrenaline and itchy to get on with our insertion. Anything was better than sitting there waiting. Right before we received the word to saddle up, I got bored with playing cards and walked over to another gunship to talk to Wilsher.

"Seav," he said. "I've got a bad feeling about today. It's going to be bad and some of us aren't coming back today."

He didn't.

The previous evening our platoon leader had assembled the whole platoon, which was a rarity, and announced that the next day's mission would be working an area on the Cambodian border, west of Tay Ninh. There was expected to be a heavy concentration of enemy troops and supporting anti-aircraft guns in the area. He stated that he didn't want anyone to feel slighted or feel that there was any doubt about their courage, but that as platoon leader he was picking the crews for the next day. We were definitely going to be in heavy contact and he wanted experienced crews on the mission. Dale and I were announced for the first crew and it was the proudest moment of my life. Recognition as one who could be relied on in combat in front of our whole platoon of brave men meant more to me than any medal.

Art Silacci and Wilsher were the other two crew chiefs

who would be going. We were told to expect heavy anti-aircraft fire and to bring along M-16 rifles for the pilots. If we went down, we'd be walking back and, since the pilots only carried pistols, everyone had better have an automatic weapon available. There would be very few clearings to land a ship, and if knocked out of the sky, we would probably fall through tall timber. He didn't have to explain what that meant: an explosion from ruptured fuel tanks.

I doubt if any of us really gave the mission much thought or lost any sleep over it. I don't believe most of our platoon cared what our mission was or where we were going on any given day. Most of us preferred heavy contact to a quiet day, anyway.

The call came over the radio for the guns to saddle up, interrupting Wilsher's discussion about his premonition. I turned and trotted toward my ship, thinking that we'd talk about his feelings later that night in the 116th's NCO Club and laugh about the mission. But for now, we were on our way to the border.

I don't know where we went exactly, somewhere northwest of Tay Ninh, where the border looked like a boundary between separate dimensions or eras of time. The Vietnamese side of the border was triple-canopy jungle, interspersed with natural clearings. Everywhere we looked, the landscape on our side of the border was pockmarked with bomb craters from B-52 strikes. The Cambodian side, however, consisted of harvested rice fields stretching for miles with no signs of fighting or of warfare. There were houses in the distance, which looked different somehow. Probably because they still had tile roofs without gaping holes from artillery shells. Off in the distance, we saw a large pagoda towering above a small hamlet, which gave the landscape a peaceful and serene look. It was like a postcard. What didn't look peaceful, however, was a large convoy of military trucks heading south on a highway parallel to the border. There they were. The NVA, hundreds of them. They were heading south for us to fight tomorrow and the next day and there was nothing we could do about it. Cambodia was their sanctuary and we could not touch them.

We had only been over the border for several minutes when our FM radio started clicking. A radar-controlled flak gun was tracking us. Immediately, our ships dove for the trees and safety. We wouldn't have a prayer against a 37mm antiaircraft weapon if we stayed high. It was much better to eat tree limbs with our rotor blades than to face a radar-controlled gun. Diving down, I could see the muzzle blast of the flak gun next to the pagoda. While the shells were bursting high in the air, none exploded anywhere near our ship. In escaping the antiaircraft gun, we had become disorganized. After regrouping to the east, we flew toward Tay Ninh to meet our slicks and guide them into the LZ. Our C&C ship stayed low over the trees northeast of the LZ to await our return.

After joining our slicks, two gunships took up their defensive positions on the flanks of the flight of ten ships loaded with infantry that followed the lead gunship toward the clearing in the jungle. As I flew along on the right flank, I watched the artillery impacting in the clearing near the border. Within seconds of the last artillery round hitting the ground, our three gunships pounded the perimeter tree lines to cover the landing infantry. We were into the landing zone before any enemy troops could recover from the artillery barrage. The entire mission was conducted at treetop level in order to hide from the 37mm antiaircraft gun. Our commanders were hoping that the antiaircraft crew could not depress their gun barrel low enough to hit us since the weapon was designed to fire at targets high above the horizon. Apparently they couldn't, because we didn't receive any flak. C&C did, though.

The landing was a classic event. The troops were jumping out of each helicopter while they were still two meters off the ground and their helicopter was still moving forward to land. None of them wanted to be caught in an exploding helicopter in the LZ. Everyone knew the landing was when they were the most vulnerable because enemy weapons would be concentrated on the helicopters. The slicks were in and on their way out in seconds, their gunners blasting the tree lines with thousands of rounds. Our infantry had made it into the landing zone. But could we get them out?

Our position didn't seem very secure. We were only a few hundred meters from the border, in heavy jungle. If the ground troops found a large enemy force, it was going to be difficult for us to help them because the trees would shield the enemy from our rockets. Even if the ground troops didn't find the enemy, the nearby NVA troops knew that we would have to take our infantry out of the same clearing where they had landed. While our infantry patrolled the jungle between the clearing and the border, enemy units could be rushing in to hit us when we picked up the troops. The whole exercise had the potential to be a disaster, and I mentally estimated how long it would take to walk back to Tay Ninh.

Soon after entering the woods west of the LZ, the infantry found a large arms cache of mortar rounds with no one guarding the cache. The guards hadn't gone far, however, as we were hearing the *clack, clack, clack* of individual AK-47s shooting at us as we circled above the treetops. Actually, the jungle wasn't as thick as it appeared from a distance. At tree-top level, I could look down through the branches and watch our troops searching the area. While some troops were setting up explosives to destroy the arms cache, others slowly expanded their perimeter to ensure the enemy didn't attempt to counterattack the raid on their cache.

Our gunships continued to fly low to keep away from the flak gun and tried to cover the infantry constantly, still breaking away periodically to check the LZ to ensure there was no one trying to set up an ambush. While the LZ seemed secure, we were constantly taking fire from individual AK-47s in the woods. Enemy troops were nearby, but appeared to be scattered with no one in charge. A disciplined NVA unit would not have been randomly shooting at the helicopters if they were planning to attack our infantry. They appeared to be the disorganized guards who had fled into the timber when our infantry walked into the cache they were supposed to protect. On the other hand, they might not have been idly shooting at the helicopters. Not having many radios, enemy troops were known to communicate with gunfire. Their shots may have been calls for help, or to alert a larger NVA force nearby.

Whatever our original purpose for this mission, the commanders flying in our C&C ship must have realized we were pushing our luck staying and decided to call the raid a success and get out while we could. Explosive charges were set on the arms cache, and the infantry quickly filed back to the LZ to await their ride to Tay Ninh. Since the slicks had been called as soon as the infantry started walking back to the clearing, they were already inbound. The infantry didn't have to wait long at the clearing until they were jumping into the landing slicks and airborne out of trouble. Everyone was out in minutes. The slicks were flying over the treetops, headed for home, while my ship headed back to sweep the pickup zone. We rode in low and fast to make sure that no infantryman had been left behind. The PZ was clean and we climbed up toward the sky knowing that we were safe and could go home. But first, we broke right, heading for the border. Approaching the border, we climbed at a sharp angle while firing our rockets toward the pagoda. Without waiting to see where they impacted, we dove for the trees and headed home.

Goddamn it. It felt good to be finished with the border. I felt light-headed and high on adrenaline. Our mission could have been a disaster given the terrain, the proximity to the border, and the possibility of running into a heavy concentration of enemy troops. We had been damned lucky that the LZ was not guarded and that the arms cache was only lightly guarded. While we had taken some 37mm flak and a good bit of scattered small arms fire, we were okay and heading home. The C&C ship was still hanging around the LZ waiting for the explosives to demolish the cache. The slicks and our second gun were headed east into Tay Ninh, while the lead gun and my ship flew south, heading back to Cu Chi.

Our two ships had passed Trang Bang and were coming up

on the village of Go Dau Hau, when I turned from idly watching the scenery and saw that our pilot appeared to be in shock. He was talking, but I couldn't hear him because I had AFVN radio on full blast, listening to civilian music. Hitting the radio switches, I heard him say, "Nine Six went down." *So what?* I thought. Wilsher was on Nine Six's ship and he had a lot of practice going down. I'd watched him get shot down three times in the previous two weeks. He should be used to it. Every time they went down, Wilsher and his gunner would each pull the ring on a smoke grenade and trail smoke along the way until the pilot bounced them through a rice paddy to a stop. Showing off, letting us know how cool they were.

This time was different. I hadn't seen it since I'd been looking to the left out the open door, but I was told that the rotor blades had swung out of control and had cut off the tail boom. Their gunship dropped like a rock, while Wilsher and his gunner, Scotty, trailed colored smoke from each door until the gunship exploded on impact with the earth. We were right behind them and were instantly over their wreckage, but couldn't do a thing to help. The ship was crushed, burning and exploding on the southern edge of Go Dau Hau, while wisps of red and yellow smoke dissipated along the near vertical flight path the gunship had traveled after losing the tail boom. The wreck had landed upright, slightly east of the main road, in a vacant lot of bamboo thickets and palm trees. I could see most of the ship even though flames were shooting ten meters into the air, creating a giant column of black smoke reaching up for us to breathe as we circled slowly above our friends. By sheer luck, their ship hadn't landed on top of a family, but people were running from the nearby hooches, attempting to flee the site before the entire wreck disintegrated in a bigger explosion.

We circled helplessly above them, watching our comrades burn, while rockets and grenades exploded in the flames. I thought it ironic that Pete Polak, the only person in our platoon who wore fire-resistant Nomex clothing, was trapped in the flaming wreckage. No one was walking away from this fire, but we couldn't leave. Maybe someone had jumped or had been thrown out of the ship upon impact with the ground. A nearby mechanized infantry unit had been called and they were on their way to secure the site, but we weren't leaving until we were positive our people were dead. It wasn't long before APCs started pulling up and forming a perimeter around the wreck, but no one was going to get close to the funeral pyre. There was nothing anyone could do: the ship was being consumed by the raging flames and ripped apart by the exploding ordnance. It was twilight when we circled our friends for one last time, then headed for Cu Chi, silent and lost in thought. I recall wondering if a few of our men might have lived if the Army had issued parachutes to helicopter crews like some of the other services. But I knew, even if given parachutes, we would ride our ships down when they fell from the sky. I couldn't help trying to imagine what Wilsher and Scotty thought on their quick ride into oblivion. They surely knew that the ship would explode in seconds, but they both thumbed their noses at death by pulling the rings on smoke grenades and trailing smoke all the way down to the ground. Those two boys had more courage than we realized. I wondered why anyone would ever go back up in a helicopter after seeing one explode. Flying on a gunship didn't seem like such a great job.

Approaching Cu Chi, our AC flew straight down the main runway to land at home instead of going to POL. I suppose we skipped refueling because 440 was due for her one-hundred-hour inspection and would be in maintenance for a couple of days, but perhaps he really didn't care and just wanted to get us home as quick as possible. Bouncing into our revetment, we landed to find our entire platoon waiting to help mourn our loss. Art and Garcia were at my open door as soon as 440 touched down, offering help with the ship and the guns. Everyone seemed lost, not knowing what they should do. While Wilsher and I were good friends, having been in Texas and Di-An together, I was surprised that everyone felt so concerned. What the hell did they think was going to happen in the field? Not all of us were going to come back every day. "Screw the ship," I told Art. "It's down for inspection, I'll take it apart in the morning." Throwing my helmet into the ship, I walked to the NCO Club.

I wasn't in the club very long when the rest of the Stinger NCOs came in and joined me at a table. Lost in our own thoughts, we silently sat together and drank whiskey. No one got drunk, however; we were too damned sad. This made eight dead since the beginning of January in our small platoon of twenty-six people. And we were only partway through February. Maybe we were only drinking and mourning for ourselves, however. No one mentioned it, but we knew how to count. The odds didn't look very good.

Losing Wilsher was especially hard because he was probably the most popular enlisted member of the platoon. Everyone would miss him. While most of our platoon thought that I was his best friend, I knew better. His best friend was Pop Heck, an old man in our eyes—he might have been thirty years old. Pop was the company handyman and carpenter, but I'm pretty sure he had been a machine gunner when he was stationed with Wilsher and me at Di-An. Pop came into the club as soon as he learned about the crash and joined us at our table. He wanted to know what had happened. He was broken up about Wilsher's death. I was still in denial. I had seen death every day, but it didn't make losing one of our own any easier. Eventually, we ran out of things to say. Most of the group drifted off and the club closed. Pop, Garcia and I spent several hours sitting on the wooden sidewalk outside the club, talking a little and thinking a lot. In forty-five days, Wilsher and we three were to have gone home together.

Early the next morning, Garcia shook me awake. I'd thought I'd spend the day taking 440 apart for maintenance. It had never entered my mind that someone had to fly in Wilsher's place. I have no idea where we went or what we did that day, but I remember coming back in the evening and finding Pop Heck waiting for me. He had gone out with a team to retrieve the bodies. He was crying and upset. The whole crew was listed as missing in action, since there isn't much left to identify after a helicopter burns. But Wilsher was definitely dead; Pop had found his head. It wouldn't be until mid-March that the crew was taken off the MIA list and the Army conceded they were dead. Nothing was making any sense.

Several days after the crash, we had the typical military religious service: boots, rifles stuck into the ground by their bayonets, and helmets resting on the rifle butts. Some damned chaplain droned on about the courage of Jesus to become a man and die. I couldn't help thinking, *What courage?* If Jesus was God and knew he was to be resurrected in three days, then no courage was involved. It took a lot more courage to die if you didn't know what happens after death. Our whole platoon could show the chaplain something about courage.

I always wondered why none of the chaplains at military services ever brought up the verse, "He who lives by the sword, shall die by the sword." It would have been more fitting in our situation. I thought that it was ironic in Wilsher's case: he had been a rotor repairman before becoming a crew chief; it was the rotor that caused his death. Just like Jesus: live by the nail, die by the nail. The whole New Testament in a nutshell.

I believe that what really disturbed me most about our loss was when the military officially determined the crash to be an accident and the crew were not listed "Killed in Action." "Died as a result of non-combat cause" was the way, as I recall, their deaths were officially listed. Someone had been able to determine that mechanical failure had caused the gunship to tear itself apart. What about the 37mm anti-aircraft rounds bursting in the sky? What about the AK-47s, each throwing thirty rounds toward us as we flew over the treetops? The flight controls could have taken a hit anytime at the LZ and held together long enough to fly to Go Dau Hau. The Army wouldn't give our fellow soldiers the respect of listing them as "KIA."

By the way, I did see Wilsher again. For quite some time, I had trouble sleeping and would get up in the middle of the night and walk around or sit on the sandbags outside the hooch and think. Mostly, I would think about extending for an additional six months to keep flying, rather than get out of the Army in April. I liked what I was doing and couldn't imagine what I would do as a civilian. I was perfectly happy being a gunship crew chief, but everyone I had discussed extending with said that I was crazy. Two older NCOs whom I respected tried to talk me out of the idea whenever I mentioned it to them in the NCO Club. They were both on their second tour of duty in Viet Nam and they considered the war a waste of men and material. Besides, they'd seen the bullet holes in our gunships. I had mixed feelings and didn't know what to do. One night, when I was sitting on the sandbags surrounding our hooch, I looked over to the right and there stood Wilsher, leaning against a pile of sandbags about ten meters away. He looked right at me, waved, and then walked toward the hooch where Pop Heck slept. I never did ask Heck if he saw Wilsher again.

I suppose it was only natural that I felt sad and disturbed about Wilsher dying; I had known him for almost two years. Living and working together twenty-four hours a day creates a bond between people. I knew I would miss him. I couldn't help thinking the same fate awaited me. Neither one of us had been forced to fly; we could have stayed in the maintenance platoon for our entire tour if we had wished. We had both begged our way into positions in the gun platoon. I had to wonder if we had made a wise decision.

XI

The pilot and gunner who died with Wilsher were men I had flown with, but I didn't know them very well. The AC who was flying that day was our platoon leader, Nine Six, and while I didn't fly with him very often, we had shared a heartbreaking mission together several days prior to his death.

We started the day as the lead gun working north of Duc Hoa, hunting infiltrating troops from Cambodia and not having any luck. My ship was rarely used as the lead gunship because it took longer to reload our minigun armament system and was therefore slightly slower to return to the field whenever we had to rearm. Generally lead gun was one of the ships armed only with rockets, but that day our platoon leader had decided to fly 440. He had left our other two gunships parked at Duc Hoa while we went out with our C&C ship to recon potential landing zones for the insertion of infantry. Our two ships had flown over hundreds of abandoned rice fields and woodlots without finding a promising LZ when Nine Six saw a group of men running down a trail in a large expanse of scrub forest. Quickly notifying our C&C ship he had running men in this free-fire zone, he began yelling over the intercom, "Kill them! Kill them! There they are! They're running! They're running!"

"Where?" I hurriedly asked, jolted alert from my boredom. There were numerous trails crisscrossing throughout the scrub and I couldn't see any running men.

"They're running down the trail!" he shouted.

"Which trail are they on? I don't see them," I answered,

knowing that I should have been paying attention to what I was doing. It had just been one of those uneventful mornings when nothing was happening, and after looking at endless acres of swamp and brush in the bright tropical sun, I had become drowsy and had failed to concentrate on my job. I was wide-awake after Nine Six yelled, but I had no idea which trail was the one where he had seen the men running.

"Damn it! Just fire your gun, I'll adjust your fire," he gruffly replied.

Picking random trails, I'd fire quick short bursts at each one and he'd then yell at me, "No! No! You're not even close. The main trail! The main trail!"

Where the hell were they? I couldn't spot them or the trail that he meant; there were trails everywhere and they all looked alike. "I don't see them," I yelled back at him. *Damn it. If he can see them, why doesn't he put some rockets or minigun fire on them?* I thought to myself. Since both of our other ships were sitting at Duc Hoa while we reconned this area, we were flying much higher than normal. The extra altitude gave me a much wider field of vision, making it easier to see more trails but harder to pick out the trail with men. I guess that he didn't want to do low-level gun runs without a backup, but yelling at me wasn't accomplishing anything.

"Give me a landmark," I asked irritably.

"The main trail!" he shouted.

"What main trail? There are trails everywhere."

He was getting angry with me, but before I could spot the enemy, a call came over the radio ordering us to abort our reconnaissance and to fly north of Cu Chi. We were needed to help an infantry unit in contact. Nine Six was pissed. Because I had not been paying attention to what was happening, we were going to lose the runners.

Our two guns at Duc Hoa were called to saddle up and were given the coordinates of our next mission. We were briefed about the situation over the radio while flying to our new mission. After listening to the radio transmission, Nine Six made it very clear to me that I'd better get my head out of my ass and start paying attention to my job. It was his opinion that I'd just screwed up badly, and I had better not screw up where we were going, since things were going to be hot. We were going to rescue a wounded soldier lying in front of a machine gun. Apparently, the NVA had let a point man walk right up in front of a camouflaged bunker before shooting him in the stomach. They knew that the Americans would try everything possible to recover wounded soldiers, and they were using the gut-shot soldier as bait. He was also being used as a shield against artillery or jet strikes.

We knew that rescuing the soldier was much more important than shooting running men. We all had it drilled into us: never abandon your wounded. How can anyone expect someone else to come to his aid if he was not willing to recover others who are wounded? There was more to it, however, than just reciprocity. Maybe it was our feeling that in Viet Nam, and in 1969, no one except our fellow soldiers cared about us. We certainly didn't think that anyone back in the States gave a damn. We had to take care of each other.

After reaching the ground troops who had called for help, we made a few low passes to familiarize ourselves with the terrain and the situation. The area looked like a thousand other places we had worked in—abandoned, overgrown fields surrounded by scrub jungle. A line of old rice fields two hundred meters wide stretched for twenty-five hundred meters, with a limb of fields jutting north from a point about five hundred meters west of the northeast corner of the main fields. The eastern boundary of the main line of fields abutted a tangle of jungle through which numerous trails ran for several hundred meters to an obviously well-used landing spot on a small river. Men and supplies were being transported to this area from Cambodia, and somewhere within the scrub jungle, the enemy was resting and waiting.

A small force of Americans had entered the scrub along a trail heading out of the rice paddies about two hundred meters east of the intersection of the main fields with the limb of small fields jutting north. They intended to patrol parallel to the limb for several hundred meters, then hook to the right toward the river. Several hundred meters to their front and slightly left of their line of march was a long-range reconnaissance patrol (LRRP). The LRRPs were hidden in the scrub brush, with orders to observe enemy movement but not to engage. They had rolled out several bright orange panels on the ground to indicate their position to us, and to ensure not only that we wouldn't shoot them, but also that we wouldn't give away their position by needlessly flying over their heads. The infantry patrol we had come to help didn't need panels. They were easy to see. They lay to the right and left of the trail. NVA machine-gun bullets raised a dust storm on the beaten dirt path that divided their group into two sections. Looking down at the men, I watched bullets rip leaves and limbs from the surrounding brush, showering shredded vegetation around their prone figures.

Their point man had walked up the trail a hundred meters from the field to a T in the trail and had been shot while he stood next to a low, camouflaged bunker at the head of the T. He was lying slightly left of the firing port of the bunker, which we were going to silence. The ground troops had made an effort to flank the bunker but had received heavy small-arms fire from hidden positions on both sides of the bunker. The bunker had to be taken in order to save him.

It was going to be close work. Rockets aren't very accurate weapons, and we had to hit the bunker without killing the wounded soldier. Rolling in hot, Nine Six put rockets on the eastern side and the back of the bunker, but the NVA machine gun never paused. When making our rocket runs, we flew as low and slow as possible to ensure that our rockets would not miss the bunker and hit the wounded soldier. On our second gun run, we had fired our rockets and were flying low over the top of the bunker when another NVA position to its north started firing rocket-propelled grenades at us. The infantry platoon leader immediately started yelling over the radios: "Cease fire! Cease fire! Stop your rockets! You're hitting us!"

"We're not even close to you!" Nine Six told him. "RPGs are missing us and impacting around you."

Since our rockets weren't accomplishing anything—and

to prove to the infantry that RPGs were hitting near them and not our rockets—Nine Six decided we were going to knock the bunker out with hand grenades. We would be going in low and slow from east to west, flying level with the tops of the shrubs screening the bunker. Nine Six expected me to put a hand grenade into the bunker.

Making a practice run, I machine-gunned everything to the right and left of the bunker, hoping to hit men hidden in spider holes on its flanks. Dale fired at the NVA positions that were firing RPGs and small arms at us from our right. Passing over the bunker, we immediately made a hard left, coming back toward the front of the bunker, so that I could duel with the enemy machine gun. Gunships cannot hover, but we seemed to be suspended over the infantry as our ship crawled through the air above the trail until we passed two meters above the heels of the wounded soldier. The pulsating hypnotic glow of the NVA machine gun had made time irrelevant, and our ship inched its way through the thick gelatinous mass of semifrozen time over the bunker. With all the time in the world, I leaned forward out the door and poured machine-gun rounds into the bright muzzle flash throbbing from the gun port. Ignoring the enemy entrenched in the fighting positions north of the bunker, I concentrated on putting bullets into the face of death, grinning at me in the flame dancing out of the firing port. Our two other gunships were firing rockets into the area from where we were receiving the RPG fire, but each time I glanced north, the twinkling muzzle flashes of enemy guns sparkled in the low brush.

After passing the bunker on our practice run, we flew east, did a quick turn over the river, and, with our skids in the brush, headed back to kill the bunker. Going in on our first grenade run, Nine Six told me to throw the grenade at my discretion and to attempt to put it in the rear entrance. Fatalistically taking a fragmentation grenade out of its black cardboard container, I wished for a miracle—anything that would stop or change our attack. We fought bunkers until someone was dead—and sometimes it wasn't the occupants of the bunker. I would never have volunteered to throw grenades next to a wounded soldier, but I had no choice. I would have given anything to trade places with one of the crew chiefs on our other ships. I would never forgive myself if I put the grenade in front of the bunker and killed the young man. Leaning out of the open doorway to my left, grenade pin pulled, I held the spoon tightly and gazed at the wounded boy lying directly in front of my target and waited stoically for an NVA bullet to hit me. No matter what happened, I had to keep my grenades away from the front of the bunker and the wounded soldier. Forgetting everything else I looked down through the smoke trails of RPG rounds and tried to judge our airspeed, the possible location of the bunker entrance and the arc of a grenade thrown from a moving helicopter. As always, when trying to destroy a bunker, I felt vulnerable hanging out of the ship holding a hand grenade. I would be unable to shoot back if an NVA soldier popped up the camouflage cover of his spider hole and emptied his AK-47 at me.

This can't be happening, I told myself, hoping to wake from a bad dream. *Why me?*

I was scared. But more than that, I didn't want the responsibility of knocking out this bunker. Not with the wounded boy so close. I was not confident I could keep a grenade from exploding near the wounded soldier. On the other hand, I might be shot as we approached the bunker. The NVA soldiers in the nearby spider holes were not going to ignore me while I dropped grenades on their friends. I couldn't win. Releasing the grenade spoon, I got ready to throw the armed grenade—ready to explode in seconds. In those few seconds, I reminded myself that I had volunteered for my job and wondered why.

The grenade floated over the top of the bunker, exploding on the far side, raising a cloud of dirt and shredded vegetation. "Close" doesn't always count when throwing hand grenades. Turning left, Nine Six brought us around, trying to draw the machine-gun fire away from the infantry. Flames erupted from the bunker's firing port as we slowly swung suspended over the heads of the prone infantrymen. I concentrated on placing bursts of fire into the firing port, determined to get some bullets into the bunker. If I didn't kill the machine gunner, I would have to do another grenade run. Passing the wounded soldier, we broke toward the river and received a call from the LRRPs asking for help. An enemy machine gun had opened up on their position and they needed us to quiet it so they could withdraw to another position. Our other two gunships flew over to their position and quickly poured rockets into the area from which they were taking fire. Nine Six made a wide turn at the river and went back to our bunker.

Two or three more passes were tried with me making the determination when to throw the grenades, and I hit slightly past the bunker on all of my attempts. I was close but not close enough. "Can you try lining me up, sir," I asked Nine Six. "Maybe you can see the bunker better?" Approaching the bunker, Nine Six would wait until the bunker appeared in the chin bubble below his feet, then shout, "Mark!" Throwing on his command seemed much better; our following passes had grenades going off on top, behind and next to the bunker. As soon as a grenade exploded, we'd immediately spin to our left again. Every quick turn put us over the infantrymen sprawled to the sides of the trail and directly in front of the bright muzzle flash of the NVA machine gun. The pulsating light in front of the gun barrel was acting as a visual narcotic. As soon as we passed by the flame spurting out of the bunker's firing port, I couldn't wait for us to come around on another pass. I knew that sooner or later Nine Six was going to drop a little bit lower on a pass and then we'd see who was the better machine gunner. I had taken off my seat belt so that whenever we swung left into the front of the bunker, I would lean out and shoot into the firing port before my counterpart in the bunker reacted. When my first rounds hit the firing port, it was like waking up a sleeping dragon—flames erupted from the machine-gun barrel facing me. My ship concentrated on the bunker and the wounded soldier while our other two ships alternated covering the nearby LRRPs and us. Eventually we had to start our rotation for refueling and as one gunship left to refuel, our other gunship was busy working over the enemy positions firing at us from the brush north of our bunker. I suppose the other ship also made grenade runs on our bunker, but I really don't know. I was so involved with my own work, I really can't say what else was occurring. I was totally absorbed in throwing grenades and couldn't afford to lose my concentration, as a near miss might kill the wounded soldier.

After about twelve grenade drops, we flew a few circles over the river while Nine Six took a little time to consider the situation. I heard him tell our C&C there was no alternative to our grenade runs. But I knew of a way to get this bunker. Since we were getting low on fuel and ammunition, our ship was much lighter and more maneuverable. I'd bet anything that Nine Six could slow our ship enough so I could jump out behind the bunker. Even if I broke a leg jumping, I could still get a grenade into the bunker. I knew my idea would work. I could get this bunker, but I couldn't make myself volunteer to do it. I really believe Nine Six would have tried it if I had had the nerve to say something, but I didn't have the guts. Keeping silent, I peeled the tape from a grenade canister as we dropped down to the bunker again.

Every time we'd come toward the bunker, I would lean out, grenade in hand, and see the wounded soldier lying there in the hot sun. He was lying with his head toward us as we made our grenade drops and his eyes were following each grenade as if his life depended on it. He would slowly lift his head slightly and I was close enough to see that the left side of his face was muddy from his sweaty face lying in the dirt. The wind from our rotor blades and the muzzle blast of the NVA machine gun combined to ripple his blond hair and clothing, which made it appear that he was trying to move. His hands would move slightly but I never saw his feet shift. I guessed that he was hit in the spine. He wasn't going to crawl away from the bunker on his own. After dropping the grenade on the command of Nine Six, I'd quickly grab my machine gun and spray everything to the sides of the bunker. As soon as the grenade exploded, we would then make another quick hard left turn and I'd fire rounds into the firing port of the bunker. As my rounds hit the firing port, I'd occasionally watch the wounded soldier try to move. He was still alive, but hurt badly.

There was never any doubt that we would knock out this bunker, but eventually our twenty-minute warning light came on to notify us we had approximately twenty minutes of flying time left until our fuel tanks would be empty. We had to head for Cu Chi and refuel fast. Leaving our platoon to deal with the situation, we flew at maximum speed at low level, never speaking to each other, each of us on board keeping our thoughts to ourselves. The situation seemed hopeless. Throwing grenades on the sides and on the back of the bunker sure wasn't working. A hand grenade in front of the bunker might stun the occupants, but it would also surely kill the wounded man. I knew that if a person dropped from a helicopter behind the bunker, with two grenades and a pistol, he could take the bunker. Why didn't I say something? I knew that I should at least mention my idea to Nine Six because I was certain that I could take the bunker. But I kept my mouth shut and my thoughts to myself.

Flying back to Cu Chi for fuel, I kept thinking about the situation. I realized the wounded soldier had to have been shot from a spider hole somewhere near the bunker. Each time we passed the bunker and made our sharp left turn, we were vulnerable to the machine gun in the bunker only for a short time. As we approached the bunker, the machine gun in the bunker was tearing away the roof of the firing port when it fired at us and it couldn't have been able to shoot the wounded soldier in the stomach while he had been standing in front of the bunker. It might have hit him high in the legs, but even that was doubtful because, from the position of his body, he had been standing to the left front of the machine-gun crew when shot. In order to hit him in the stomach, the gun would have had to engage him prior to his getting to the position where he lay. Someone on the left flank of the bunker had to have shot him. Since our infantrymen were still receiving sporadic fire from that area, there must be several enemy positions flanking the bunker. There was no weapon next to the wounded man, so someone in a fighting position near the bunker must have it. We were a perfect target for the men in the flanking positions as we continued our grenade runs. I realized that when we returned to the bunker, if I continued to lean out of the ship to drop grenades, I would probably be shot. Those men in the spider holes were not going to let us continue to fly three meters above them and drop grenades on their friends. Eventually one of them was going to throw his overhead cover off and point his AK-47 at the belly of our ship as we approached his position. Hanging out the left door with a grenade in my hand, I would be unable to stop him from shooting. I could either lean out and machine-gun the area in front of our nose or lean out and throw grenades, but I couldn't do both. If we were going to grenade the bunker when we returned to our little fight, I would have to remember to lean out far enough so that when I was shot, I wouldn't drop my grenade into our ship.

Landing at Cu Chi, we refueled and rearmed our rocket tubes in minutes. Dale and I tossed several cases of fragmentation and concussion grenades into the ship and we were soon on our way back to work. We had flown only a few kilometers from the Cu Chi bunker line when we flew over twenty or thirty NVA troops in uniforms. They were sprawled along a ditch, lying in the sunshine, taking a well-deserved break from life in the tunnels. We were only five or six meters above them, but we were flying so fast neither they nor I reacted by shooting. What a target of opportunity. But we had better things to do that day and we left them alone. Our pilot did mark their location on a map, however. We'd be coming back.

Arriving back at work, we found things hadn't changed much in our absence. The two gunships that stayed on station had been busy trying to knock out the enemy positions north of the bunker, and as soon as we were in sight, one ship quickly left to rearm at Cu Chi. Our smokeship had flown out to join the fight and made several slow smoke runs around the bunker, but received so much enemy fire and took

so many hits it ha⁻ to leave before it was shot to pieces. As
soon as Smokey left, ⸱ve flew into the white smoke that hung
in the air surrounding the bunker while our other gunship
suppressed the enemy weapons on our right side. We made
another grenade drop on the bunker and as it exploded, an infantryman tried to take advantage of the combination of the
smoke and the blast of the grenade while the NVA gun crews
were momentarily distracted.

I watched as he quickly sprinted from the bush along the
right side of the trail and dove onto his belly near the feet of
the wounded man before the machine-gun crew could react.
Twisting in his prone position, he loosened his pistol belt,
reached forward and quickly wrapped his belt around the
wounded man's ankles. The machine-gun crew immediately
realized that he was trying to steal their shield and opened
fire on him. I watched NVA bullets, which had passed mil-
limeters above his spine, tearing up the dirt trail behind his
heels. The machine gun could not be depressed low enough
to hit him, but if he moved backward he'd be torn to pieces.
As we swung left and came in front of the bunker, I kept the
trigger pulled back, pouring maximum machine-gun fire into
the muzzle blast of the NVA gun, doing my best to help the
rescuer. While my rounds were on target, hitting the firing
port, it was pretty obvious that, while I was tearing up the firing port, I wasn't hitting the occupants of the bunker. NVA
bullets continued to churn the dirt behind the rescuer's heels.
On the next pass, we would have to come in a little lower so
my rounds could go straight into the bunker. The machine-
gun crew just ignored my fire and kept their fire going over
the rescuer. They were determined to kill him and we were
determined to kill them. We all knew we were going to have
to make a wider left turn after our next grenade drop in order
to draw the machine-gun fire toward us. If we made a wide
low turn, we would be a perfect target for the men in the
bunker, and if they lifted their fire away from the men on the
ground, the second man might be able to roll to his right,
dragging the wounded man with him. Nine Six said that he
was going to bring us in front of the bunker as low and slow

as possible to give the NVA machine-gun crew a target they couldn't resist. I took a deep breath and held it, mentally readying myself to see who was better and quicker with a machine gun. When we made the next low left turn, someone was going to die.

Flying past the bunker, we had just done a tight left semicircle over the river to line up to make another grenade drop when a radio call from the infantry broke our hearts. The rescuer had been shot. As soon as we had passed by their positions, an NVA soldier had jumped out of a spider hole on the east side of the bunker and had sprayed the rescuer with an AK-47. Now we had two wounded men in trouble.

Hearing the call that the brave young man with the pistol belt had been shot did something to me. I felt emotionally drained and stunned. This was not the way things were supposed to happen. This never happened in books or movies; brave rescuers saved people and never, ever, were harmed in their attempt to save someone. We were the good guys and therefore things had to go our way. It seemed unfair that the young man's courage was rewarded with a burst of AK fire. I have often wondered where this soldier had found the strength and fortitude to crawl into the face of certain death. I couldn't believe his courage. I wondered what the wounded soldier had meant to him, a friend perhaps. Maybe it was only his sense of duty to his comrade that made him attempt the rescue, but where inside of you do you find such courage? What could possibly make a young man jump directly in front of a machine gun? Why couldn't I even find the courage to ask Nine Six if he would slow our ship down behind the bunker so that I could jump out behind the gun? There wasn't a doubt in my mind that I could have taken that bunker, but I couldn't find the courage to even ask Nine Six to let me try. Thirty years later, I still know I could have taken that bunker.

My whole world was that bunker and the wounded men. I could hear Dale firing away at the enemy positions on our right, but I had no idea what he was shooting at. Our other gunship had returned from rearming and was also hitting

those positions while we made our grenade drops. I don't
know what Dale was seeing from the right door but the
smoke trails of RPG rounds were between our skids and the
bunker roof. There was obviously much more going on than
I knew, but I could concentrate only on my portion of the
fight. Leaning out the door, I held the grenade, memorizing
everything in front of me—shrubs, bunker, wounded boy,
pistol belt on the ankles, hands locked onto the pistol belt,
another wounded boy, bullets raising dust, dirt trail, hidden
infantrymen. I can close my eyes and see it today. I threw the
grenade. As it blew more vegetation from the bunker, Nine
Six made a low wide left turn. We were behind the patrol,
much lower, but not low enough. The enemy machine gun
still couldn't raise his muzzle high enough to hit us, but I
couldn't get my rounds straight into his firing port either. We
went back to our original plan of taking out the bunker with
grenades. Somewhere on the side or on the back of the
bunker was an entrance hidden by vegetation and I had to
drop a grenade into it. Time after time we flew along the
shrubs, dropped another grenade, then swiveled around to
fire into the muzzle blast again. After each attempt to shoot
into the bunker I would shift my fire and shoot everything
around the bunker, trying to kill anyone in spider holes before we had to come back to make another grenade drop. I
suppose I should have been shooting at the positions to our
north, but they didn't seem as threatening as the men in the
spider holes next to the bunker were. The NVA soldier who
had jumped up to shoot the rescuer could have just as easily
shot me as I leaned out with the hand grenades. Going in on
the drop was when we were most vulnerable, because I
couldn't fire my machine gun straight down and still hold an
armed grenade. As soon as the grenade left my fingers, the
gun would be in my hand and firing, but our belly was exposed with each slow approach to the bunker. I was tense
with anticipation, knowing for certain that I was going to be
shot if we kept drifting slowly to throw grenades, mere meters above the spider holes guarding the bunker.

We continued dropping grenades, but daylight was fading

and something had to be done soon. The LRRPs seemed to be all right. They were well hidden in new positions and thought we had silenced the enemy position near them. They were planning to stay right where they were for the night to observe the area and would call for artillery support if the enemy came near their position. Our infantry along the trail could not spend the night in their positions, however; they were too vulnerable lying scattered throughout the brush on their bellies. They'd have to regroup and set up a defensive position back in the open rice paddies to their rear before darkness fell. Our wounded men would have to stay in front of the bunker.

We made another low pass over the two boys to satisfy the ground commander that nothing more could be done for his men. After we lied to him and said that his wounded boys were dead, the infantry pulled back through the brush to the abandoned rice paddies behind them. They believed us, or wanted to believe us, and slowly crawled backward under the bullets flying over them while we fired into the bunker and nearby brush to keep the NVA occupied. As soon as a secure area was set up in the fields, two of our slicks flew in, bringing the infantry their packs, water and ammunition from their home FSB. We had left the wounded to cover the re-supply and, as the slicks took off, we headed straight back toward the bunker. Our two severely wounded boys lay in front of the bunker, still sprawled in the dust. The shirt on the first man was burning. Something—probably a spent tracer that had ricocheted or possibly a piece of hot grenade shrap-nel—had ignited his clothing; he was burning and twitching with pain. Both men's eyes opened and closed, an indication that, while they were perhaps dying, they were still alive. I could see the slight gleam from a gold wedding band flicker as the second wounded boy slowly flexed his left hand and I wondered why a married man would forsake his spouse to save a friend. As we turned slowly above them, the words came over the radio, "Don't let them suffer." I machine-gunned both of them.

Only Nine Six and I knew what happened. Our pilot and

gunner, on the right side of our ship, didn't have the view we
had as the ship slowly turned with our left side downward.
Nine Six would soon die and I alone would know what happened to the wounded. I alone would also know that I could
have saved them, but I didn't have the courage. All my life I
wanted to be a soldier and, in my mind, I'd failed a basic responsibility of soldiering: Don't abandon your wounded.

The human shield protecting the bunker was gone. So we
turned around at the river and dove on the bunker, firing all
of our rockets. Air Force jets had been called and arrived on
station to finish our work. As we flew east over the river to
get out of their flight path, I could hear our C&C identify the
target: "Drop everything on the small fire north of the strobe
lights." The small fire was the burning clothing on the point
man's body and the strobe lights marked the infantry position in the rice paddy. The point man was the only spark of
light in the low gray shrubs, as twilight disappeared into the
coal-black darkness of the tropics. I watched the jets drop
out of the sky. The small fire disappeared, smothered by the
detonating bombs. We turned and went home, beaten mentally and physically.

What a goddamned day. Our ship was quiet all the way
back to Cu Chi. Nobody spoke or looked at another person.
Perhaps we didn't want to recognize what had happened. I
sat and thought about what I had done. I also thought about
what I hadn't done. I knew damn well that I should have suggested to Nine Six that he let me jump out of our ship to take
the bunker. I knew without a doubt I could have taken it, but
I hadn't the courage to volunteer. I still believe that, if I had
offered to jump, Nine Six would have ignored the RPGs and
dragged our ship through the brush behind the bunker to let
me jump. The incident was made more tragic by my shooting
the two wounded boys I didn't have the courage to save. I felt
personally responsible for the disaster at the bunker and
waited for Nine Six to say something. We refueled, rearmed
and settled into our revetment without a word. After shutting
down, I tied down our rotor blades and started my postflight
inspection with the AC and the pilot. Finally, Nine Six spoke:

"You'd better start paying more attention, you cost us a bunch of kills this morning."

Stunned, I answered, "*Xin loi,* sir, I just couldn't see them. I'll do better."

What the fuck! I couldn't believe what he had just said. After what had happened at the bunker with the wounded men, he brought up the morning's screwup. The officers walked away, leaving Dale and me to clean up the ship, without mentioning the bunker. After finishing our work, Dale and I headed for the NCO Club and talked about everything except what we had done that day. Neither of us wanted to think about it, let alone discuss it. I had never considered the possibility that I might have to shoot our own wounded. I guess I thought we always won the fight, sweeping over any enemy positions near our wounded. We didn't win all our fights and circumstances didn't always allow us to recover wounded or dead, but having the enemy shoot our wounded was one thing. Our doing it was another matter. We had a few drinks and returned to a quiet hooch. No one who had been out in the field felt like talking. I was ready to lie down and go to sleep when Garcia called me outside. Nine Six had told Garcia he was angry about my failure to see the running men in the morning and he had considered throwing me out of the platoon. Garcia warned me I'd better not do anything to piss off Nine Six for the next week or two, because he seemed serious about getting rid of me if I messed up again. I asked him if Nine Six had mentioned anything else about what we had done that day. "No," he answered. "Why?"

XII

Daylight found us back at the bunker again. It was still there. The goddamned Air Force had missed an easy target. The only fire burning in the darkness. The nearest bomb crater was about fifty meters west of the bunker and, while it might have shaken up the bunker's occupants, it probably hadn't killed them. The nearby LRRP team joined our infantry and together they slowly and cautiously flanked the bunker. There was no opposition and no one home. The bodies of our men were recovered, and after a sweep of the bunker and surrounding area failed to find any trace of NVA bodies, our infantry carried the two dead boys back to the open rice paddies. Our slicks were called; they soon landed to extract everyone. We left them at their firebase and went to work with another infantry unit. Another day, another dollar.

A few days later, we happened to be in the vicinity of this insignificant little fight and noticed someone had been busy. The southern edge of the main line of rice paddies had a freshly dug trench line, with fighting positions starting at the eastern edge of the fields near the river running approximately five hundred meters due west. Somebody was getting ready for the next helicopter assault into these paddies. Obviously, there was something nearby that the enemy was interested in protecting. I recall talking to Wilsher that evening about the new fighting positions and hearing him say, "Oh well, we'll go back there and get them some day." But he wouldn't; the next day he was dead.

After we lost our platoon leader and his crew on Wilsher's ship, there seemed to be a change in everyone in the platoon.

Some people seemed to be more irritable and touchy, wanting complete perfection on a mission, while others seemed to relax and tried to be friendlier. Maybe our immortality was wearing thin as we aged. As First Sergeant Deal always told us, no one was irreplaceable and our platoon had a new Nine Six immediately; Capt. Randall Ford, another Texan, would now lead us into battle. He was a competent, experienced officer and the platoon continued its daily work, never missing a beat. Life, and death, went on.

I was changing, however. I was getting harder and getting a "give a shit less" attitude. Wilsher's death had affected me more than I expected. I did not want to lose more friends and started withdrawing from close contact with most of the platoon. I was civil to everyone, but I spent most of my free time with Gilchrest in the NCO Club. If something happened in the field, Dale and I would be going out together. Not really knowing someone would make it much easier if they died. I was also getting tired of seeing the enemy die. The novelty of being in combat had worn thin a long time ago and the day-after-day killing was affecting me. Death was the price for the euphoria of a firefight, but there was no honor or glory in anything we did. It was all senseless brutality—to which I was becoming numb.

I was the cause of a particularly bad episode of brutality two or three days after the loss of our guys. I lost control. We were working near some hamlets east of Cu Chi early one morning and Art had shot a VC suspect running out of a village ahead of the infantry. Eventually, the infantry would check out the kill and confirm it on their sweep, so we moved out a kilometer or so in front of them to look for trouble. A short time later, the C&C radioed: "Stingers, there are two men stealing your kill. Go get them."

I had never seen this happen before—no one ever touched the dead if we were still in the area. The local Vietnamese always buried their dead after we had left. It was extremely rare to see a body still around on the day following a fight. Somehow, they all seemed to disappear overnight, but I'd never had anyone police up a body in broad daylight. My ship returned to the kill and found two men trying to put the body on a makeshift stretcher.

Someone shouted over the radio, "Get them! Get them!" I fired a quick burst and missed both of them. They separated and took off running. One ran across the open rice paddy while the other ran to a tunnel entrance in a nearby hedge-row. Instead of diving in, however, he turned and went into the tunnel legs first, which slowed him down. As we came over the entrance, I looked straight down and, from three or four meters away, I could see his face in the tunnel looking up at me. I fired a short burst and a tracer hit him in the fore-head. Our AC, Pat Ronan, didn't even realize that I had shot the man in the tunnel. He couldn't see the man from his po-sition when I fired. He thought I'd missed, so he quickly turned our ship toward the other runner.

This young VC was running like the wind to his favorite tunnel. We followed, tearing across the dry rice paddies, two meters off the ground, coming up behind him swiftly. I leaned out the door firing madly, spraying bullets every-where, but not hitting him. I wasn't aiming, and felt com-pletely out of control, urged on by some bloodlust. I was as berserk as any Viking ever had been in battle. I was just shooting to shoot. I wasn't controlling the gun at all. I had my finger on the trigger, filling the air with tracers. I didn't know or care what I was doing. Our runner dove toward a hedgerow on his left and crawled as fast as he could into a tunnel entrance. As our ship turned over his position, all I could see of him were the back sides of his legs. I pointed my machine gun down, gripped it tight and methodically wove bullets left and right across his legs. The entire episode had been a display of piss-poor shooting and bloodlust.

"Nice shooting," Ronan said, sarcastically.

"Xin loi," I replied.

The infantry were almost up to our position by then, so we marked the body that had almost been stolen and the leg-shot man with smoke grenades. I didn't bother telling anyone that I'd shot the other man in the head. While waiting for the in-fantry, I started to feel very guilty about shooting those men.

Maybe they were brothers or friends of the first man. I didn't think picking up a body for burial should automatically make a man guilty of being Viet Cong. I doubted if most Viet Cong would have exposed themselves during our operation just to recover a body. I had a bad feeling that I'd just shot two IC (innocent civilians). What a way to win the hearts and minds of the villagers.

The infantry checked the first body, finding nothing on it, but when they pulled the leg-shot man out of the tunnel, they radioed their commander on the C&C. I was listening to the infantry radio net and heard someone say, "This guy has an ID card."

The commander instantly replied, "It's a counterfeit; throw it away."

God, the C&C crew must have great eyes to tell the difference between a real ID card and a counterfeit while flying five hundred meters above the ground. Since the man was still alive, a slick was brought in and he was medevaced to the hospital at Cu Chi, where he died. He would be our platoon's only recorded prisoner in the first three months of 1969.

While the slick carried the wounded young man to Cu Chi, we left the infantry and flew to Duc Hoa to refuel. After filling our fuel tanks, I told Dale to fly on the left side of the ship in my seat. I was plain disgusted with myself, both for the poor shooting and for the idea of shooting men retrieving the body of their comrade. I couldn't imagine what had come over me. I had never felt anything emotional when I had been shooting at someone. It was part of the job, and I usually felt indifferent about either shooting or being shot at. I suppose I was not over losing my friends a few days before and was probably killing to avenge them. My bloodlust had been more than satisfied. I was ashamed of the whole episode. Dale could fly left side down and do the shooting for the rest of the day. I was mentally burned out and didn't care if I ever fired another machine-gun burst. I knew I had mentally passed the emotional barrier that divides the soldier from the killer. I had lost control of myself and knew I shouldn't be trusted to use a weapon any longer. No matter what happened in the field, the final decision to determine who lives and who dies is made by the person doing the shooting. The majority of our kills were during brief contact with small enemy units or individuals that were usually engaged by the door guns. Our officers only determined the target, the crew chiefs and gunners knew they were the ones who decided if the target was hit. We all stopped our rounds short or hit high whenever we chose. When bullets hit low, they were an honest miss: good shooters know that a low shot can kill on the ricochet. Bullets that hit above a man indicated the shooter consciously or subconsciously wasn't interested in killing. The saying "Aim high" meant more than most people realized. Good machine gunners knew where every burst would hit and would always "aim low."

In the middle of the day, we stopped again at Duc Hoa and shut down for a short lunch. It was rare for a gunship crew to shut down for lunch, so whenever we did, we immediately tried to get something to eat at the nearest compound. No matter what size the compound was, it seemed that we could always count on the NCO Club to be open. Dale and I walked to the club to buy sandwiches for the crew. I always thought it odd that no matter where we were, the Officer's Club was always closed, so it was Dale and I who bought lunch. We had just returned to the ship with four baloney sandwiches, when two slicks from the 173rd Assault Helicopter Company landed nearby. The whole Duc Hoa compound emptied as the local ARVN soldiers ran out to meet the slicks. Both ships were loaded with NVA prisoners dressed in spotless green uniforms and wearing web gear that looked new. The ARVN soldiers swarmed over the prisoners, beating them and kicking them as they passed the punishment cells of the ARVN. These cells were small barbed wire cages used to discipline their own troops and were built so a man had only enough room to squat or lie in a fetal position in the hot sun or pouring rain. Seeing how they treated their own troops, it wasn't surprising to see them beat other soldiers. Sitting there eating my sandwich, I couldn't help but wonder how the NVA soldiers had managed to be so clean. They must have just crossed the border from Cambodia before being captured. I thought back to an article I had read about helicopter warfare that implied the sight of fresh, clean troops wearing spotless uniforms jumping out of helicopters into battle would be psychologically devastating to weary, dirty enemy soldiers. Most of our infantry wore dirty, ragged uniforms, however, and it was the enemy troops, fresh from the supply depots in Cambodia, who were wearing new, clean uniforms. Whoever wrote that article didn't realize that clean uniforms were the sign of green troops, and neither side feared new people. They were dumb and easy to kill—in both armies.

After eating lunch, we went back to work and the rest of the day was pretty much uneventful until our last assault of the afternoon. We were going to put troops into the area near Cu Chi where I had seen the thirty NVA lying in the ditch on the day of the wounded man at the bunker. The flight of ten slicks was following our new Nine Six into the LZ. Second gun was on their left, and we were on their right, slightly behind them. I was still flying on the right side and, while watching the brush, I saw a man's hand about four hundred meters away on our right. The lighting was perfect. The late afternoon sun on a moving hand caught my eye and held my attention. As we flew by, I looked behind us at the hand and saw a face slowly appear alongside a nearby tree. Someone was watching us flying into the LZ. Even though I'd had enough killing that day, this was different, and I calmly reported my sighting to Pat Ronan. "Got a man back here."

"Keep him in sight. We'll get him when the flight lifts off," he replied. Pat radioed Nine Six that we had a man in sight behind us and was directed to lead the guns back to the man after the slicks cleared the LZ. The slicks went into the LZ, machine guns blazing. The troops were off and the slicks on their way out of the landing zone in seconds. As the last slick lifted out of the LZ, Pat asked, "Still got him?"

"I have him," I said. Couldn't lose the guy as he stood with the evening sun in his face next to a lone palm tree, off to the side of the only group of palm trees bordering the entire length of rice paddies. Pat turned our ship in a tight circle and headed back toward the hand and face in the brush, fifteen hundred meters to our rear.

Unfastening my seat belt, I got up from my seat to kneel between the two pilots' seats to guide them. "One thousand meters, eight hundred meters, six hundred meters, see the palm trees, go to the palm tree fifty meters west of the field. There's a man standing on its right side."

"Got him," said Pat. "Get him, Dale."

Dale hit him with machine-gun fire, but didn't drop him. As the other gunships flew in behind us, they reported numerous men running. Now we'd get them with the miniguns. We started our gun run but when Pat told the pilot, "Make me hot," the miniguns started turning right, left, up and down. The guns had an electrical malfunction and were flexing every which way out of control. Something was wrong with our electronics and we couldn't fire the guns while they were running amok. We made the attack using Dale's machine gun on the running NVA soldiers. While Dale was busy shooting NVA soldiers, I kept changing electronic circuit boards, not sure which board controlled the positions of the guns. Our other two ships fired rockets into the running men while we flew circles off to one side of the fight. After getting the guns to stop flexing and to stay pointing forward, we joined our platoon and rolled in. But now the miniguns wouldn't fire at all. Dale and I used our machine guns going in and coming out of the gun run, then Pat radioed Nine Six that we were going to land at a nearby ARVN compound to clear our miniguns. We landed quickly, and after unloading the guns we found that they spun fine by hand, indicating we had an electrical problem, not a mechanical malfunction. After tightening everything electrical that had anything to do with the armament system, Pat tried dry-firing the guns and they worked. Quickly loading the guns, we were off again, ready to chew up everything with minigun fire, but we were too late. While we had been working on our miniguns, our other two gunships had been busy. The infantry had also walked up from the LZ in our absence and were confirming kills and throwing grenades into the numerous nearby tunnel entrances. I don't recall how the infantry decided to divide the kills, but they gave us nine—all because I had seen the sun shine on a hand moving in the dense tropical brush. I thought that nine was plenty, but Dale said he alone had dropped five and thought we should have been credited with more. I didn't really care one way or the other about the count, as my two of the morning still bothered me. I was feeling good about being the one who had initiated the fight, however. A couple of months earlier, I wouldn't have been able to spot a whole man, let alone see a hand.

Twilight was fast approaching, so the infantry moved back into the rice paddy for pickup. They'd been brought in only for a quick insertion, look for trouble and leave, not to spend the night. Slicks came in, troops were loaded, and the slicks were out, nothing to it. As the third gun, we would make sure the pickup zone was clean, then head for home. Riding into the PZ, a couple of meters off the ground, Pat was tempted to try out the miniguns. It was a good thing he didn't. The PZ was not clean. One lone soldier stood there waving at us. Maybe he was napping or relieving himself in the bush, but he'd missed his ride home. A slick turned back for him and I imagine that the man, his squad leader and his platoon leader took a real ass-chewing that evening.

XIII

Even though we had some easy kills that afternoon, working relatively close to home, there was something drastically wrong with the Big Picture. What were those enemy troops doing out in daylight next to the Cu Chi base camp? For that matter, why were there all those abandoned rice fields so close to our camp? Evidently, civilian farmers couldn't be secure working these fields, even with four thousand Americans living less than a mile away. If we couldn't control what was happening a mile from our barbed wire, how were we ever going to pacify a country? It seemed ironic that the U.S. military preached that persistence and determination were the attributes of a winner: we seemed to ignore the fact that the Viet Cong were the only political and military power in Viet Nam who had persistence and determination. While the average Vietnamese was probably neutral in his political philosophy, they were caught in the middle and had both the VC and us bothering them. If we were winning this war, why couldn't our troops go into Cu Chi village? We weren't even secure in the village attached to our compound, let alone in the fields next to our camp. Something told me we had picked the wrong side in this civil war.

Men and women were living in tunnels, in malaria-ridden swamps, in the mountains, in the nipa palm thickets, the mangrove tidal jungles, and in the triple-canopy rain forest. We found them and fought them everywhere and couldn't help but wonder why these people refused to give up and acknowledge our superiority. But we were superior in only some things—such as air power—and nobody ever won a war by air power. Dedicated ground troops win wars and the enemy had the dedication, not us. Most of us were in Viet Nam for a year; the soldiers who opposed us were going to be there all their lives. They were willing to suffer because of their certainty of prevailing. They would take the worst that we could throw at them and come back for more.

Following an air strike by B-52 bombers, we went on an assault of an NVA base camp near Dau Tieng. Our company was airborne with ten slicks loaded with infantry and three gunships minutes away from the landing zone as hundreds of tons of bombs tore apart the jungle near a rubber tree plantation. As the last bombs exploded, we flew into an impenetrable dust cloud and quickly turned around. It would have been suicide to continue the assault; we couldn't see a damn thing and might have flown into each other. Every ship except the C&C ship flew to Tay Ninh to sit and wait for the dust to settle.

After an hour of loafing along the Tay Ninh flight line, the call came over the radio from our C&C for us to saddle up and get our rotor blades turning. The crew chiefs quickly untied the rotor blades on their ships and the pilots started the turbine engines whining. Our three gunships dragged their skids down the runway, passing the infantry as they started to climb back on the slicks for another ride into another landing zone. In minutes, we were on our way and headed for the impact area. We were going straight in without first reconning the LZ, as we didn't expect any opposition. This LZ was going to be an easy mission for the guns, but difficult for the slicks. They had to land in the fine ankle-deep powder of pulverized earth, vegetation and people. As the slicks were on their final descent into the LZ, their pilots were cautioned not to fly into each other in the expected dust cloud. Ten ships flared to land and we momentarily lost sight of them as each slick churned up its own separate tornado of dirt and debris, which screened the troops jumping out better than any smokeship could do. It was a cold LZ; there was no opposition as the infantry jumped from the slicks. As the empty slicks departed to pick up another load of infantry, our gun-

ships flew quick figure eights over the infantry and over the
hundreds of bomb craters to determine what damage the
B-52s had done. Our first loads of infantry wandered beneath us through a barren moonscape of craters and debris,
searching for signs of the enemy. As we flew slowly over the
landscape, shredded and torn by bombers who never saw the
destruction they caused from miles above the battlefield, I
wondered what bomber crews thought of their work. I suppose they rationalized everything by assuming only trees and
shrubs were vaporized in the dust clouds beneath them. As
we circled the devastation, our pilot mentioned that the Air
Force was also using B-52 strikes on population centers in
North Viet Nam. Dale and I didn't believe him. As hard and
callous as we were, we could not believe anyone could be
found to fly such missions.

A quick look showed the bombers had obviously hit in the
right place. Concrete slabs of bunker roofs could be seen
twisted on the edges of bomb craters. Our first impression
was that hundreds of men must have died here. Then we
noticed that the fallen dust covering the impact area was
churned with the footprints of separate individuals, which
then converged into trails, all heading into the rubber plantation. The infantry found no dead or anything of value. We
flying overhead found no signs of men within or around the
bomb craters. A lot of North Vietnamese had survived the
bombing and disappeared into another sanctuary, a Michelin
rubber plantation.

These plantations owned by the French were normally
large swaths of trees, planted in straight rows, with few signs
of battle damage. We were limited when taking offensive action in the rubber plantations because our government paid
for every individual tree damaged by our weapons. While
our government condoned the wholesale destruction of farms,
villages and families without compensation, the assets of a
multinational business could not be harmed. It was pure capitalism in action and we were on a crusade for Capitalism.

A week later and several miles away, we would fight an
NVA unit that used a Michelin plantation as concealment to

ambush an American convoy on its way to Dau Tieng. We
had been working nearby with ground troops hunting NVA,
flying at treetop level, peering down through the branches,
watching for any signs of men or fortifications ahead of our
infantry. From high above the trees, nothing could be seen
except a thick carpet of lush, green vegetation, but if we
skimmed the treetops, it was surprising how much could be
seen through the gaps between branches and tree trunks. We
had been burning our eyes out trying to locate the enemy in
the jungle and were relieved to get a break by being called to
fly in aid of the convoy. As we climbed skyward after leaving
the trees, our height allowed us to see a black column of
smoke coming from burning vehicles at the ambush site.

We arrived at the highway in minutes to find a burning fuel
truck sitting along the road in an area where the engineers
had cleared a swath of trees several hundred meters from the
sides of the road. I wondered why the enemy had struck the
convoy at a place where the trees had been cleared and not at
the tail of the convoy where trees came right to the edge of
the road. Perhaps the clearings worked to the enemy's advantage as they had a much larger field of fire across the clearing and could engage multiple targets from their position. A
quick look showed that enemy automatic weapons continued
to fire from the edge of the clearing, but vehicles in the convoy were not sitting still waiting to be shot. Every vehicle behind the burning truck hugged the opposite shoulder of the
road and drove past while two military police jeeps engaged
the enemy with machine guns. I suppose there was the danger of the fuel truck exploding as the other trucks drove by,
but the convoy drivers realized there was more danger in letting the whole convoy stack up behind it, becoming easy targets.

We made a few gun runs, firing rockets into the enemy positions, and were getting ready to make another run when a
quad fifty came up from the rear of the convoy and positioned itself near the burning truck. We held off our gun run
while the quad fifty started dropping trees like grass under a
lawnmower. The quad fifty was a five-ton truck with four

.50-caliber machine guns mounted on a turret. When it fired, rubber trees fell like matchsticks. Its sheer firepower broke the ambush. After it had literally destroyed the edge of the tree line, we finished our gun run, catching quick glimpses of men running away. Once the enemy dispersed into the rubber plantation, they were safe. Flying over the rubber trees, we took sporadic small arms fire, but couldn't shoot back unless we saw a definite target. Afterward we wondered if the crew of the quad fifty was reprimanded for thinning the expensive trees bordering the highway. We left the ambush area knowing the NVA were still out in the rubber trees waiting for us. We had broken their ambush, but they escaped and we'd fight them again and again.

Early in the morning of February 27, the mortars started landing. "Karumph!" "Karumph!" "Karumph!" By their loud heavy bass sound, we knew that they were 82mm mortars, not the little 60mms. These mortars had some power. They could disintegrate a human body, not just maim it. Listening to the sounds of impacting rounds, we knew that the rounds were being walked through another company's area and that we were safe. But the heavy thumping sounds were the music of fear, and the adrenaline flowed through our bodies and made us subconsciously grin. We always expected a mortar crew to make a quick adjustment to the weapon and spin it to point at us, but they never did. They were too predictable and disciplined. Thirty years later, I find myself periodically singing the song of falling mortar rounds and give myself a short rush: *Karumph, Karumph, Karumph*.

Then came the rockets. Big ones: 122mm rockets that some poor souls had carried for miles through heat and rain and mud, then had quickly set up and fired in the general direction of the sprawling Cu Chi base camp. While the mortars tried to saturate a target, the rockets landed haphazardly. Louder than the loudest crack of a lightning bolt ever heard, individual rockets impacted around us and among our helicopters.

Out of the corner of my eye I caught the brilliant light of a rocket impacting across the road from our hooch and, as I turned to look where it hit, shrapnel whistled through the air above us from another rocket exploding. At the same moment the whole sky to our far right lit up as muffled explosions and leaping flames erupted from the Muleskinner Corral, the area where our Chinook helicopters were parked. These were the huge twin-bladed helicopters used to ferry artillery and infantry, retrieve crashed helicopters, and pull armored vehicles out of the mud. They were similar to a flying bus; it looked as if there'd be no more Chinook rides out of Cu Chi. It was pretty obvious the VC were on the compound and were using hand-carried satchel charges to blow up Chinooks. Since the crews of the Chinooks slept on their ships, we knew there were a lot of Americans dying in the fires lighting up the night sky.

Our platoon was sitting on our wooden sidewalk watching the fireworks when our platoon sergeant came running from our TOC bunker. He quickly told us to get to our helicopters. All flyable ships were to evacuate before the VC sappers could blow them up. As we were fully dressed, Dale and I hurried to our ship and stood with our machine guns, watching figures scurry through the dark. Luckily, the people running around our flight line were Americans, not VC. It was a perfect situation for a disaster. There was mass confusion; no one in charge, explosions, semidarkness lit by the glow of helicopters on fire, armed men running, the certain knowledge that the enemy was among us in the darkness. It's a wonder no one started a firefight with their own troops.

Dale and I hadn't been sitting next to our ship more than a couple of minutes when two pilots showed up, wearing only pants and flip-flops. "Untie the blades and let's get out of here," one shouted. As soon as our blades were turning, Cu Chi control tower was radioed that we were lifting off. We were told to fly out over Cu Chi village and not toward the tower. "Puff the Magic Dragon" was en route and was going to work the bunker line at the tower end of the runway. Puff was an Air Force fixed-wing aircraft that could carry enough ammunition so that its three miniguns could fire at the maximum rate of ten thousand rounds per minute. It was rare to see Puff in action, as it was generally used only against massed troops during a concentrated ground attack on an American compound. Puff was now going to work over the bunkers where we had spent many nights on guard. I wondered if the guards were in the bunkers or on top where I always sat. Anyone on top of our bunkers would stay on top for the rest of his short life if Puff flew over him.

Our AC gave the ship full power and we struggled to hop out of our parking revetment. We were about to line up along the runway for takeoff when the night air vibrated with a huge explosion. The whole sky lit up and rockets could be seen flying skyward from the helicopter rearmament point. They'd blown up our ammo dump. Flying down the runway, I watched the huge fire leap skyward while hundreds of tracers and rockets shot out of the flames in every direction. Our own rockets were now impacting throughout the sprawling base camp and would continue to do so for hours. A few more Chinooks went up in flames, telling us that the VC sappers were still running around the camp using satchel charges. Looking back into the camp as we flew over the village, there were so many large fires raging I could see almost as well as if it were daylight. I wondered if we were going to turn around and try to shoot running sappers in the light of our burning Chinooks.

Once airborne, all gunships were told to stay west of Cu Chi and wait for further orders. All the slicks were told to head for any other secure base and shut down, but to keep in radio contact. As we flew around in the darkness, I wondered what we could do. Massive fires were burning in the Chinook compound and the ammo dump was burping explosions as the raging fires found more piles of rockets and ammunition. Puff was working over the bunker line, sending a solid wall of tracers that, according to rumor, would put a bullet into every square inch of a football field. Our guys in the bunkers and those behind them waiting as a reaction force had frontline seats for a Puff the Magic Dragon show. I couldn't imagine what our gunships could do, as no one on the radios seemed to be reporting any enemy concentrations. There were other gunships to the east and north firing into mortar positions, but they weren't asking for help. Apparently no one could figure out what to do with us and we were told to head for any friendly base and to shut down there.

We went to Di-An where, for some unknown reason, our pilot landed us at a military police helipad instead of along the runway. We sat there until dawn, then decided that as long as we were with the MPs, we might as well join them in their mess hall and get something to eat. After breakfast, we refueled and went back to Cu Chi. I'll be damned if I can remember what we did when we got there, but I'm pretty sure we sat around all day waiting for a mission that never came. I seem to recall everyone checking out the ships for shrapnel damage from the previous night's rockets, but that should have been done before we'd flown out of Cu Chi. There was talk of VC sappers hiding in culverts and drainage ditches and everyone was walking around armed. Sandbags were being filled and fighting positions were being built along our flight line. While we had plenty of bunkers along the flight line, they were shelters to duck into when rockets and mortars started impacting, not fighting positions. In a ground attack, going in one would be going into your grave since VC sappers could run up to the bunkers unobserved and toss in grenades. New bunkers were being built with firing ports. While those of us who had spent many nights on the bunker line knew that the line was not secure, now the higher-ups apparently knew as well. Wonder what was their first clue? The exploding Chinooks, or the exploding ammo dump?

For the next couple of nights, we'd spend all night next to our ships on the flight line. After flying all day, we'd get a quick meal at the mess hall, then Dale and I would set up our machine guns in a ditch next to the runway. One evening some of the slick crews were set up in a bunker about a hundred meters behind us. They called out to us, "Don't forget to yell if you guys have to run for our bunker; we don't want to shoot you."

"Don't worry about shooting," I told them. "If somebody is running toward your bunker, it won't be us. We're holding that ditch even if the whole North Vietnamese Army comes here." We shot NVA for a living, and no NVA was going to chase Dale and me out of our ditch.

Officially, we were on 100 percent alert and no one was supposed to be sleeping at our flight-line fighting positions, but everybody did and no one checked on us. If it wasn't safe to sleep in the middle of the headquarters compound of the 25th Infantry Division, then we should have conceded defeat and gone home.

Several days following the Cu Chi sapper attack, we were engaged in a routine firefight. The other two gunships on our mission took hits from small arms fire. Those two ships had to land at the 116th maintenance area for repairs while we went to refuel, feeling lucky and invincible. After refueling we were getting ready to take off when a hovering slick moving toward the refueling point blew a galvanized roofing sheet from the nearby destroyed ammo dump right into our rotor blades. There was a blizzard of metal scrap in the air as our rotor blades ate the metal sheeting in seconds. Knowing that chewing up a large sheet of galvanized metal couldn't have done our blades any good, we flew over to maintenance and joined the rest of our damaged platoon. Inspecting our ship, we found we had major damage. Both of our main rotor blades were severely cut and gouged. There were no spare blades available for my ship so we had to wait until two new blades could be borrowed from another unit.

With nothing to do until the new blades arrived, we went back to the company area to loaf. Joining the other crews at the hooch, we were sitting around bullshitting when the door opened and the battalion commander entered. Shouting and yelling, he demanded that we get our helicopters back in the air and get back in the field. No use arguing that we were waiting for parts; we walked back to the flight line and loafed there until he showed up yelling at the maintenance crews. I guess he thought that screaming could get ships fixed even though there were no spare parts. When our maintenance officer, Cecil Johnson, flew into the maintenance area on the Beekeeper helicopter, we knew our ships would soon be back in the air. The Beekeeper was the maintenance platoon helicopter that delivered mechanics and parts to us out in the field or went hunting spare parts when we needed to repair ships fast. Wherever Cecil had gone looking for parts, he had been successful; we could see spare rotor blades had been loaded sideways across the cargo area of his ship and were hanging out of each doorway as he landed in front of the company hangar. Once the necessary parts were unloaded, the gunships were repaired quickly. Our maintenance people didn't need a lieutenant colonel shouting at them to get our ships flying. They were good at their jobs and had every gunship flying in a few hours. While no one in either our platoon or the maintenance platoon really talked about it, all of us felt hurt that our battalion commander thought we were purposely delaying our return to combat.

XIV

For several weeks prior to the sapper attack, things appeared to have been heating up. Following the sapper attack, there seemed to be even more contact with small groups of VC and NVA. Nothing serious, but we seemed to hop from firefight to firefight every day. Insignificant little skirmishes, but good men, American and Vietnamese, were dying at every point of contact. On March 4, 1969, we finally got in way over our heads.

March fourth started as an ordinary day: up before dawn, ship ready, and blades turning as the dark sky slowly gave way to the first sign of light. Lifting off, we were en route to do a quick assault on a village east of Trang Bang, attempting to catch the villagers and guerrillas at breakfast before they scattered to the rice fields and hiding places.

We expected that it was going to be an easy day: troops would land and sweep the village while we circled low, watching for men trying to escape the infantry sweep. We joined our C&C ship in the AO and had the village pointed out to us. From the air, it looked like a wooded island in a sea of barren, harvested rice paddies. While there was another large square wooded area of several hundred acres nearby, it was separated from the village complex by two hundred meters of dry, bare rice fields. Lead gun would mark the LZ for the slicks in the fields south of the village while we on the other two gunships guarded the flanks of the landing party. There would be no shooting or any type of artillery preparation since the only obvious target was the village itself. After landing, the slicks would depart to the east, avoiding the large woodlot to the west. As our slicks landed along the southern edge of the village, a squad of infantrymen would break from the main assault party and head for the paddies on the west to block any possible escape to the woods. The main force would work south to north while our gunships would stop anyone from leaving by the east or north. We could do this mission in our sleep.

The landing was made without any surprises, and our infantry cautiously advanced across the open fields to enter the village. We flew circles above the houses to their front but saw nothing unusual. Everything appeared to be normal. It was another typical morning in a little agricultural community. We left the main body of troops and flew over to check the blocking force on the western perimeter of the village. We found our blocking force on the west, walking slowly northward, keeping a rice dike on their right for protection from the village. We were flying directly above them about ten meters high when a single shot from a .51-caliber machine gun flew over their heads. But it didn't come from the village; it came from the woodlot on the west. The infantry jumped over the dike and faced the trees, leaving their backs exposed to the village while we on the gunships immediately turned to engage the tree line with rockets and minigun fire. Someone in the woods had really screwed up.

There had been no intention of bothering with the woodlot, and that single shot had now alerted us to the enemy's hiding place. Fifty-one-caliber machine guns did not operate alone; when we found these heavy machine guns, we always found concentrations of troops. As the lead gunship flew along the tree line, firing rockets through the limbs, enemy tracers flew up through the leaves beneath his skids. The muzzle flashes of AK-47s were everywhere. The entire eastern flank of the woodlot was honeycombed with fighting positions. My ship ran into the same wall of fire as we flew down the perimeter of the woods with our miniguns roaring.

Leaning out, I was firing slightly behind us, and from the corner of my right eye I could see that our lead gun had made a tight left-hand turn at the end of the woodlot. Lead gun was quickly returning to cover the third gun laying down rockets behind us. With no one covering his tail until lead finished his turn, the NVA poured their rounds into third gun as he flew by their positions. As I watched the rockets from our third gun explode behind my ship as he provided cover for us, I heard their AC on the radio: "We're losing controls and all gauges and putting this ship down."

Damn it! They were losing altitude fast, headed for a landing in the dry rice fields where the infantry had landed. The crew chief and gunner were both holding smoke grenades out the doors and trailing multicolored plumes of smoke. Once again I watched our boys showing they were cool by riding their crippled ship down to their deaths, trailing smoke, recognizing that when their ship hit the hard-as-concrete, dry rice paddy, they might erupt into a giant fireball.

Having just seen everyone on Wilsher's ship die, I felt numb watching another crew go down. Their ship hit the paddy and skidded to a stop in a cloud of dust. No explosion! God, I felt so relieved. Lead gun then radioed, "Heading back to Cu Chi, we're full of holes, two wounded and leaking fuel, be right back with another ship."

Our pilot, Jim Barre, then told us that a bullet had gone through the floor next to him and put shrapnel in his foot. When asked by our AC, Hesse, if he was hit bad, he calmly replied, "Don't worry, no big deal. I'm okay."

We flew over to our downed ship to cover the crew, wanting to make sure they hadn't landed near enemy positions that had stayed hidden during the initial landing. We were flying low over our disabled gunship, watching the pilots take out the radios, and the enlisted crew set up their machine guns on the nearby dike when our C&C ship radioed for us to go back to the tree complex. *What? Go back alone!* I thought, wondering if our commander knew what he was telling us to do. It would be suicide for a single gunship to take on all of the troops hidden in the trees. We were told to fly straight at the woodlot on an east-to-west run to determine the extent of the enemy positions hidden in the trees. They were obviously on the eastern perimeter, but we had to determine how far into the woods their positions extended. There wouldn't be any fancy aerial maneuvers or fancy gun runs; we were to go straight into the enemy positions, firing all our weapons, and take whatever was thrown at us. We were being sent to die.

Our AC made several circles to gain altitude for our probe of the woodlot. Climbing higher gave me time to think about what we were to do and I knew there was no way possible for us to fly straight into the trees and live. We had lost two ships by flying along the perimeter of the woods. Flying straight at these positions would allow every weapon on the perimeter to pivot toward us. Besides the people on the perimeter, there had to be scores of troops behind them waiting for us with their automatic weapons. Glancing around the ship, I saw no signs of fear on the faces of the rest of the crew and I wondered if they realized what we were about to do. They looked calm and resigned. No one said a word. Hesse lined up on the center of the woodlot and dove toward the tree line eight hundred meters to our front, straight into the fire of the enemy machine guns.

Since I was on the helicopter, I was committed to the ride, but if I had been on the ground, I would have run for my life. I'm not sure many pilots would have done what we were told to do, but I knew that Hesse wouldn't hesitate. My impression of Hesse was that he must have been a Nazi SS trooper in a previous life—he looked like a blond German soldier and was fearless in battle. While enlisted crews joked and kidded around with other officers, Hesse was never mistaken for one of the boys. But he was the type of man we wanted to be with if there was going to be gunfire.

As we approached the woodlot and were coming into range of the trees, muzzle flashes sparkled along the entire eastern side of the perimeter. Normally, we flew into a fight with our shaded helmet visors down in order to be able to pick out single muzzle flashes more easily, but today the shaded visor allowed me to see too many flashes to count. My legs were shaking in sheer terror and I pressed my machine gun on my thighs to keep my feet from banging the floor like a drum. I have never been so scared in my life. I distinctly remember thinking, *This is what you wanted. You're shaking all over and scared to die. You're a phony and you know it because you can't face combat when it's a real battle.* I knew for certain that we were going to die. Our daily missions of hunting guerrillas and small bands of NVA were a joke. We were not really elite gunship crews; we were nothing but cannon fodder. We were being sent to our certain deaths for no other reason than to probe the enemy line to determine its depth. We were a tool to use and throw away. I told myself, *If we ever land, I'm walking away. I'm through with this shit.* I was terrified and shaking with fear, feeling we were going to die for nothing.

Much later, I would realize that the men on the C&C ship had made the right decision by telling us to probe the woods to determine the extent of the enemy's positions. Someone had to do it and we were available. They needed to learn where the enemy was positioned in order to conduct the battle.

As we roared into our battle, the minigun firing a few feet away from my head made my teeth ache and stopped them from chattering from fear. Targets were everywhere. I forced myself to fire at one separate muzzle flash at a time. My resolve calmed my shaking legs.

Tracers were everywhere. And every fifth round was a tracer! How much steel was really in the air? We were putting down over fifty-five hundred rounds a minute and there were more tracers coming up than going down. We flew over the entire wooded complex and received fire from one end to the other. Who the hell was down there? The entire North Vietnamese Army? We broke left and circled around, then made another run down the eastern perimeter south to north. Everybody seemed to still be home. We received as much fire as the first time through.

Out of ammunition for the miniguns, we rolled right and flew low between the trees and the infantry in order to draw fire toward us and away from the infantry. Gilchrest now faced the enemy fire and his machine gun fired constantly as we moved parallel to the tree line. Looking straight down, I could see the ground troops sprawled a few meters beneath me and watched as they lifted their rifles to the top of the dike and pulled the triggers. Most of their rounds were hitting in the field between them and the trees. No one in the infantry squad was willing to raise his head above the dike to take an aimed shot, not with enemy bullets chewing away the dike protecting them. None of our infantry appeared to have been hit by enemy fire, but they were not in a very secure position. They were hopelessly outnumbered and outgunned. Their only chance was to lay low until the enemy guns in front of them were silenced. As long as helicopters were nearby, the NVA would probably not chance rushing across the paddy in force to annihilate the squad. Looking down at them, I wished that I was behind a meter-thick rice dike too.

Breaking left, we flew over to cover two of our slicks bringing in troops to protect our downed gunship and to pick up our crew. I had no idea where our main assault force was located, but I imagined they were working their way through the village to protect the rear of the trapped squad. Several Cobra helicopters from the 25th Aviation Battalion soon arrived on station and started pouring rockets down on the positions in the tree line. While we had flown right over the treetops firing into enemy positions, the Cobras came diving in from an altitude of a thousand meters and pulled out of their gun run at 150 meters. There was quite a difference in tactics between our units. We rarely flew as high as their lowest altitude and never when engaged with the enemy. Their theory was that height equaled safety, while our theory was that by being low, we were over the enemy so fast they didn't have much time to shoot at us.

With the Cobras on station, my ship headed back to Cu Chi to rearm and refuel. We might have shut down to determine battle damage after a normal firefight, but this fight was too big. The only obvious damage appeared to be a few bullet holes around the pilot and a bullet hole behind my head. We loaded fuel and ammo with blades turning and were joined at the rearm point by our lead gun crew in another ship ready to return to our fight. They had landed their first ship full of bullet holes next to our maintenance area and jumped into another gunship. Their lightly wounded crew were also returning to the fight again, though they could have stayed at Cu Chi—Stingers didn't quit because they were bleeding. The crew of the third gunship radioed that they would join us shortly in another gunship. The slick that had brought the infantry to secure their ship until a Chinook could carry their wounded bird home had returned our crew to Cu Chi. Not satisfied with being shot down once, they threw their gear in another ship to do it again.

All day long we would take turns hitting the NVA troops in the trees. Artillery would pound them for a while, Cobras would expend their armament, then maybe a couple of jet strikes, then us. No matter what was done to the woodlot, every time we went in we received heavy automatic weapons fire. Dale and I fired continuously at separate muzzle flashes without any regard for conserving ammunition. We both knew that as soon as the rocket tubes and minigun trays were empty, we'd be heading back to rearm. The tactic of the day seemed to be to expend all armament as quickly as possible, then go back for more.

Following one of our numerous refuel/rearm runs, we were eating our lunch in the air, watching the Cobras expend their entire ordnance, when we noticed an armored unit driving up. We were going to be treated to an armored attack. The tanks lined up across a broad front parallel to a portion of the eastern perimeter with the armored personnel carriers behind them. They intended to assault the eastern perimeter of the woodlot just south of the infantry squad, which was still sprawled behind their rice dike waiting to be rescued. I had never seen an attack by a large armored unit, and it was impressive to see a long line of steel armored vehicles move out on line toward the enemy. Tanks and APCs climbed up over rice dikes, exposing their soft bellies to the enemy, then down the other side and across the paddy to the next dike. I expected the NVA on the eastern perimeter to break under the assault, abandon their positions and run for their lives.

Who in their right mind would stand up to a line of tanks coming toward them? I naïvely expected the armor attack to go through the woodlot like a hot knife through butter. The NVA would then be running ahead of the armor out into the exposed rice paddies, where we would greet them with our miniguns. I forgot who we were fighting.

The armored vehicles were firing their heavy weapons into the tangled woods, but they didn't intimidate the NVA. The tanks were about four hundred meters from the tree line when RPGs started flying toward them. Numerous smoke trails from these slow antitank rockets soon hung over the bare rice fields. RPGs were exploding everywhere around our tanks, but I don't believe that any tanks were hit. The tanks immediately started backing up out of RPG range and let the APCs move ahead of them. All of the machine guns on the APCs were tearing into the brush while the tanks stayed back out of RPG range and fired high explosive rounds into the woods. The APCs stopped short of the trees and fired everything they had as they attempted to shield a "Zippo" maneuvering toward the trees. The Zippo was an APC using a heavy-duty flamethrower, which had a large fuel supply carried inside the APC. The Zippo drove to within a hundred meters of the tree line and poured liquid fire into the enemy positions. But even the flames of Hell couldn't stop the enemy automatic weapons fire coming from the woods.

The frontal assault was called off and the armor pulled back while artillery and jet strikes hit the woodlot again. All during the afternoon, mechanized units joined us and extended our lines around the southern and western sides of the woodlot. Our slicks had also been ferrying in more infantry during the afternoon to face the eastern and northern sides, so the NVA were effectively surrounded. No one was moving to assault the woods, however, as heavy fire still met any aircraft attempting to neutralize the enemy. The woods were going to be pounded to pieces and the NVA troops torn apart before any ground troops entered the woodlot. We had the enemy trapped and, whoever was in charge, flying overhead in the C&C helicopter, had wisely decided not to waste lives with an infantry assault. The NVA soldiers weren't going anywhere. Many commanders would have sent infantry straight across the open rice paddies into the enemy machine guns, but the 25th Infantry Division did not squander the lives of infantrymen.

By twilight, the only positive thing achieved for certain was that the infantry squad trapped in the rice paddy had somehow managed to rejoin its unit along the village perimeter. Obviously, the tons of ordnance expended in the woodlot during the day had to have done something, but heavy fire still poured from the area every time we flew over it.

I'm not sure how many gunships our platoon had flyable in the morning, but 440 was the only one still able to fly as darkness covered the battleground. Our other two crews kept trading ships during the day because the NVA kept filling them with bullet holes. Somehow, nothing important had been hit on my ship. Enemy fire had put down the rest of the Stinger gunships. Just after dark, we were told to make a couple of gun runs to expend our ammunition and then go home. A company from the 25th Aviation Battalion would take our place during the night.

We ended the day by flying low over the tanks and APCs, making the exact same gun run that we did in the morning when I knew we were going to die. After a whole day of bombing, artillery and gunship strikes, there should be nothing left in the woods, but I knew the enemy was still waiting for us. As our miniguns roared, their muzzle flashes lighting up the inside of the ship, Dale and I fired at muzzle flashes twinkling in the darkness surrounding the light of numerous individual small fires burning throughout the woods. The sky was full of tracers, both green and red, when Dale's voice came calmly over our radio, "Seav, I'm hit." All of us turned toward Dale as he calmly said, "I'm hit in the back," while still firing his machine gun at NVA muzzle flashes.

Quickly unbuckling my seat belt, I put my machine gun on the floor. Sprawling across the minigun trays, I loosened Dale's body armor to determine how badly he had been wounded. As I lay across the ammo trays, bullets were ripping through our floor between the minigun trays and our cases of grenades. I distinctly recall wondering what would happen if a bullet hit one of our white phosphorus grenades. I suppose we would have exploded in midair. It was just a passing thought. I checked Dale. He had a fragment of shrapnel in his back, not a bullet. Tightening up his body armor, I told our crew that Dale wasn't hurt badly and then slid across the ammo trays, picked up my machine gun and went back to work.

Shooting short bursts of machine-gun fire at every muzzle flash possible, I could tell that my rate of fire was slowing down because of carbon buildup on the piston. As we left the woodlot and started turning to make another gun run, I took advantage of the break to change machine-gun barrels, grabbing an extra barrel that didn't have a flash suppressor. Entering the woodlot again, we continued to receive heavy automatic weapons fire and, as I fired short bursts, I learned why a flash suppressor was installed on automatic weapons. Backes hadn't lied when he had trained me. The flash suppressor had not been installed to keep the enemy from seeing my muzzle flash; its purpose was to suppress the flash so that the shooter could see while he was firing. When I pulled the trigger, there was an area of white-hot light three feet in diameter at the end of the barrel; not a flame, exactly, but almost. The whole left side of the ship seemed to glow when I'd shoot and, as we came out of our gun run, I quickly changed barrels for one with a flash suppressor.

On these last gun runs, it seemed as if we were receiving as much enemy fire as earlier in the day, but I felt no fear whatsoever. Maybe I was numb. Way back in the morning, a hundred years ago, I had been mentally shocked that the bastards in the C&C ship were sending us into certain death. But we'd made gun runs all day long and were still alive. I knew I could only go into so much automatic weapons fire before a bullet hit me. Perhaps I was resigned to fate. But after the initial fear, I did my job without concern. If we went down in flames, so be it.

Time after time that evening we would make a firing run,

turn around and go back toward the enemy. In those short intervals of inaction on the turns, I'd glance around the ship.
There were bullet holes in the floor and ceiling and, as a crew
chief, I had to wonder if any vital controls were hit. Control
rods might only be hanging together by a metal splinter, the
failure of which would send our ship out of control until it
exploded into a ball of flame on contact with the ground. I
wasn't really worried, however; I was way past that stage. We
were committed to the fight and we were going to fight to the
end. I felt absolutely calm and indifferent to our situation.
My hands were dry as they usually were when in combat. I
always noticed how dry my hands became and had wondered
if a human body shuts down the sweat glands in a person's
hands so that he doesn't drop his weapon: evolution? Taking
advantage of our short breaks on the turns, I'd lean back
against the bulkhead and think about what we were doing.
There wasn't any honor or glory involved; we were going
into a meat grinder of NVA fire, trying to grind them apart
with our weapons. It was really no different from men trying
to club each other to death. After completing our turn, Hesse
would straighten the ship to fly back into the wall of tracers
and I'd take a few short, deep breaths, lean slightly forward
with the machine gun and pick individual muzzle flashes as
my targets. Some of the guys swore they took a deep breath
before a fight and could remember exhaling after the fight,
thereby proving that we don't have to breathe in order to live.

After dark, gunships from another company arrived. We
expended the last of our ammunition and were released to
Cu Chi. God, what a relief. I was physically and mentally
drained—but still exuberant we had made it. Barre and Dale
had relatively minor wounds, while Hesse and myself were
fine. What a day!

Flying back to Cu Chi, I was high on adrenaline. But we
weren't safe yet. Everyone knew we had taken plenty of hits.
We knew many helicopters escaped hot areas only to fall out
of the sky heading for home. While we were in a state of ex-
hilaration, laughing and joking to relieve the tension, I think

all of us were watching our gauges and listening for any slight difference in the normal helicopter noise.

Coming into Cu Chi, Hesse didn't even bother taking our ship to POL to refuel and rearm. We had enough bullet holes to keep 440 in maintenance for a long time. We landed at the 12th Evac Hospital, where Dale got out to get the shrapnel removed from his back. Jim Barre stayed with us, ignoring his shrapnel wound. After the ship was sitting in its revetment and shut down, we started counting bullet holes and were surprised we had only forty hits in the ship plus a few in the rotor blades. I had expected to find hundreds after the wall of fire we had flown through. I suppose the NVA were just spraying the sky. A lot of the tracers probably weren't even near us. I don't think most people with an automatic weapon really aim at a target, anyway. A good example of typical automatic weapons fire can be found by looking at the bullet holes in a building after a firefight. You know damn well that the windows and doors were the targets, but the entire building will be pockmarked. Sometimes it appeared as if the windows and doors were not even hit.

We were the last of our platoon to return home. We wrote up our combat damage in the logbook hurriedly. Maintenance would start their repair work after they received our daily logbook pages and prioritized the work to be done. Cecil Johnson and his repair teams were going to be busy. Having been in maintenance, I didn't envy those guys. No matter how badly our ships had been damaged, maintenance would be expected to have twelve slicks and three gunships flyable by morning. My ship wasn't going to be flying for a while. Not with forty bullet holes in it. Leaving the ship and the guns dirty, we hurried to the company area.

The Stingers had a platoon party scheduled for that evening and we were ready to celebrate. There were several of us heading home within the next month. But while this was a going-away party, it was also a celebration for coming home alive. I'm sure I wasn't the only one who had not expected to be alive at day's end. About half of the platoon had been wounded, but no one seriously. Everyone seemed to be mentally and physically high on adrenaline. Alcohol wasn't having any effect on us. We laughed about the day, forgetting some of us were going out again in the morning.

Our platoon leader came to the party and told us the company commander was recommending the Distinguished Flying Cross be awarded to all crewmembers for the day's action. Even if the recommendations didn't go through, he thought the crew of 440 should definitely get the award because our crew had been the only one to spend the entire day in action. Everyone else had been getting shot down or getting shot up and returning to Cu Chi for repairs, but we had only left the fight for fuel and ammunition. I later heard the two pilots and Dale received the Air Medal with "V" for valor.

Garcia shook me awake in the darkness of another early morning and told me to get dressed—our platoon was going to the site of the previous day's fight. I hadn't expected to have to fly so soon. But our maintenance platoon surprised us once again. They had worked hard and repaired three gunships overnight, so we were ready to rejoin the fight the morning of March 5. At our platoon party the previous evening, we had joked about having a day off from work, never expecting that Cecil and the night maintenance crew would have our ships flying so soon.

Having worked in the maintenance platoon, I knew how time-consuming it was to do repair work in the dark with only the weak glow of small flashlights lighting the helicopter. Visiting the piss tube between our hooch and the road next to our parked ships in the middle of the night, I had idly glanced over to the flight line and seen the twinkling of the flashlights hovering like fireflies above the roofs of several helicopters. I had gone back to sleep, not really expecting the company to be able to send out a heavy gun team until late afternoon at the earliest. As always, the overworked mechanics and officers of the maintenance platoon knew there were infantry out in the bush counting on helicopters. Our guys were not going to let them down. It would have been easy for the men out on the flight line in the darkness to slack off. No one would have known or questioned why the ships weren't flyable by daylight. Cecil and his sergeants had performed their triage on our bullet-riddled ships, and then had their teams strip other helicopters of parts to get the least seriously damaged birds back into the air. They were the men who ensured that the helicopters of the 116th AHC were flying over the heads of our infantry again. A lot of the enemy would die on March 5 because of the dedication of our maintenance platoon. Maintenance never received any glory or praise, but they were the ones who kept our company operating. The rest of us just went for a ride every day. But if the men in maintenance had known what they were sending us out to do the next morning, they might not have worked so hard.

Our three gunships were a little late taking off because of normal maintenance problems. By the time we arrived back at the AO it was already daylight. The heavily wooded complex of the previous day had been reduced to a smoldering, smoky, bomb-cratered patch of charred earth. The few trees that hadn't been toppled by bombs and artillery either leaned over waiting for gravity to pull them down or stood as bare, stripped poles. We replaced several Cobras as the onsite overhead air support and were ordered to provide cover for a mechanized infantry battalion that was starting to cross the open rice paddies along the southern edge of the smoking graveyard of the NVA. As the mechanized unit left the dry paddies and entered the shattered remains of the tree line, we circled thirty meters over their armored vehicles, anxiously waiting for defensive fire to erupt. Nothing happened. The tracks entered the splintered, smoldering woodlot without opposition and then crawled forward; APCs twenty meters apart with a squad of infantry between every two vehicles. The whole unit kept on line as it moved at the speed of a slowly walking infantryman through the debris of battle. Counting dead, shooting wounded and retrieving weapons, the soldiers conducting the sweep moved slowly toward the open rice fields to the north, where additional infantrymen waited in ambush along the dikes for any enemy survivors who would or could run out of the woodlot.

We flew over the battlefield, but had only started scanning the moonscape in front of the armored sweep when we were ordered to leave the area. Since the infantry sweeping the smoking wasteland below us were not receiving any opposition, we were told to hunt down stragglers. It was thought that a large number of NVA had slipped through our blockade during the night and were now traveling west to regroup in Cambodia. Most people have probably heard or read of a news report following a battle that states, "Troops are now engaged in cleaning up stragglers." I doubt many people have any idea what that term means. Basically, it is hunting shell-shocked, lost, mostly unarmed men and killing them. It is murder, pure and simple.

Call it what you might, we had no qualms about shooting stragglers. Because we knew, if they crossed the border, they would come back some day looking to kill us. I suspect those in charge of this operation had decided to have us hunt stragglers in order to credit the 116th with some kills. The 25th Infantry Division was keeping the tally for this battle and their units would get the kills. As I recall the final total body count was over 250 enemy bodies actually found in the smoldering woods and the 116th Assault Helicopter Company was credited with one kill. It made us wonder how someone had determined that our bullets had killed the one man. In all honesty, however, I couldn't truthfully swear that we had done any harm to the enemy concentrated in the woodlot. No matter how much ammunition we fired into their positions, the air would be filled with bullets coming our way on the next gun run. We flew into a wall of tracers every time.

Only receiving credit for one kill after what had happened on the previous day didn't seem fair, but there was nothing we could do about it. The infantry confirmed, totaled and allocated the kills with no appeal procedure. What really impressed us, however, was that twenty-seven undamaged, operable machine guns had been retrieved from the enemy fighting positions. How many more had been carried away or destroyed by bombs or artillery? No wonder the sky had been red and green with tracers. It was later estimated that an

NVA regiment of eight hundred men had been bivouacked in the woodlot and every member of the regiment had probably shot at us.

The day after the fight was another matter, however. The surviving NVA soldiers had been mauled by our firepower and had lost their interest in fighting. Most survivors were probably headed back to Cambodia. No longer a disciplined regiment, survivors of the battle could be scattered for miles to the west, either hiding or walking aimlessly. We left the mechanized troops in the smoldering woodlot and joined a nearby infantry company sweeping the adjacent hamlets to the west for lost NVA soldiers. Civilians were fleeing their homes ahead of our ground troops and numerous oxcarts were headed cross-country through the dry rice paddies. The drivers of the oxcarts did not want to use the local road, where they could easily be stopped and searched. While they might outrun our infantry, they couldn't hide from us. A quick flight a few meters above them let us see that most carts were hauling large flat rice winnowing baskets that only partially hid men in uniform. We might not even have noticed the men hiding in the back of the oxcarts if they hadn't kept lifting the edges of the flat baskets to look at us flying above them. Machine-gun fire was placed in front of the oxen to try to stop each cart from leaving the area. But I don't recall any stopping to wait for our infantry. Most men on the oxcarts were killed, but some were let go if no weapons were observed. We were flying only several meters above them and could easily see the fear on their faces as the tired young soldiers looked up at us for mercy. If no one on an oxcart appeared to be armed, it wasn't a priority target. And a few terrified young men with military haircuts were left to live another day. Not many, though.

Our infantry commander on the ground soon radioed us to let the carts alone and use our guns on possible enemy hiding places in front of the infantry sweep. He requested we machine-gun the heavy vegetation surrounding several dry streams and a small dry canal to the front of their line of march. He was cautious because he knew vegetation could conceal armed stragglers and the dry narrow canal was a perfect fighting position for hidden NVA soldiers.

Even though it didn't seem to be much of a target, we made a quick gun run down one overgrown streambed, firing machine-gun rounds into the brush without observing any sign of soldiers. They were there. As our infantry walked the streambed, soldiers would periodically drag a body out into the rice fields. Naked bloody bodies soon lay scattered in the fields next to the dry stream, since our troops stripped the dead of anything that could be used by local guerrillas. Shortly after the bodies were searched and stripped, we received a radio call from the ground troops asking if we wanted souvenirs. Our pilots were curious as to what the infantry had to give us, since they rarely shared their booty. I assumed that they were going to give us a few AK-47s because they had collected quite a few of them searching the streambed. My ship landed in the rice paddy and several men ran toward us with their arms full of captured equipment. We were handed a Tokarov pistol, numerous pairs of Ho Chi Minh sandals and a pile of belts with NVA buckles. I don't know what the other guys on our ship did with their share of the booty, but I threw mine away.

Our third gun left to refuel while we started working on a long narrow dry canal shaded by the limbs of trees planted along its edge. The green vegetation intertwined to roof the canal from the sun and effectively hid any enemy troops who might be resting in the shade. The crew chief on our lead gunship had randomly machine-gunned the length of the canal and, at the end of the trees, they had made a tight left turn to fly straight back toward us while staying on the other side of the canal. They would pass on our left, going back to where the vegetation along the canal started. Our ship would repeat the same maneuver. We skimmed the trees along the canal, our skids running through the branches. As we flew along the dry canal, randomly shooting the brushy overhanging vegetation on each side of the dry canal bed, I glanced to our front and, through an opening in the trees arched over the canal, I could see a man in an NVA uniform running along the dry canal bed. Before I could pivot my gun, I momentarily lost sight of him when some tree branches obscured my view. I thought we had lost this soldier when Pat Ronan turned our ship left to fly across the canal.

As our ship made its tight turn five meters above the canal, I looked down through an opening in the branches and there was our man. Our left turn had brought me face-to-face with the soldier. He instantly stopped running and looked up at me. Time seemed to stop. We stared at each other for hours. He was a young man, probably still a teenager. He wore a powder blue uniform and faded green battle harness, but carried no weapon. I was close enough to see his eyes blink and watched the expression on his face change from that of a hunted, harried animal to relief and resignation. He started to smile. He looked right at me from a distance of ten meters, so close that I could see a button was missing from his shirt. His hands were slowly being raised in the universal symbol of surrender, or *chieu hoi,* when my bullets hit his chest. I hadn't consciously pulled the trigger. We were probably over the opening in the trees for a split second that seemed like hours, and in that brief instant, my eyes and mind were on the young man while my fingers worked independently. I felt as if I had shot a brother, but bullets cannot be recalled. I could taste the blood flooding his lungs and spewing out his nostrils as his knees buckled. I watched him die as gravity brought him to the ground. Time started up again, and before I could make myself speak, we had made our turn and were a hundred meters away paralleling the canal.

"I got a man here," I said.

"Well, kill him!" shouted Pat.

"Already did," I softly answered.

Our lead gun had made another left turn ahead of us and was coming toward us again on the other side of the canal. We radioed that we had a kill eight hundred meters to their front and that the body was lying in the bed of the canal. A new gunner on the lead gunship machine-gunned our powder blue boy for practice, then we moved on to other streambeds. I wish I had let that young man live.

We did this type of work for two days and our new platoon sergeant flew his first mission as a gunner with our platoon on our second day of cleaning up stragglers. Later that evening in the NCO Club, I overheard him telling another sergeant he couldn't believe what the Stingers were doing in the field. The ship he was on had apparently tried to stop an ox-cart and the crew chief mistakenly hit the woman driver instead of a man hiding behind her under a basket.

"He killed the woman and nobody said a thing. I just don't believe they can do things like that," he said, shaking his head side to side.

He looked over at me and asked, "Is that what you guys do every day?"

"What the fuck did you think we did out in the field? It's a different goddamn Army out where we work! Don't you ever see our ships coming back full of bullet holes? No one shot that woman on purpose! Wait 'til you have to walk machine-gun bullets up to a person's sandals to stop them. It ain't so damn easy!"

I was so damned mad at him I was sputtering. Who the hell was he to judge another person's mistake? I believe what made me angry was listening to him discuss a screwup in the field with someone at the base camp. There was a saying at Cu Chi, "What plays in the field, stays in the field." When bad things happen, don't bring them to camp with you. Mistakes happen. Learn from them.

I walked away from the bar and went over to a corner to sit with Dale and to meditate about the guy in the powder blue uniform. Dale and I rarely talked about anything that happened in the field. Forget what happened today, tomorrow might be worse. We sat and drank and thought, until First Sergeant Deal closed the bar and told us to go home to our hooch. Sergeant Joe Deal replaced our previous top sergeant in January and was one of those rare old sergeants who would go out to work with us hunting the NVA. The three of us left the bar and sat on the wooden sidewalk outside the club for a while talking about the war. Eventually we grew tired of talking about things over which we had no control. Sergeant Deal left to visit our TOC, and Dale and I went to our hooch to get some sleep. We didn't bother walking up to the TOC to find out where we were going the next day. We didn't really care and it didn't really matter.

XV

The next morning we went out to another day of mismatched missions. Starting out before dawn, at first light the guns were sent to suppress sniper fire harassing an infantry platoon trying to eat breakfast. Flying over the heads of soldiers sprawled along a paddy dike calmly eating, we were contacted by their lieutenant. Speaking slowly and in a very polite manner, he asked, "Can you guys please put some rockets into the tree line to our November Echo? There's a couple of rifles in there."

"No sweat. Will do," our AC replied.

Rolling in on the tree line, several muzzle flashes indicated that somebody was hiding there and our rockets either scared them or killed them. After the first pass there were no more muzzle flashes when we flew by the trees.

"Thank you for the assistance," the lieutenant politely radioed.

We left our polite lieutenant and flew away to insert other infantrymen near several hamlets, where they would search for local VC. These small hamlets were nothing more than a few scattered dwellings in a lush tropical jungle of palm trees and shrubs. No streets or roads crisscrossed. Footpaths and trails interconnected backyard to front yard. The village scheme appeared to be a maze. It must have required some thinking before someone went for a walk to go visit Uncle Nguyen on the other side of the community.

The infantry landed without opposition in a large rice paddy south of the community and headed into the village walking toward the north. The vegetation was so thick that, even flying with our skids hitting tree limbs, we could see only a glimpse of our infantry now and then. Our troops slowly patrolled through the hamlet, making random stops to search homes for men of military age and for hidden supplies. We soon noticed two men running ahead of our troops but were unable to get a good look at them when they sprinted across a yard or down a path. None of us could see if they carried weapons and therefore we couldn't shoot them. Whenever they stopped, we'd drop a smoke grenade to mark their position, but as soon as the smoke grenade hit the ground, they'd scurry through the brush and down the trails. We chased these two men around the hamlets for at least an hour before they disappeared. While they probably were VC, no one would give us permission to shoot them for running around in circles. The hamlets appeared relatively prosperous, tile roofs on the houses, rice drying in the yards and no impact craters from artillery, very unusual where we worked.

After this "walk in the sun," the morning sweep ended with the infantry filing out of the hamlets to line up in the open rice paddies for extraction by our slicks. Two of the soldiers left the village carrying a large wooden bed they had liberated from a home. When the slicks took off after picking up the troops, the bed stayed in the middle of the field, abandoned because it wouldn't fit into the helicopter. There went someone's hope of comfort in his firebase bunker. Our slicks flew only a few miles, then landed the troops in another area where they would spend the rest of the day patrolling toward their base camp. We then linked up with another infantry unit at Tay Ninh for an assault into the real jungle west of the Black Virgin Mountain, Nuy Ba Dinh. Talk about extremes in a day. From hunting scattered local-yokel VC in a built-up, populated area to hunting main-force NVA units in a triple-canopy jungle.

Our entire company landed at Tay Ninh to refuel and pick up infantry. Once there we were told to shut down and break for lunch. Our C&C ship left Tay Ninh and took the infantry commander out to our new AO to scout the area while we were eating. The C&C staff flew west over the jungle and picked our landing zone, an 800-meter-long, 200-meter-wide clearing of rotor-blade-high elephant grass surrounded by heavy timber. It appeared to be a great place to land troops, but the enemy knew this as well as we. It was therefore a great place for NVA machine gunners to shoot up an incoming helicopter assault. Both sides recognized clearings that made good landing zones. After getting the call to saddle up, the guns flew straight to the proposed landing zone while the slicks loaded the infantry for the assault. They would sit at Tay Ninh for fifteen minutes, then head straight out to meet us near the LZ. We made our initial pass over the LZ to get an idea what it looked like, then headed back to meet our slicks, which were airborne with the troops. The clearing picked as our LZ had a slight dogleg to the left and the lead gun was radioed to mark the touchdown point for the lead slick far enough into the clearing so that all troops would land past the dogleg. As we left to meet our slicks, artillery rounds started impacting along the tree lines surrounding the LZ.

Returning with the slicks, we could see artillery fire hitting the tree lines while we were still several kilometers from the landing zone. The call came over the radios that the artillery had ceased fire. We started our long descent toward the clearing. As always our lead gun would fly in front of our flight of ten slicks and mark the landing position of the lead slick with smoke grenades. Second gun flew along the right flank of the slicks to suppress the right tree line, while my ship flew slightly behind the slicks. My ship was to cover the left flank, firing our rockets into the edge of the woods to protect our slicks as they lost airspeed in order to land in the high grass of the LZ. As the slicks were coming in on the final approach, I distinctly recall one of our rockets hitting dead center, a third of the way from the top of a huge tree, causing the entire top of the tree to tumble off. Never saw that happen before. The landing was unopposed and quiet. All slicks had touched down briefly while the infantry jumped off and were ready to lift off when a .51-caliber machine gun started firing.

My gunship had been drifting toward the right, attempting to line up behind the second gunship when directly to my left the heavy machine gun opened fire. The machine gun was not in the tree line as expected but was located in the high grass inside the LZ, to the left rear of our slicks that were still sitting in the landing zone. Apparently, the crew of the machine gun could not see the slicks in the high grass, even though one of our helicopters had landed within fifty meters of their position. The heavy machine-gun crew had probably been crossing the grass clearing when they had been caught by surprise by artillery rounds impacting in the trees. Our inbound flight had followed so close behind the artillery barrage that the machine-gun crew did not have time to set up their gun to catch our slicks as they landed. Rather than shoot the slicks as they left the LZ, the crew made the mistake of picking our lead gunship as their first target. After marking the touchdown point, the lead gun had climbed up over the trees at the front of the clearing and banked into a left turn to come down the left side of the slicks. The machine-gun crew could see and shoot the gunship but couldn't shoot the slicks until they tried to leave the LZ. They probably figured that a bird in the air is worth ten in the bush.

Huge, green tracers floated toward our lead gun and, expecting to see it explode at any moment, I started firing short bursts of red tracers into the enemy position, trying to draw their fire toward my ship. For some strange reason, I recall deliberately trying to ensure that all of the expended empty brass being ejected from my gun flew back into our helicopter and not down into the turning rotor blades of the slicks underneath us. I suppose all my days on a maintenance crew replacing rotor blades made me wary of damaging their rotor blades. Knowing that a heavy machine-gun position always meant there were more enemy troops nearby, I was also trying to conserve ammunition by firing short bursts into the tall grass hiding the gun crew.

As the lead gun completed its turn, it now faced the fifty-one and flew head-on into its bright green tracers. Once again, in a bad situation, time seemed to stop. We were barely floating along, and for what seemed like long hours I watched the entire fight unfold before my eyes. I suppose that our gunships were each flying at least eighty knots per hour and that we could do a complete circle around the landing zone in a few minutes. While that may be true, I was there and I would swear it took at least an hour to fly each hundred meters while the heartbeat rhythm of the sound from the fifty-one ticked off the minutes. Not everyone experienced enemy fire like this. Some guys said that entire firefights were a blur to them as everything happened faster than the speed of light. Other men saw everything in slow motion as I did. What always struck me as being odd, however, was that this feeling of the slowing of time was so inconsistent. Sometimes it happened, sometimes it didn't.

We would move through the air in our predetermined maneuver, one gunship following another around the slick formation beneath us. Normally the slicks would have lifted from the ground and been on their way out of the LZ within four seconds of touchdown, but the enemy gun crew had made the mistake of giving away their position by shooting at our lead gun. Our commander flying overhead in the C&C ship had realized that the machine-gun crew hidden in the high elephant grass couldn't see our slicks and had radioed the flight to hesitate in the landing zone. From my position, it appeared that as soon as they attempted to leave the LZ and broke above the high grass, they would be in big trouble. The NVA machine gun would easily knock them out of the air as they tried to gain altitude to climb over the trees at the end of the LZ. The flight of slicks was told to hold where they sat until ordered to leave. When the order was given, they were to fly straight out of the LZ keeping as low as possible, flying through the trees if necessary, while the gunships engaged the enemy.

Lead gun was the first target in the shooting gallery and it appeared to crawl through the air toward the enemy. Green tracers surrounded it while its rockets tore out of the tubes and barely moved as they flew toward the machine gun.

Everything was happening so slowly that it appeared that the air must have turned into gelatin. For hours I watched our lead gunship slowly ride the roadway of bright green tracers toward the place in the high grass from where the tracers originated. My AC, Hesse, was as cool as always, calmly telling me, "Cover Nine Six, keep hitting that gun." He didn't have to tell me that. As soon as I saw the first green tracer and heard the sound of a fifty-one, I had been firing short bursts of machine-gun fire into the grass surrounding the NVA position. I wasn't firing to cover Nine Six, however; I was firing to save me. I knew damn well that I would soon be flying into those big green tracers.

Rockets from our lead gunship were impacting all around the fifty-one, but its slow, heavy fire, like a heartbeat, continued sending a steady stream of green tracers toward the ship. As Nine Six broke over the enemy position, our second gun had made the left turn around the flight of slicks beneath us and lined up on the machine-gun position. The fifty-one immediately focused on it, rather than try to follow our lead gun as it passed over the heads of the machine-gun crew. As second gun rolled in to engage the fifty-one, the slicks broke out of the LZ, flying low and skimming over and through the trees at the front of the clearing. The crew of the enemy gun must have had target fixation on our second gun since they failed to take advantage of the easy target of ten slow fat slicks breaking out of the LZ.

I suppose there may have been other enemy weapons firing at us, but our eyes were on the fifty-one. Subconsciously, we all knew that the fifty-one posed the largest threat to our existence and its demise was our first priority. As in any fight, when a .51-caliber machine gun opened up, our weapons concentrated on it, ignoring any lesser and weaker enemy weapons. I always thought that its steady thudding sound drew us to it. A fifty-one sounded like death calling your name.

Second gun finished its gun run, and it was our turn to line up into the sights of the NVA heavy machine gun. The NVA crew refused to swivel the gun to track a target. Why should they? We were going to trace each other's path, straight down the machine-gun barrel. They didn't have to move or swing the gun. We were giving them a shooting gallery situation where one target followed another as each gunship drew the fire of the enemy gun so that our slicks could escape from the LZ.

Big, green tracers were coming straight at us as we flew directly at the "eater of helicopters." Glancing left, I could see that all slicks were out of the LZ, the infantry were sprawled throughout the LZ, and tracers were flying by us. I leaned out of the open doorway to my left, butt stock on the outside of my right shoulder, firing a stream of red tracers straight ahead to the place in the elephant grass from where the green tracers were being sent to drop us out of the sky. My machine-gun barrel was almost next to the left front door window and Hesse was receiving the muzzle blast two feet from his head, but if it bothered him he didn't complain. Time seemed to almost stop again. It was our turn to crawl down along the line of green tracers slowly coming toward us. I couldn't see exactly where the gun was positioned in the high grass. I watched the tracers materialize in the air above the vegetation as they began their slow crawl through semi-solid air, taking long hours to reach the magical point, about twenty meters in front of my face, where human eyesight cannot focus on the hot green glow coming straight into the eye. I consciously ignored the tracers approaching my face and estimated where behind the first sight of green the gun was positioned. It was tempting to try to hit the fat, sluggish, green balls of death coming straight at us, but I placed my red tracers fifty meters behind the place from which the green tracers materialized out of thin air.

Hesse would yell, "Coming hot," and I'd immediately stop shooting. Unlike our other gunships, my ship fired individual rockets instead of pairs. Rockets left our tubes, alternating from right rocket pod to left, and every second rocket fired would roar out of the tubes next to me, blasting the small, metal firing contact back into one of my legs. Watching it chug along at the speed of a glacier, I'd estimate when it was far enough ahead of us so that I could shoot without having my bullets hit the rocket motor, then squeeze a long burst of red tracers at our target until I'd hear "coming hot" again. As soon as we flew past the left side of the fifty-one position, both Dale and I would immediately turn around and fire behind us at where we thought the machine gun was hidden in the high grass. Once we had passed their position the enemy gun crew ignored us to engage the next gunship as it came down the pathway of tracers.

We made several gun runs, flying our tight circles so that as soon as one gunship flew by the machine-gun position another was starting a gun run toward it. We had just flown by it for the third or fourth time, when leaning out of the door and firing behind us I could see six or seven men milling around a large machine gun mounted on a tall tripod. I had only a brief glimpse of them before they disappeared into the grass, but could see that they were grabbing the tripod of the gun and starting to carry it away. They were in view for a second, then the grass swallowed them. Spraying the area, I noticed the fifty-one had stopped firing. Had I got it?

When the heavy machine-gun fire had ceased, we returned to our normal routine again. As the third gun, our ship immediately left for Tay Ninh to rearm and refuel. Jumping out at the POL point, I looked down at our armament system and said to myself, "What the hell, our rocket pod is gone!" It had been there when we had been dueling the fifty-one, but it had somehow disappeared during the fight. Maybe a big .51-caliber bullet had knocked it off. Who knows? I do know that when we replaced the rocket pod back at Cu Chi that evening, we jumped up and down on the new pod and couldn't get it to fall off. There were many times we pulled tree branches from the rocket tubes or from the miniguns after hunting men in the bush, but the limbs had never knocked a pod loose. I still think that an enemy bullet knocked the rocket pod off our ship, but can't explain how it could have disappeared without my noticing.

Quickly loading up the remaining rocket pod on our right side and dumping belts of ammunition on the floor for the

miniguns, we were soon back in the air. It took only minutes
to return to our firefight. Dale and I finished reloading our
minigun ammunition trays just as we arrived back at the LZ.
As second gun left to refuel, they advised us that nothing
much had happened in our absence. The infantry were still
slowly and cautiously working their way through the four-
meter-high grass toward the machine-gun position. They had
good reason to be cautious. Heavy guns never worked alone.
There were people hiding here—armed people. As we flew
above the infantry, we were tense as we waited for the enemy
to initiate contact. Without a doubt, this LZ would soon turn
into a battleground.

My body one big tense muscle, I braced myself for a hail
of enemy bullets as we joined our lead gun flying "low and
slow" around the perimeter of the clearing, looking for the
missing fifty-one crew. *Come on, where is everyone?* I
thought to myself, *Somebody shoot!* I was tense with anticipation, waiting for bullets to start hitting me. Less than an
hour before I had thought that we were going to litter this LZ
with burning helicopters. Now there was nothing.

The ground troops finally made their way through the
thick grass to the site where the machine gun had been positioned and were on the radios. They had found an area of flat-
tened grass littered with empty brass cartridge cases and
reported that pools of blood covered the ground. Blood trails
in the grass showed where wounded or dead had been dragged
along the ground toward the nearest tree line. We had been
hitting men on the machine-gun crew on our gun runs but
apparently there were other men hiding nearby in the grass
who quickly replaced anyone we hit. Guessing the blood
trails led to an NVA complex hidden in the tall trees, the
ground troops decided to smash the woods with heavy artillery fire before following the blood trails any further. We
were told to return to Tay Ninh while the Red Legs worked
on the jungle with high explosives. Once back at Tay Ninh,
however, we were diverted to another mission and never
found out what happened at our jungle LZ. Another typical
day at work.

Day after day we went out to search and kill. And to look for our own deaths. Hours of boredom, scanning and watching. Where's our infantry? Where's the point? Watch the flankers, don't look for people: look for parts, hands, faces. Watch the bush and tree limbs. Scan the hedgerows, trails, streams and riverbanks. Look into the holes in the roofs of hooches and into the open windows. What's on the porches? What's in the garden? Watch the bright tracers floating up to kiss us. We became eyes.

We worked the swamps, jungle, scrub thickets, nipa palm thickets, rubber plantations, rice paddies, pineapple fields, villages, hamlets, friendly areas, contested areas and free-fire zones. We might stay in a certain type of terrain all day or we might bounce from one extreme to another several times during the day. We worked all over III Corps, wherever we were ordered to go. Infantry units were given "blade time" and they used us any way they wished for the hours they had us assigned. If nothing much was happening, they might conserve their allocated blade time by letting us sit for hours while the C&C monitored the ground troops without us. If trouble started, we'd be on site in minutes. If real trouble started, no one counted how much blade time was used.

Some days we went from LZ to LZ, as we checkerboarded troops around the terrain looking for trouble; other days the first landing found enough action to keep us busy all day. Some days the enemy was everywhere, other days we saw no one at all. Most missions just blurred together, but in early '69 we seemed to be in contact with NVA or VC troops quite often. Generally, they were found in small units; several men here, several men there. Some of them were smart, some foolish. Sometimes they made mistakes and sometimes we made mistakes.

We once had an enemy soldier make the mistake of shooting at an infantry patrol walking parallel to an isolated bunker built on a rice dike. It was nothing more than a large pile of dried mud, surrounded by several hundred acres of wide-open, dry rice paddies. It was one of those little hiding places that was so obvious that no one would have even bothered checking if the man inside hadn't started shooting. While he wasn't hitting anyone with his shooting, the infantry wasn't hurting him either as they returned fire with rifles. His bunker was one of the solid dry mud and timber bunkers commonly found on the dikes, but rarely occupied. He had no way to escape: it was only a matter of time until the ground troops flanked his blind sides and put an end to him by tossing a grenade into his bunker. The C&C wanted to try something different, though, and had a slick bring in a man with a flamethrower. The guy just calmly jumped off the slick, put the tanks of chemicals on his back, walked across the rice paddy toward the bunker and gave it a long shot of liquid fire. He turned around, walked back to the slick, and was on his way back to Cu Chi before the infantry stood up and finished brushing the dirt from their clothes. I wondered how many times he put on his flamethrower show. He was either very brave or very foolish.

We seemed to be finding more and more enemy troops in small groups that appeared to be high-ranking VC rather than local infantry. They were armed because all soldiers are armed. But they didn't act as if they were prepared to use their weapons and some died with their AK-47s still slung across their shoulders. One afternoon, we were returning to Duc Hoa for fuel and saw three armed men walking along a road, each carrying a little Swedish "K" submachine gun. Apparently these men were not average guerrillas and carried the light lime-green guns as a sign of their importance. They should have learned how to use their weapons, however, instead of carrying them for status. They might have lived.

We were finding armed men out in broad daylight near populated areas more and more often. Dressed as local peasants, they generally carried the more easy-to-conceal, folding stock version of the AK-47 rather than the standard issue assault weapon with a wooden stock. The enemy appeared to be more confident. We assumed they were building up strength for a reason.

For several weeks it seemed every mission would be interrupted: we would be providing gunship cover for one infantry unit when we'd be called on the radio to fly somewhere else to support a different unit in contact. Usually, it was just sporadic fire that was being taken by the ground troops and we would low-level their area looking for targets and trouble. What was unusual was the frequency. We were constantly being radioed to support units in contact. Nothing big was happening, but there were a lot of little actions. The frequency of contact made us tense and suspicious. Was something building up to explode, or was it just coincidental? Why were the natives restless?

Late one afternoon, we were ending a day of little skirmishes by flying overhead cover for a platoon of infantry finishing a long walk in the sun. This infantry unit had been searching for enemy troops all day, while we had bounced around so many places north of Cu Chi I had no idea where we were. We were working above another nameless expanse of scrub brush, where nothing looked familiar. All we could see was stunted trees, less than two meters high, growing in scattered thickets interspersed with small clearings and trails. Everywhere I looked were well-used trails showing signs of recent heavy use by enemy troops.

Someone had fired a quick burst of automatic weapons fire at our guys, then disappeared. The infantry platoon leader could hear our rotor blades nearby, and after radioing his HQ to determine which helicopter unit was working adjacent to him, he called to ask if we'd do a quick aerial recon of the area in front of him. Responding to his call, we circled the area slowly, scanning the brush for the man who had shot at them. Every little thicket could hide a bunker or two, and some patches of scrub brush were large enough to conceal a company of men easily, but there was nothing obvious. Flying low-level circles around the area produced nothing, so it was decided to fire some rockets in front of our troops. Maybe some high explosives would flush out any exposed NVA troops who might not have jumped into a bunker before we arrived.

There was no obvious target; we were just going to put a

few random rockets into the brush. Nine Six put a couple into the shrubs, then my ship rolled in to do the same thing. Pat Ronan fired two rockets as we dove out of the sky, setting off a huge secondary explosion. *What the hell did Pat hit?* I wondered. Black smoke and flames roared out of a large rectangular hole; he had obviously hit an ammunition cache. He must have been lucky and put a rocket straight into the entrance of an underground bunker.

The explosion scared us. If we had been at the end of our low gun run when it occurred, chances are we would have been blown out of the air. I was damn glad to be flying with Pat and not one of the pilots who had the habit of splattering mud on his windshield from the explosions of his own rockets. Staying away from the billowing plume of black smoke, we continued flying circles, looking for signs of North Vietnamese soldiers. An ammunition cache this large must have guards. Someone noticed that interspersed throughout the scrub brush were large rectangular areas where no vegetation was growing. Once the areas were pointed out, they were obvious. The rectangular areas were actually large mats of woven vegetation being used to cover something of value to the enemy.

None of us had ever seen anything like this. We had discovered some type of NVA supply dump consisting of three-meter-wide by ten-meter-long excavations in the earth. Each hole in the ground had wooden supports holding up the vegetative mat covering used as a roof. There were at least ten of these pits and, while we were naturally curious to find out what was hidden in them, we were tense with the anticipation of fighting the soldiers guarding this cache.

Smoke grenades were thrown near the cache closest to the infantry to mark the location. They made their way through the brush, slowly and cautiously, expecting to be greeted by automatic weapons at any instant. The infantry platoon came upon the first cache and immediately circled it, setting up a defensive position. Watching a few soldiers search for an entrance to the cache, we suddenly heard the sound of auto-

matic weapons fire. Our infantry were on their bellies looking outward instantly, but who was firing the weapons?

Twenty meters in the brush, near the southern edge of the
cache, two men were engaged in a machine-gun duel. Flying
toward a trail, we saw an American soldier standing in the
middle of the trail firing an M-60 machine gun from the hip.
I distinctly remember he had no shirt on. It seemed odd at the
time since everyone else was fully dressed. This guy stood
there, bare-chested, legs braced, firing down the trail. About
ten meters from him and slightly to his left stood an NVA
soldier firing an RPD light machine gun at our man. It
seemed impossible, but neither man was hitting the other.

Pat started yelling. "Get him! Get him!" It was the first
time I heard Pat get excited. He kept shouting at me to kill
the NVA soldier but I couldn't shoot from our position. We
were too low and were directly behind the American. As Pat
shifted our ship to the right slightly, I found that I could fire
at the enemy machine gun but my rounds were going to be
awful damn close to our guy. I was worried that I might hit
him, but I pulled the trigger and my tracer rounds started
going over his right shoulder alongside of his head toward
his left front. At my first burst, the NVA soldier jumped to
his right into the brush. Not knowing if I had hit him, I continued putting fire into the area where he had disappeared.
The machine gunner on the ground and I kept hosing down
the sides of the trail with machine-gun fire until it was appar-
ent no one was returning our fire. I felt mentally drained and
totally exhausted. God! That had been close shooting. I
hoped that I would never again have to fire so close to our
troops and wondered if I had done the right thing. While no
one ever mentioned my shooting so close to our machine
gunner, things might not have gone so well if one of my bullets had been a little bit to the left.

Now that the shooting had stopped, I was curious about
two things: Had I shot the NVA machine gunner, and what
was in those caches? I never did learn the answer to either
question. Several minutes after the machine-gun duel, our
radio started blurting out another mission. Someone had

observed a large group of men walking through the rice paddies north of the village of Duc Hoa and had called for gunships. Since we were the nearest gunships to Duc Hoa, we
were told to check them out. *Damn it!* I said to myself. *Who
the hell is making this stupid decision?* We had known caches
protected by enemy troops right under us and we were being
ordered to check out some damn rice farmers.

Reluctantly leaving the infantry to guard and search the
caches, we informed them that we'd be back as soon as possible and flew as fast as we could for Duc Hoa. Hopefully, we
would check out the farmers and then be released to return to
the caches. It didn't take long for us to fly to the area we were
to recon. We were disappointed to find that it was just a typical, flat, open area of unharvested rice paddies with no sign
of bunkers or fighting positions. While there were no men in
sight, any men seen in the area would have to have been local
farmers. No experienced enemy troops would be caught in
an open farming area like this in daylight. While one lone
man could be seen standing on a rice dike in the distance,
there weren't any obvious signs indicating that a large group
of men had recently been here. I thought whoever had called
us out must have been seeing things.

Flying over the open fields to take a quick look at the soli-
tary figure walking slowly along the top of a small dike, we
noticed that he was wearing a Sam Browne belt. He was no
farmer. Nine Six quickly notified our C&C, who was still flying over the cache site, that we had found a man in uniform.
"Kill him" was the reply. Instantly machine-gun bullets were
on their way toward him. As bullets flew around him and
landed in the rice paddies, men started jumping up out of the
tall green rice plants. Everywhere I looked, there were men
in uniform running for their lives. They had dropped or
thrown away their weapons and were definitely not interested
in fighting us. These boys were probably fresh, green troops
who had just walked into Viet Nam from Cambodia and had
never faced helicopters before. A veteran NVA force would
not have been caught in a position like this and would have
stood and fought if they had. Running away was suicide. If

they had stood their ground and fired their weapons, they might have inflicted some damage on us.

As it was, however, their only hope was that we'd miss individual soldiers as we strafed the rice paddies with rockets, miniguns and machine guns. We were flying so low that Pat had 440's skids in the rice. He sprayed the runners to our front with the miniguns, while Dale and I mowed down rice and men to the sides with our machine guns. A lot of men died in the rice of Duc Hoa that day. To save time in the field and to lessen the number of times we would have to rearm, we had thrown extra cans of minigun ammo onto the ship. As soon as a row of ammo trays was emptied, Dale and I reloaded them in the air so that our ship could stay on target longer.

I had never had a day like this and I was high on adrenaline. It was an unbelievable afternoon. After spending months constantly trying to find well-hidden guerrillas in the vegetation, we now had men in uniform running through the wide-open rice paddies in broad daylight. Coming out of Duc Hoa after refueling and rearming for our last gun run, I was trying to share my happiness by tossing C-rations into the village yards for the local kids. We were flying only about five meters high and I had just thrown a can of beans and franks down toward a shack when a little boy of five or six slowly appeared at the open door. He walked out of the doorway and into a large can of C-rations coming out of the sky. The can hit him in the middle of his face. The poor little guy was knocked off his feet. If it didn't kill him, it probably broke his nose. Damn it. I couldn't even do something nice in this war.

As we returned back on target, Nine Six left to refuel. We had been back only a few minutes when our C&C radioed that our slicks were inbound with infantry. The C&C ship had left the site of the cache and had joined us near Duc Hoa shortly after we had notified them about the running men. While we had been refueling, the C&C staff had radioed the slicks to pick up infantry from a nearby artillery FSB and then bring them here to sweep the fields. My ship would lead them in, as Pat was the senior AC in the two gunships on site. It would be a piece of cake. We had shot everything in the area of the LZ and had received no return fire. We'd put the lead slick down near the body wearing the Sam Browne belt and then let the infantry police up our kills. We flew out several kilometers to meet the inbound slicks, then turned left to lead them into the LZ. Dropping rapidly, we were going to take the slicks into the LZ flying low-level, right above the rice. On Pat's command, Dale and I each pulled the ring on a smoke grenade, let the spoon fly and thrust the arms that held the grenades out the open door. With a grenade trailing smoke in my left hand, I fired bursts of machine-gun fire to our left as our skids skimmed through the rice plants. Leading the slicks to their landing point, I saw several men jump up and start running through the rice. I swiveled the machine gun lying across my legs toward them and fired a quick burst. I released the trigger, but the gun wouldn't stop firing.

I had a "runaway gun." Every now and then, a machine gun would "run away" and not stop firing when the trigger was released. Ordinarily, it was no big deal. I just twisted the ammo belt with my left hand and broke the belt. But this time there was a hot, smoking grenade in my left hand. I couldn't toss the grenade until Pat gave the order to do so. It was to mark where the lead slick would land and I couldn't break the belt without tossing the grenade. The grenade was so damn hot that I thought that my fingertips would melt, but no one in our platoon ever threw a smoke grenade to mark a landing zone until told to do so. Trying with all my strength to control the runaway gun with one hand, it vibrated loose from my grip. Before I could get it back in control, two rounds hit the structural column between the cargo door and the pilot's door.

I was mortified. I would never live this down in the platoon. Guys had shot rotor blades and rocket pods, but I had never heard of anyone shooting the structural wall before. Thankfully, I heard the command "Mark," and tossed the grenade and then broke the belt of ammunition. I replaced the feed cover and barrel in seconds and was back in action with an operating machine gun. I decided that I had better confess to my screwup and get my reprimand over with. I sheepishly announced that I had just shot the ship and Pat just laughed. He called Nine Six to report we had some crew chief combat damage. No one ever said another word about it.

Our slicks were off and out of the landing zone in seconds. They would land at Duc Hoa to wait until called to extract the ground troops. The infantry spread out through the waist-high rice, then walked toward the dike where the body of the man with the Sam Browne belt lay. They quickly counted fourteen bodies, searched them, and called for extraction. I couldn't believe it. They had just got here and were going to leave already. There were enemy bodies everywhere in the rice and we wouldn't get credit for any unless the infantry confirmed them. We weren't happy with their total count, but at that time and place, the infantry confirmed all kills. In fairness to the infantry, the sun was lowering in the sky. Keeping them there in the wet rice paddies overnight would serve no purpose. The numerous dead in the rice weren't going anywhere.

The infantry slowly waded through the rice and set up in position to load onto the slicks when they returned. All three gunships were once again on station so, while Mike O'Conner on third gun flew circles around the pickup zone, Nine Six and our ship were told to sink sampans along a nearby river. These boats probably had brought these NVA troops across the Cambodian border. We amused ourselves by tossing grenades into them. Most of the boats were half submerged in the water already. We ensured that they couldn't be refloated to ferry more troops into the area. The pickup of the infantry was uneventful and we left as darkness covered the dead. We expected that we would return the next morning to either Duc Hoa or to the caches, but we would be sent to other places and to other fights.

After we had refueled and rearmed our ship back at Cu Chi, we landed at our revetments to perform our postflight inspections and then call it a day. Our pilots had left after helping Dale and me clean out the thousands of empty brass cartridge cases and links that covered the floor. A jeep pulled up next to our ship. Shining my flashlight toward the occupant of the jeep, I recognized the executive officer of our battalion. *Now what?* I wondered. Since battalion officers generally thought we were really in the Army, I yelled, "Attention!" Dale and I both saluted and stood at attention, but the XO immediately told us to be at ease and shook our hands. He had been flying near Duc Hoa late that afternoon and, after hearing our radio traffic, had flown above our ships watching what we did. He claimed our ship had put on the best display of minigun use in a combat zone that had ever been done. He wanted to know who the pilots had been and asked how we rearmed in flight. After we answered his questions, he promised that our crew would get an award for the day's action, then left to find the pilots, Pat Ronan and Mike Ward. Dale and I both laughed at the idea of an award because it was relatively rare for anyone to receive one. We cleaned our guns in the dark, then I went looking for some friends in maintenance who would repair the bullet holes in my ship and, more important, keep their mouths shut about the holes. That night, Dale and I bought drinks at the NCO Club for anyone who would sit with us and listen to us talk about our day in the field. And, of course, a lot of the guys listened to us and then said, "That was nothing, you should have been here when . . ." Things were always tougher in the old days—the monsoon seasons were wetter, the dry seasons were hotter, the NVA were more numerous, the old guns never jammed and the guys never missed a target or shot their own ship. No matter what happened, there was always someone with a better story.

XVI

Several days following the slaughter at Duc Hoa, we were sent southeast of Cu Chi to provide gun support for an unusual small military unit known as Sherlock Six and the Bandits. I'd worked with them a few times before but no one had ever explained to me who they were or who they worked for. Sherlock Six dressed as an American Army captain, but everyone claimed he was a civilian. The Bandits dressed like ARVN soldiers, but were supposedly all ex-VC or ex-NVA soldiers. While rumor had it they were a CIA operation, I always thought that they were a local MACV unit because we never inserted or extracted this unit by helicopter. Since they were walking into the hamlets they patrolled, I guessed they were probably living at a MACV compound nearby. They apparently picked their own missions, did what they wanted and answered to no one. A small mobile unit, they usually worked in a group of ten or twelve, small enough to maneuver quickly and quietly, but large enough to defend themselves if trouble occurred.

Most of the guys in our platoon were glad we rarely worked with these people, because spending a day with the small group was usually boring. We seldom did much other than fly low-level reconnaissance ahead of them as they conducted their own specialized method of patrolling. We were only there to keep any local VC from overwhelming their small force as they roamed villages and hamlets in their search for guerrillas. Flying twenty meters above their heads, it was easy to tell these guys were professionals and knew what they were doing. They patrolled with the confidence that came with experience. American troops entered a hamlet cautiously, slowly searching for booby traps and hidden weapons. The Bandits would immediately spread out and move through a hamlet fast and confidently. Being ex-VC, they knew that mines weren't everywhere; certain areas had to be safe in order for the local residents to function in their daily life. The Bandits also seemed to know who and what they were looking for. They might walk by thirty village men, then grab the next man for reasons only they knew. They seemed to pick the right person, and their prisoners usually showed them something of value.

On this mission, they had roamed through several hamlets without finding anything interesting, except for two local men who were thought to be VC and were made to join their group. Coming out of the maze of thatched huts and gardens into a large area of harvested rice fields, the group stopped to interrogate their suspects. While most of the Bandits sat on the rice paddy dikes, the American captain stood in the open paddy watching two Bandits interrogate the prisoners with their fists. The interrogators must not have heard what they wanted to hear, because they pushed one man to the ground, quickly tying his hands together behind his back. His ankles were then trussed and his hands drawn back to be tied to his ankles. He lay on his belly, his back arched while the Bandits stood around him. We watched as the Bandits shouted at him and kicked him. Then we saw a Bandit place a plastic bag over the head of the prisoner and secure it around his neck. I wondered what they were doing: scaring the man or killing him. We flew in closer to the group, fifteen meters above their heads. Sherlock Six called on the radio. He told us to leave the area, to do a low-level recon over a large woodlot about a mile away. They would be going there after they ate lunch.

I expected our officers to say something about the prisoner, but nothing was said. I had never seen or heard of treatment like this, but if the Bandits were ex-VC, they were probably using VC tactics. Our gunships left for a half an hour or so to do our recon of the woods and returned to find

Sherlock Six and the Bandits finished with lunch and ready to leave. Sherlock Six radioed to say that they planned to check out a possible weapons cache in another nearby small woodlot, several hundred meters to their right. As we circled over their heads, I could see, lying in the paddy behind the group, a body with a plastic bag over the head and ropes on the hands and ankles. During our absence one prisoner had died, but the second prisoner had apparently remembered something about a weapons cache he wanted to show to the Bandits.

We were told to fly low circles over the small woodlot they would search and warned we should expect this cache to be guarded. Flying in our normal low left circles, we searched the woodlot thoroughly and, even though it was not very thickly vegetated, but rather sparsely timbered with some low shrubs, we saw absolutely nothing. Visibility was excellent, and if there were men guarding a cache in this area they were underground. We would have had no trouble seeing anyone hiding in the shrubs. All of the trails appeared well used but this meant nothing; we would have expected the local villagers to frequent these trails when cutting firewood.

Doing a quick recon, we reported no evidence of guards or enemy activity to Sherlock Six as he and his Bandits stood outside the woods in the rice paddy. Entering the scattered timber, their prisoner-guide directed them to a trail, then took them on a branch of that trail, and another branch and so on. It soon became obvious they were not being shown the way to a cache. It appeared more likely they were being made to wander the trails so they could be led into an ambush. The whole group stopped in the middle of the woodlot. Flying over their heads, we could see they weren't happy with the prisoner. Four or five Bandits started shouting at him and hitting him. They apparently convinced him he had better pick the right trail.

The group started moving down another trail. Soon afterward I could see the prisoner had stopped and was pointing toward the ground several meters in front of him. Two or three of the Bandits circled the area where he was pointing, then the man behind the prisoner pushed him toward whatever he was pointing at. Whatever was there, he wanted nothing to do with it. He jumped back and refused to go forward. Circling low overhead, we wondered what was happening on the ground, but our radio was silent. I suppose Sherlock Six figured it was none of our business.

Leaving one man near the place the prisoner had pointed out, everyone else moved back ten meters and lay down. The lone man went down on his belly and crawled up the trail. Using the bayonet on the end of his rifle, he slowly pried up the camouflaged cover to a tunnel entrance. *BLAM!* An explosion erupted from the tunnel. The tunnel entrance had been booby-trapped, which apparently the prisoner had forgotten to mention. No wonder he had been unwilling to go near it. Everyone came up the trail and surrounded the tunnel entrance, waiting for the black smoke to clear. Suddenly, the radio crackled, "Prisoner escaping! He's running! He's running!"

What the hell? I thought. Looking down, I could see him standing right next to the Bandits. He wasn't doing anything. One of the Bandits brought up his M-16 and fired an entire magazine into the chest of the prisoner. The quick ripping sound of an M-16 rifle burst came over the radio. We heard the words again: "He's running." All four of us in the gunship looked at each other. No one said a word. What could we say? We weren't on the ground and we didn't know the whole story. If the Bandits were ex-VC and NVA, maybe this was the way they had been taught to act. Also, it wasn't one of us who had to lift the cover to the tunnel. Better not to judge someone when you were not in the position he was and you didn't know the facts. Even so, I don't understand why they bothered to radio us that the prisoner was escaping.

We watched several Bandits enter the tunnel and then pass various unknown items out, which the others piled near the entrance. Sherlock Six radioed that he and his men were staying near the tunnel to set up an ambush for any local VC who became curious as to what had happened at the cache.

We weren't needed anymore and were released to Cu Chi. I never saw or heard of Sherlock Six and the Bandits again.

Soon afterward, we were working near an abandoned village in one of the many free-fire areas near Cu Chi. We were just flying around at low level, looking for trouble, while our C&C ship inspected nearby clearings for use as possible landing zones. Suddenly, our C&C radioed, "There's a man running down the road, several hundred meters to your front, go get him." Someone on the C&C ship happened to be looking toward us and spotted the runner. Normally a single running target would be engaged by one of the crew chiefs, but for some reason Nine Six decided to shoot him with a rocket. Nine Six quickly climbed up from the tree limbs, gained altitude and dived toward the running man, firing rockets onto the dirt road. Rockets exploded all around the man, throwing up dirt and clouds of dust, behind, beside and in front of him. Out of the billowing dust cloud the runner emerged and continued down the road. The second gunship was Silacci's ship, a 40mm cannon on the nose. His AC went in firing a long burst of 40mm rounds straight down the road. Once more the runner appeared out of the cloud of dust and explosions and continued running straight down the middle of the road. My ship was the third gunship—armed with two miniguns capable of throwing out eight thousand rounds a minute. We dove toward the runner spraying bullets. He didn't have a prayer. We missed him.

Son of a bitch! Why doesn't he just jump into the hedgerow and hide? I thought to myself. I would have let him go, but I wasn't in charge. All three of the crew chiefs had held their fire on the previous gun runs, but as the lead gun came up on the runner again, the crew chief's machine gun stopped his running. He should have aimed high and missed. I would have. That guy deserved to live.

On another quiet day, we were finishing our work for the day by making a quick twilight landing outside of a fairly secure village complex west of Cu Chi. The infantry were going to unload from our slicks, then spend the night adjacent to the village. Once the slicks were out of the LZ, we would head home for supper. Everyone was bored and hungry. We had been out since before sunup and were tired of staring into the bright tropical sun.

The slicks were inbound, led by the lead gunship, while the rest of us flanked the inbound flight. We just watched the tree lines, our guns quiet. The village was considered fairly secure and it had been decided that there was no need to lay down any suppressive fire. The slicks were in the LZ and the infantry was jumping out when mortar rounds started impacting the paddy between the slicks and the western tree line.

"Get the mortar! Get the mortar!" the C&C commander yelled. The slicks were leaving the LZ as fast as possible, while the infantry hugged the ground. The mortars were not being fired in support of NVA ground troops: no automatic weapons fire came from the tree line. The mortar tube was set up somewhere in the village and had been preregistered to have its rounds impact in the rice paddy our slicks used for the landing zone. The VC and NVA knew what a good landing zone looked like as well as we did. Fortunately for the slick crews, they hadn't landed as close to the tree line as the enemy anticipated they would. The mortar crew had followed their instructions to the letter and walked their mortar rounds on the preset course, even though the slicks weren't sitting where the rounds were impacting. All rounds impacted along a line parallel to the line of helicopters in the LZ. Apparently the mortar team didn't have a forward observer to adjust their fire.

As the slicks flew northeast out of the LZ, our gunships flew down the western tree line at treetop level looking for VC, but found nothing. Coming to the southern end of the tree line, we broke to the right and flew over the village looking for the mortar. This village was not an American village laid out in a grid of rectangular streets but instead was a haphazard scattering of homes separated by gardens and small woodlots. A dirt road winding through the wooded village like a crippled snake served as our only obvious reference point. The homesites looked pretty much alike.

We had just started flying over the village complex when someone shouted over the radios, "There they go, they're running down the main trail, heading north." Since no more mortar rounds were impacting at the LZ, the crew must have quickly hid the mortar tube and were running away to hide in the village. Looking down the road ahead of us, I could see four figures wearing white, running north on the trail.

I thought white was an unusual color for a guerrilla to wear because the runners—surrounded by green vegetation—were as obvious as a cue ball on the green felt of a pool table. As our lead gun flew up parallel to the runners and the crew chief started firing his machine gun at the runners, I leaned out my doorway and fired my machine gun to the front of our ship, walking my bullets straight down the dirt road toward them. As soon as bullets started churning the road dust, the runners split into two pairs. One pair turned left onto a trail into the woods while the other pair ran straight up the middle of the road. I mixed my tracers with the tracers coming from the crew chief on the lead gun into the two runners that had stayed on the road. As the lead gunship passed these two, the crew chief pivoted and faced backward, his tracers flying into the road in front of the runners, while my ship came up parallel to them and I fired straight down at them.

The two runners caught between our guns were soon sprawled on the dirt road and I swiveled to my rear to fire at the other two runners. They had broken to their left and onto a footpath through a grove of trees but were easy to see in their snow-white clothing. "Kill them! Kill them!" someone was yelling over the radios. I had no idea who was yelling because I had too many radios on at the same time. I was listening to the C&C, the other guns, the infantry and our internal intercom system.

"They're getting away! Get them! Get them!" the radios crackled. I leaned out and fired away, shooting behind us and walking tracers down the westward trail after the two runners. The third gunship was almost up to them and tracers poured out the left door as the crew chief fired his M-60. We were losing daylight quickly and I fired until the white runners were stopped. Someone radioed, "They're all down. Let's break for home." Done for the day, we headed back to Cu Chi while the infantry settled into positions along the tree line for the long night.

The encounter with the four runners had happened too fast for things to register. It had been getting dark and everything had been done without much thought. While flying back to Cu Chi, I thought the whole episode seemed odd. Why were the four runners dressed in white, and why were the last two runners women? Their long, black hair had flowed behind them as they ran for their lives, and while VC women were not uncommon, runners were always men. Women could easily blend into the civilian population.

After landing at Cu Chi and taking care of our ship, Dale and I walked back to the Stinger hooch to find one of the other crew chiefs sitting on his bunk, looking mad as a hornet. "What the hell, Seav! Why did you kill those women?" he shouted. "Why didn't you let them go?"

"What the hell are you talking about?" I replied. "You were firing at them too."

"I was shooting in front of them to stop them. Not to kill them."

Rather than argue, I went to the mess hall for supper with Dale, then to the NCO Club. When we returned to the hooch, the rest of the guys were talking and listening to music. As always, Dave Nancarrow had his stereo blasting, making too much noise for anyone to talk. No one seemed interested in discussing the four runners that night and the subject never came up again.

A day or two later, we found out the four Vietnamese in white had been a "psy-ops" team or psychological operation team, who had been putting on a government-sponsored propaganda program for a group of villagers. When the mortar crew had started firing, the psy-ops team immediately concluded their program and ran for their lives before the VC came. We didn't hear another word about the incident, but one crew chief thought about this episode a little bit harder than the rest of us and quit flying.

It was now mid-March, and I had only a few more weeks left to serve in Viet Nam. In April I would go back to the United States to be released from the Army because I would have less than ninety days left to serve in my three-year enlistment. The Army didn't believe it was cost effective to ship a soldier to another base for less than ninety days; might as well let him go home. I was having a hard time deciding what to do. Leave Viet Nam and the Army; extend my tour of duty in Viet Nam for six months; reenlist for three more years. I really didn't want to commit myself to another three-year enlistment, but I was seriously thinking about extending for six months to stay where I was. While I had always considered making a career of the military, I was no longer sure what I wanted to do. It wasn't serving in combat that changed my mind, but the certain knowledge that a career in the Army meant years and years of the frustration and boredom of duty at Fort Hood. Viet Nam and the excitement of combat would not last very long. It was no secret the U.S. Army was already making plans to decrease the number of troops in Viet Nam. The entire 9th Infantry Division was rumored to be getting ready to stand down shortly for redeployment back to the States and, once they left the country, other units would soon follow them home. A six-month extension might be all the time left for anyone to serve in this war. On the other hand, any time I mentioned the possibility of extending to other NCOs in the company or to an officer I was flying with, I received no encouragement. They thought it was foolish to stay to fight here; we were fighting over the same ground time and time again and, while we weren't losing, we sure didn't seem to be winning.

Except for our first sergeant, Joe Deal, and my previous platoon sergeant, Johnny Holman, most of our NCOs didn't seem very interested in going out with us where the bullets were flying. The general attitude of our NCOs surprised me. Where was their warrior spirit? We seemed to be an army of technicians, not soldiers. I guess it was because, unlike other

units in combat, our NCOs usually stayed at the base camp
while their subordinates went out to fight. I thought that the
Army made a big mistake by making all pilots officers.
Maybe flying sergeants would make more sense, at least
from the standpoint of unit cohesiveness and function. It
never made any sense to me that an NCO could be a tank
commander and lead a multimillion-dollar formation of
tanks, but in order to fly a relatively cheap aircraft, an officer
was needed. In hindsight, I can see it was a mistake asking
other NCOs for advice: they were not engaged in the same
war I was. I'd been out in the field with the Stingers for
months hunting men and had forgotten the drudgery of life
at the base camp. Talking about extending with my fellow
enlisted men was a waste of time. While some had extended,
most did so in order to ensure that they could get an early out
by returning to the States with less than ninety days left to
serve in the military. Dale had extended several times, but
only so he could pursue his goal of getting married and taking his wife back to the States. Most men wanted out of the
Army and back to civilian life as soon as possible. We were
missing out on the booming economy in the States, where
our civilian friends were getting way ahead of us, either in
college or in civilian jobs.

I couldn't visualize what I would do when I was discharged. I didn't want to go to college because I couldn't
think of anything I was interested in learning there. College
meant becoming a teacher. Teachers were my only contact
with people who had college degrees. I wasn't interested in
becoming a schoolteacher and hadn't taken the time to in-
quire what other professions needed a college education. I
was perfectly happy doing what I was doing, but couldn't
make the decision to extend my tour, partially because I
didn't want to be thought of as a sucker and partially because
I was scared. I hadn't been wounded, though a lot of bullets
had come my way, but no one's luck lasts forever. Going out
to face machine guns every day may be exciting, but it's also
dangerous. The closer it came to the end of my tour, the more
nervous I became. I was checking everything mechanical on

the ship several times a day, worrying about crashing due to mechanical failure. I constantly listened for any odd noise when flying and felt every slight vibration different from the norm. I didn't want to become another story of someone who almost finished his tour.

If I had wanted to do so, I could have quit flying when I had two weeks left to serve, but I told my platoon sergeant I'd keep flying and quit when I had one week left. During this week of my "day 14 to day 7" left in country, we performed our normal missions. Other than catching a VC mortar crew dropping mortar rounds on our slicks in a landing zone, nothing unusual happened. During this week, one of our new gunners did manage to blind himself by not paying attention and shooting a rocket as it left the tube next to his feet. Because he had been in the platoon only two or three days, most of us didn't even know his name and could only sympathize with his being blinded by calling him a "dumb shit" while secretly wondering if anyone in the platoon had taken the time to warn him about shooting rockets. Roger Backes would have.

Seven days left to serve in country and in the Army, and I quit flying. Garcia and I came over together and would go home together. We now started our out-processing together. Picking up our pay records, medical records and filling out paperwork only took a couple of hours and then we were free to loaf around the company area. Unless the first sergeant put us on daytime bunker duty, we would be free to do whatever we felt like for the next week. We were counting on Joe Deal to erase our names from his guard roster. The next morning we made the company's first formation, then went back to the hooch to sleep. After lunch, I went to the PX and, as I was walking back to our hooch, Garcia met me and told me that our platoon sergeant was looking for me.

"What does he want?" I asked, wondering if I'd been put on guard duty.

"They need a gunship crew chief ASAP," Garcia replied.

Now what? I thought.

As we walked through the company area, I had a feeling

something wasn't right. It was a feeling of impending doom. It didn't take long to locate our platoon sergeant and find out what he wanted. Another helicopter company, working west of Cu Chi, had two of their gunships shot up and the lone gunship on site had requested assistance ASAP. Our three Stinger gunships flying that day were working too far north to assist, and battalion operations had called our company operations to get a crew together and a gunship out. Pronto!

"Sarge, I only have six days left," I said. "Can't someone else go?"

"You're the only crew chief here right now," he replied meekly.

I could tell that, while he didn't really want to send me out on this mission, he also wasn't volunteering to go himself. For the first and only time, a mission had come up I didn't want to go on. I had a feeling this mission was going to be bad and I didn't want anything to do with it. I was mentally debating whether I should refuse to go, but then I reluctantly said, "I'm going on this flight, but then I'm done. No more!"

After throwing my PX purchases in our hooch, I ran over to our revetments where the "volunteered" pilots and gunner were waiting for me. We did a quick preflight inspection of the gunship, while the pilots briefed me on our mission. We were going to take on a bunker that had killed eight Americans: two helicopter crew chiefs and six infantrymen. *Oh boy, another damned bunker,* I thought as I put on my chest armor. I didn't feel confident or comfortable with this mission. I was used to going out with Dale on 440. Going out with a different ship and a different gunner increased my foreboding.

I knew it was not going to be fun. Flying out to our work site, I was scared and trembling. I kept thinking about the bunker two months previous and I prayed that this was not going to be a similar situation. The pilots had said that we were going to an area of overgrown, abandoned rice paddies along an infiltration route from Cambodia. The entire area was known to contain numerous bunkers used as resting places by NVA troops, and our infantry had walked up on a bunker that was occupied. The man walking point had been allowed to walk out into the bare rice paddy until he was approximately seventy-five meters from the bunker with seventy-five meters of open rice paddy behind him to the nearest protective dike. An NVA machine-gun crew in the camouflaged bunker killed the point man with their first burst of fire and then wounded several men behind him. Gunships had been called and had tried to silence the bunker with rockets, but succeeded only in blowing away the camouflage. The helicopters then flew in front of the bunkers, letting the crew chiefs pour machine-gun fire toward the bunker's gun port. Apparently the NVA machine gunner was the better man with a machine gun, as two crew chiefs were killed. While the helicopters had been attempting to silence this bunker, several soldiers jumped over the dike in an attempt to rescue their wounded. Their bodies joined the others in the field, as the NVA gunner swept the rice paddy with bullets. Six Americans lay dead in the field and two dead crew chiefs were on bullet-ridden helicopters returning to their base camp.

It didn't take long to fly out to the site of this small fight, another insignificant abandoned rice paddy. There wasn't much to see: six dead men in an open rice paddy, an obvious bunker in a shrub-covered dike, several scattered fighting positions in the shrubs, and a patrol of our infantry lying behind a dike about 150 meters to the front of the bunker. The men in the bunker had been smart enough to allow sufficient room in their firing port to be able to engage anything in the rice paddy and low-flying aircraft. Almost every time we circled to the front of the bunker, a line of tracers would reach out to touch us.

We joined the other gunship on station and circled for fifteen or twenty minutes, waiting for the C&C ship of the assault unit that had lost the two crew chiefs to return from refueling. We had plenty of time to think about the situation. I thought we would repeat the previous attack: pound the bunker with rockets, then fly in low and fight the machine gun, one-on-one. After arriving at the fight, I wasn't really afraid anymore, but I wasn't looking forward to it. I recall looking at the parched, dusty paddies and thinking they didn't look worth fighting for. Eight men had already died here and more were going to join them. Either the bunker team would die or some of us would. No matter who won this fight, the battle site would be abandoned. Tomorrow, other teams of tired NVA infiltrators would continue to rest in this or other nearby bunkers and other teams of American troops would continue to patrol the area trying to intercept the infiltrators. Both sides would hold the territory only for the brief period they were physically on this little portion of Viet Nam. Once either army walked away, the land would once again be contested territory. We controlled the dirt under our boots, but we knew we were not fighting to possess the land: we fought only to kill each other. Nothing else mattered. We never thought of trying to justify possession of real estate by the price of soldiers' lives. We were there to kill the men in the bunker and, even if they had not killed any of our troops that day, we would have tried to kill them with just as much determination. This is what we did for a living.

I must admit that flying around in circles over the six dead men wasn't very good for morale. Sometimes anticipating the fight can be worse than the fight itself. There was no talking or joking among our ship's crew; we sat and circled and kept our thoughts to ourselves. My "imminent doom" feelings were not going away; I wasn't afraid, but I couldn't shake my thought that the mission was a one-way trip.

The C&C ship returned and we went to work to earn our two dollars and sixteen cents per day combat pay. I wish I could say what happened and what we did, but I honestly can't remember. I do know the bunker was taken, as I recall a soldier coming up on its left flank and tossing grenades into the firing port. I believe that the machine gun had been silenced prior to his grenades, but I don't recall how. I seem to remember a slick landing in the field to pick up our dead and our ship being relieved from the mission. I don't know how we performed.

We landed back home late in the evening, and after performing the normal maintenance tasks, I headed for the NCO Club. Our platoon sergeant was there and tried to apologize for sending me out when I had only six days left in country. Cutting him short, I just said, "No sweat, Sarge, sorry I made a big deal out of it. I'll go out tomorrow, if you need me."

XVII

At daybreak the next morning, I was in the air east of Go Dau Hau, firing into a tree line as our slicks landed in the first LZ of the day. Within minutes of landing, the infantry was being mortared and we were firing rockets into the remains of a once-prosperous village of clay tile-roofed homes. The village had been hit with artillery at some time in the past and numerous houses had gaping holes in their roofs. I recall looking down through a roof opening and seeing an obvious mortar pit, but no mortar and no sign of people. We must have frightened the mortar crew into their tunnels since mortar rounds had ceased to impact near our troops. Five more days to go and I still couldn't decide whether to extend or leave.

I didn't fly the following two days, and on the second day, a new crew chief was shot. As usual, he had been with us only a couple of days. I didn't know his name. Those two days were spent just hanging around the company area, killing time. I had finally made up my mind I was not going to extend for six more months. Having gone from high school straight into the military, I had no idea what civilian life was like. I was going to get out of the Army and join the crowd living the good life. Besides, I could always enlist again and come back. We had a couple of guys in the platoon who had been discharged and were back in the Army and back in Viet Nam. None of them ever talked about their reasons for coming back. But then, no one ever asked them. The monsoon season would be starting soon; I could try out civilian life for six months and skip the rain and mud.

I saw Mai each day I didn't fly. We would sit and talk when she wasn't busy. I hadn't told her that I was returning to the States, but she had found out. She finally asked me if I was leaving. "Yes," I told her, "but I'll be back."

"For sure?" she asked, as she visibly brightened up.

"For sure!" I said, knowing I had no idea what I was going to do with my life. Maybe I'd be back, maybe not.

Time was going too slow sitting around the company with nothing to do, so I went back to flying my last few days in country. The evening before my last day with the Stingers, I told our platoon sergeant to put me on the flight roster because I had to follow platoon tradition and fly my last day wearing a bright crimson "Stinger" shirt.

"Come on," he said, "you don't have to do that. You know the guys talk about doing it, but most of them don't."

"Put me on the roster. I'm doing it," I replied, as I walked over to the NCO Club to buy drinks for everyone in the club. Dale and I were sitting at the club drinking and wishing each other well, when Garcia came in and said, "Hey, man! Why are you flying tomorrow? You and me are going to Long Binh, then home."

"Got to fly the last day, wearing a red shirt," I told him.

"No, you don't. I'm a Stinger too, and I'm not going out wearing a damn red shirt on my last day."

"Fine, you don't have to, but I'm going to do it."

Garcia joined our "going home" drinking party and, when the club closed, we sat on the sandbags outside the NCO Club talking. We avoided talking about how we were going to miss each other. We might not have gotten along with each other all the time, but we had made a great team. Bonded in combat, we knew we could trust and depend on each other. We were literally going out to die with each other every day. Every morning, as our gunships lifted in the darkness, we knew we might not return. Some days were easy and some days were hard, but we faced them together. Where and when would we ever be part of another group like this? Eventually, we ran out of things to say and wandered back to our hooch. I spent most of the night awake, thinking about my decision not to extend for another six months. I had not expected to feel so sad about leaving Viet Nam. From their first day in country, all everyone talked about was going home. I wondered if I had made the right decision. Now that my year was finished, I wanted to stay.

An hour before sunrise, Dale and I were sitting on 440, waiting for my last mission. Everything seemed unreal. While doing the normal morning chores—unwrapping the shelter half from my minigun and arming the rockets—I had been overwhelmed with sadness, realizing I would never do any of these things again. Dale and I sat in the dark, knowing we would never see each other again, but not willing to admit it. Trying to look busy, I turned on the interior lights and inventoried our grenades, then lubricated my machine gun. I was wasting time because our ship had been ready to go the previous evening as always, but I wanted to go through the motions of checking the tools of our trade one last time. There was nothing for me to do but relax in the cool darkness, smoke a cigarette and watch the flashlights of other crews bob about while they were getting their ships ready. Turning out the interior lights, I sat there quietly in the dim light of false daybreak, pondering why I was leaving.

Pat Ronan and another pilot walked up and seeing me, Pat said, "Sever, you're crazy. You don't have to go out with us."

"Sure I do," I replied. "Last chance for a free ride in a gunship."

The pilots did their preflight inspection quickly and I untied our rotor blades while Dale loaded the miniguns. Jumping into the ship, I buckled my seat belt and leaned back, thinking this would be my last time to watch the sun come up from the open doorway of a gunship. Pat started the engine and we were soon dragging our skids along the runway, slowly gaining altitude as 440 became a real flying machine. I had worn my normal green jungle fatigue shirt until we were airborne, but once we cleared the barbed wire bunker line, the green shirt and chest armor went off and the red shirt went on. Whatever the day brought, it was my last day. I was going to do it the Stinger way, flouting both fate and the enemy. No chest armor today: let them shoot at my bright red shirt. No one who had gone out on his last day wearing a red shirt had been shot. I didn't expect to be.

Daylight found us west of Trang Bang searching for possible landing zones and flying low-level looking for NVA infiltrators or signs of enemy activity. Our lead gunship soon radioed that, when flying over a small creek, they could see numerous oil drums submerged in the water. There was no possible reason for these containers to be hidden in the stream unless the enemy had put them there. They could have held fuel for NVA vehicles or, maybe, they were waterproof containers for weapons and explosives. Whatever they held, we definitely were interested in retrieving them.

Our C&C radioed for us to go down lower and get a better look at our find. We quickly found out the cache of drums was guarded. As each gunship flew by, numerous AK-47s fired at us from the trees on both sides of the creek. We returned fire only with our machine guns. We were trying to find out the size of the enemy force by drawing their fire before we started to rocket their positions. When we continued to draw automatic weapons fire on each pass, I did miss the solid comfort of my chest armor. But wearing a red shirt didn't make me feel any more vulnerable than normal.

We had been returning the enemy fire from the tree lines with our machine-gun fire for quite some time and, as the third gunship, we soon had to leave to refuel. Damn it. I was disappointed—the other two guns would get the fun of the first gun runs while we were gone. We headed for Cu Chi as fast as possible. Instead of landing to refuel, Pat landed at the company area where another crew chief was waiting to take my place. Someone in the company had decided that I'd met platoon tradition. I'd gone out, wearing red. Pat had been radioed by our TOC to take me back to the company when we returned for fuel. There was no platoon requirement to stay out all day wearing a red shirt and let the NVA shoot at me. They had their last chance. Getting out, I shook hands with everyone, wished them well, but didn't say good-bye. Soldiers never said good-bye. We always used some other phrase of farewell. Generally, we said, "I'll see you," ignoring the fact that we would never see each other again. Walking away, I glanced back to watch 440 bounce along the runway, taking off for the refueling point. I leaned against a revetment and watched it fly a long semicircle to POL. I knew I should be riding back to the fight with my friends. Knowing they were going straight into a firefight made leaving more difficult. I felt like a coward, abandoning my platoon. I should not have gone out with them that morning. It would have been easier to leave not knowing they were in a fight.

Taking my flight helmet, chicken plate and gloves, I walked slowly over to the company area and returned them to the supply room. Turning in my M-16 to the armorer, I symbolically broke my final tie with the company. Without a weapon, I was no longer a soldier of the 116th.

I found Mai and said good-bye. She tearfully wished me well, then ran away crying. Our platoon sergeant found me standing on the wooden sidewalk watching Mai depart. He shook my hand and told me to get my gear and report to operations. A jeep was waiting at the TOC bunker to take me to battalion headquarters where I could catch the daily flight to Hotel Three. I ran into the hooch and threw a few things into a small AWOL bag. Leaving my locker open, I told the guys loafing in the hooch to take whatever they wanted. Looking back, I wonder why I hadn't packed my stuff the previous evening. Perhaps I thought I might change my mind about leaving at the last minute.

Running to operations, I first made a quick stop at the company orderly room to say good-bye to 1st Sergeant Deal, a good soldier I would miss. Shaking my hand, he said, "Don't do anything stupid like coming back. You come visit me at Fort Bragg. I have a daughter that I want you to meet." He knew how I felt about leaving and knew I felt I should stay with the company. I told him I would see him in North Carolina some day, then ran toward the jeep parked next to our TOC bunker. After jumping into the jeep, I rode to the battalion helipad, still wondering if I was doing the right thing. I was torn between leaving and staying. I felt like a deserter leaving my friends to face the fire of the enemy without me, but I knew how foolish it would be to stay. I almost told the driver to take me back to the company when we pulled up to the helipad, but I climbed out of the jeep and threw my bag into the helicopter instead. When the pilot of the battalion helicopter learned I was headed home, he was kind enough to detour to Long Binh, instead of leaving me on my own at Hotel Three. Things seemed to be moving too fast. I'd been shooting at enemy muzzle flashes in the early morning and now, at lunchtime, I was at Long Binh, the last processing point in Viet Nam. Ready to go home, but leaving home.

As I entered the gates of the 90th Replacement Battalion at Long Binh, I found Garcia standing inside the compound. He had caught an early flight out of Cu Chi that morning and had checked everything out at Long Binh while waiting for me to arrive. Both of us had expected to sit around the 90th Replacement for a few days waiting for a flight, but he told me that, for once, the military processing system seemed to be working. We had both been placed on flight manifests to leave the country. We would not be on the same flight, however; he was leaving that evening and I was leaving early the next morning. Shortly after he had arrived at Long Binh, Garcia had met a bunch of guys who had come to Viet Nam with us from Texas, but most of them had left before I arrived. Apparently, anyone who made it to Long Binh early was put on a flight manifest immediately. The Army wasn't making people stay in country until their year was done to the exact day. If we had known, we could have left the company the previous week and been home already. But I doubt I would have left our platoon a week early.

Garcia and I sat around until evening, talking with a few of the guys we knew from our days in Texas. Then they all had to catch their flight. Trading addresses, Garcia and I promised to keep in touch. Even though I doubted he would be heading for Pennsylvania, I thought maybe I'd find my way out to California some day and would look him up. As always, no one said good-bye. It was always "See you around" or "See you later." While we all knew in our hearts we would probably never see each other again, we couldn't say good-bye to those who meant so much to us. It seemed too final. Like the majority of the troops in our army of loners I would be going home on a plane full of strangers, leaving my friends behind. I had no idea I was going home to a country of strangers, where I would soon find that old friends had nothing in common with me. The boys from high school who had gone to college would soon be seniors, while I would feel like a senior citizen. I was lean, tan and could see in the bush, an old man at twenty-one, with scar tissue on my emotions. A shooter, not a shaker. Just another good soldier leaving the war.

Several hours after Garcia left, it was time for my flight. When I boarded a bus for the airfield, I felt again how unreal it seemed to be leaving. For the past year, I had counted the days on my calendar, marking every single day. All of us on the buses were now at zero days and, unless we ended up in jail someday, we'd never mark another calendar. While I felt a sense of relief that my year was finished, I had a nagging feeling I had accomplished nothing in the year and was leaving something unfinished behind. It was with mixed emotions that I boarded the plane that would take me from my friends, my platoon and the job I had learned to do well—hunt men from a gunship.

Several busloads of thin, tanned, tired soldiers shuffled on board and sat in silence in the early morning darkness waiting for the plane to take off and fly us back to "The World." We taxied down the runway in silence. Then, as the airplane left the ground, most of the passengers shouted and screamed with joy. I stared out the window into the darkness. Gaining altitude and flying east, we flew over a few firefights, and having watched similar "Freedom Birds" periodically fly over us near Cu Chi, I wondered if I was over old familiar terrain still being fought over. As I looked out the window watching the tracers mixing together thousands of meters below us, I knew I had made a big mistake. I should have extended for six months; I wanted to be back where the tracers mixed in the darkness, where every day could be your last. I felt like a deserter, abandoning my friends at Cu Chi. Someone else would have to take my place and he would have to learn the things that I already knew.

Sitting in the air-conditioned environment of the civilian jet, I felt guilty and uncomfortable. I leaned back in my seat, thinking about the fighting, the fear, the excitement and the boredom. It seemed like I was giving up too many good things just to be safe. Never again would I hear the heavy, loud "Karumph" of the enemy 82mm mortar rounds being walked though the compound at night. There would be no more lightning cracks of exploding rockets jolting me instantly awake and filling my nostrils with the hard metallic smell the flying shrapnel left lingering in the air. Dawn would never again bring the twinkling muzzle flashes in the ground fog to greet me as I went to work. The clacking sounds of the AK-47s hidden in the fog were early morning sounds I'd no longer hear. I would never ride another crippled helicopter out of a battle, smelling its strong gut-shot horse odor as leaking jet fuel mixed with the sealing compound in the fuel tanks. What in civilian life would be equivalent to landing a bullet-ridden ship in a cloud of dust, then running smiling to jump into another ship to return to the fight? Would there ever again be anything so emotional that would equal my feelings after those landings that were actually controlled crashes—the AC struggling with our dying ship while I sat quietly thinking last thoughts waiting for my ship to explode?

There would be no more fear- and adrenaline-filled moments when .51-caliber machine guns floated green tracers toward me while their heartbeat sound spoke the somehow familiar poem that I strained my ears to recognize. Its siren song of death drew us with magnetic attraction to the muzzle flash, while its magical ability to stop time made the world slow down to listen to the sound of death and destruction. I wouldn't be hearing this music again.

Damn it. I knew that I was going to miss Viet Nam, but more, I was going to miss the Stingers and the daily rush of adrenaline. *What the hell am I going to do as a civilian?* I wondered. I couldn't imagine spending my life in a factory or office. But I told myself I had better adjust and forget the war. Even if I extended, the war couldn't last much longer. Eventually I would have to become a civilian. I suppose I rationalized that it might as well be sooner as later.

While typical flights back to the States took about eighteen hours, our flight took much longer. When we were several hours from California, we were diverted to Alaska because of heavy fog at the California airport. Sending us to Alaska made absolutely no sense to us because we grumbled that we could have been diverted to Seattle and out-processed at Fort Lewis, Washington. But we were marked for out-processing at Oakland and Oakland was where we were going. After landing in Alaska, we sat on our aircraft for hours until the airport in California was clear of fog, then started on our way again. I have no idea which airport we landed at, but the bastards at Customs had no right to confiscate our photographs. Except for photographs we had mailed home, most of us lost irreplaceable pictures of friends who stood by our sides when things were tough. I suppose it was a symbolic "Welcome Home" to have government officials steal our most prized possessions within minutes of landing on American soil.

After clearing Customs, we boarded buses and were driven through the early morning blackness along deserted streets, as if the Army was sneaking us back into the country. Eventually we arrived at the processing center in Oakland and, while everyone wanted to start into the normal military paperwork of out-processing, we first had to receive our "Welcome Home" steak dinner. "Screw the steak dinner," we all said, "let's get started on our processing." Steak was mandatory, however, and our bitching fell on deaf ears. Those in charge at Oakland were not going to let anyone start through the processing center until our entire planeload of men ate their homecoming steak.

We all ate and then sat sleepily, barely paying attention to speeches telling us about veterans' benefits. We were then fitted for Class A dress uniforms and our financial records were reviewed. Finally, after ten or twelve hours of paperwork and standing in line, we were issued the new uniforms, paid and either released to civilian life or to the next military assignment. Running out of the room, we all made a rush for taxis to get to the airport—away from Oakland and the Army.

All I remember of the San Francisco Airport in early April 1969 is that the garbage cans in the men's restroom were full of brand-new Army uniforms. A high percentage of troops chose to pay full fare for their flight home in civilian clothes rather than pay half fare and travel in uniform. I think that says a lot about the attitude of the troops toward the Army and the attitude of civilians toward the troops. A lot of guys were not proud of having served in Viet Nam and were not going to draw any attention to the fact that they were soldiers—as if the bronzed faces and hands, the short hair and haggard looks didn't give us away. Even though they might not wear their uniforms, it was not unusual for returning troops to have SKS rifles slung over their shoulder as they waited for flights. The military and civilian airlines frowned on passengers carrying assault weapons on board their planes, but they didn't stop soldiers. Why didn't a person carrying an SKS around an airport raise a fuss back then? I saw many a soldier walk through airports and board a plane while holding a captured weapon. Was everyone so innocent they automatically knew it was a war trophy and the man carrying it was no threat?

I was one of the guys who wore my uniform on the flight out of San Francisco, however. Several hours later, upon arriving in the dirtiest, filthiest airport in the world, Philadelphia International, an ex-soldier bought me a beer in the airport bar and welcomed me back to Pennsylvania.

It was hard to believe I was "back on the block." Two days earlier I had been machine-gunning the tree lines near Trang Bang, AK-47s were clattering away and life had been good. Now, I was home, out of the Army, and had no idea what to do. I figured I could collect unemployment benefits for a couple of months and loaf for a while until I decided what to do. Once I went to sign up for the benefits, however, I learned priority was being given to finding any type of job for veterans. And I mean *any* type. I couldn't refuse a job offer or I would immediately lose unemployment benefits.

Within two weeks of my return, I was working second shift in a factory on an assembly line, making exterior siding panels for commercial buildings. Eight hours of boredom and monotony every day, and some workers had been there more than twenty years. A lot to look forward to. My life was uninteresting, mainly because everything seemed to pale in comparison to the daily adrenaline rush of combat. It's been said that combat ruins a man forever; once blooded in combat, you never fully adjust to civilian life. I believe that's true.

Two weeks after returning home, I received a letter from Garcia. He had already given up on civilian life and had joined the Army to go back to Viet Nam as an infantryman. Reading between the lines, I could tell he was going back searching for his death. I never heard from him again. In May, I received a nondescript brown envelope in the mail with the return address showing it had been sent from the 116th Assault Helicopter Company. Curious as to what it might be, I tore it open and found two pieces of paper. One was an award of the Air Medal and the other was for several Oak Leaf Clusters to the Air Medal. Neither piece of paper meant anything. Perhaps if I had known they would be the only medals I would ever receive for serving in Viet Nam, I might have thought more of them. Gilchrest had also written, telling me of heavy fighting and making me feel guilty I wasn't sitting on his left side flying into the bullets. In June, he wrote again: six more Stingers, including my favorite pilot, Cliff Wright, had been killed in skirmishes with the NVA. The year wasn't even half done and more than half our platoon had died. Rather than feeling lucky that I was home, I felt I had deserted my friends. I knew that I should be back in Viet Nam; but I also knew that it would be foolish to go back. Everyone over there wanted to be back in the States.

No rational young man in the States wanted to be over there. Why would I even consider going back?

For a year I tried to adjust, but couldn't do it. I drank a lot of alcohol and accomplished nothing of value. The few girls I dated seemed afraid of me after they learned I'd been in Viet Nam. At the time, veterans had a reputation of either being out of their minds on drugs or being killers. It was hard to shake. During my last few months in Viet Nam, I had corresponded with a girl I had gone to school with, but my letters never mentioned what I was doing. When I got home, I didn't visit her. I believe I knew I would be going back. I didn't want to complicate matters by becoming involved with her or any other girl. Perhaps girls shied away from me because of my attitude, not because of my veteran status.

My old man used to probe me with questions about what I had seen and done in Viet Nam. Usually I would say nothing. He always claimed I left my soul in Viet Nam. Maybe he was right. I definitely didn't feel like a whole person. Something was missing. I was home, physically without a scratch, but I wasn't really home. "Don't mean nothing," an expression used daily in Viet Nam, seemed to apply to everything in the States. Everything seemed to be irrelevant. Over and over, I would catch myself thinking, *These people have it made*. Everything seemed so luxurious and easy. Hot water, electricity, private vehicles, air conditioning, choices of food or drinks; it was too easy. I missed the relatively spartan life of the Army in Viet Nam. We had little and needed less. Our lives had been simple, but satisfying. God, I missed it.

I wanted to be living in a hot, dirty hooch, owning nothing more than my boots, rifle and poncho liner. I wanted to go out every day in the early morning darkness searching for death on a helicopter gunship. I missed the solid comfortable feeling of a machine gun in my lap and the reassuring vibration of a helicopter beating through the air as it carried us into combat, lurching and tossing like a mechanical cavalry horse. I missed the excitement of the shooting days and the boredom of the quiet days. Most of all I missed the feeling of euphoria in the evening following a day of fighting when our helicopter skidded and slid into its revetment. Our tight helmets and awkward, heavy chicken plate would be removed and the black carbon-filled layer of greasy LSA that had been ejected from our machine guns would be wiped from our faces. We would look at the bullet holes in the ship and everyone would be smiling outwardly and inwardly, because we had made it through another day. We were happy. Every evening was a cause to celebrate being alive. We all knew why Valhalla was truly Heaven, and why Hell was reserved for those who died in bed.

In May of 1970, American troops invaded Cambodia. Watching the news on television I saw the 116th helicopters in action. The slicks were landing in an LZ under heavy fire while the Stingers roared through the treetops firing rockets into the NVA positions. I wanted to be with them. In late May, I talked to the local Army recruiter. I asked how long it would take to return to Viet Nam. He answered, "I can't get you there today, but I can get you there tomorrow."

He lied, but eight days after enlisting I was back in the land of rice and opportunity. As I walked from the plane and into the dust and stench of the war, I looked around, smiled and muttered to myself, "*Xin loi,* Viet Nam, I never should have left you."

XVIII

It felt damn good to be back. A hot, gritty wind carrying the stench of poverty and war washed over me and all illusions melted away. My senses slowly became reacquainted with reality. I had wasted the past year in an imaginary world of shadows and irrelevancy populated by civilians, a place that failed to recognize how precious and special life really is. Life was cheap in the peaceful civilized world where our days were squandered and trivialized; death was cheap in the violent Orient, where our minutes and hours were savored. I was back where I belonged, a place where I could truly live, valuing each new day as if it were my last. Unlike my arrival in country two years previously, I knew damn well what I was doing this time.

On a quest to find my soul, lost in morning mists twinkling with muzzle flashes, I was not the young kid who had stepped off the plane in 1968, but an old man of twenty-two, so damn old even my eyes were gray. Brutality and terror would once more keep my old gray eyes wide open. Honor and glory were the impossible dreams behind the eyelids of sleeping noncombatants. I had returned without any delusions of grandeur. There had been a lot of time to think on the long flight over the Pacific, and I had realized I hadn't returned to the war for the excitement and adrenaline high of another firefight, nor had I come back because of guilt or a death wish. A year away from the fighting had taught me what mattered wasn't that the war was important, but rather that everything else was so damn unimportant. I had volunteered to participate in the war again because I knew there was something I had not comprehended in the lessons taught to me in so many intoxicating, irrelevant, adrenaline-filled firefights. I hadn't paid attention and had missed something very important; something of value had been shown to me, but my mind had purposely misplaced it, not wanting to recognize truth.

My soul had withered and atrophied in my year as a civilian and needed to be cleaned and hung out to dry by once again staring into the face of death that shimmered in the soft pulsating glow of a muzzle blast. I had to look once more into the ball lightning dancing from the barrel of an enemy machine gun to see if it could still make me grin like the only kid who knows the answer to a tough question.

Coming back to complete an unfinished education, I knew my soul would be the chalkboard on which lessons would be written. Terror and brutality would be the chalk. Such lessons were lightly erased by the euphoria of survival and left a faint, blurred message like scars on the soul, barely legible but important. I had to learn these lessons. My final grade would depend on knowing them. If the message remained too blurred to read, the lesson must be repeated, over and over, until it was understood by we who were slow learners.

Naturally, once I arrived back in country, I wanted to get back to Cu Chi to fight in the Iron Triangle again, but I had been in the Army long enough to know the Army sent men where it wanted to send them: the Army did not care or ask where they wanted to go. Very few men went where they wanted to go. But it was enough for me to be in the war again. I would go wherever I was sent. Still, I requested to be sent to Cu Chi. Two days later I walked into the orderly room of C Troop, Seventh Squadron, First Cavalry at Vinh Long in the heart of the vast Mekong Delta. The Delta, known as IV Corps, formed the southernmost provinces of the country and consisted of mud, malaria and malevolence. Florida with slanted eyes. The Delta was usually considered to be the quietest, least combative part of the war in Viet Nam; it would be my home for the next year. The news media that never left Saigon always reported the Delta as being quiet or pacified. As always, they lied; it wasn't either.

The Seventh of the First was known as the Blackhawks and consisted of five air cavalry troops. C Troop, a typical air cavalry troop, was made up of a scout platoon, a gun platoon, a lift platoon, an infantry platoon, a maintenance platoon and a headquarters platoon. The scouts used light observation helicopters to do low-level reconnaissance work while Cobras from the gun platoon orbited above them, ready to unleash their firepower at any target marked by a smoke grenade thrown from a scout ship. The lift platoon flew the slicks that carried the infantry into landing zones. The infantry platoon was used for ground reconnaissance and to secure downed helicopters. Our maintenance platoon kept the helicopters flying, while the headquarters platoon did everything needed to keep the unit functioning.

Reporting to C Troop, I fully expected to be assigned to the scout platoon since their duties were so similar to my previous job at Cu Chi. The first sergeant had other ideas, however, and didn't waste any time in telling me what I would be doing: I would be given buck sergeant's stripes and serve as the platoon sergeant of the lift platoon. I tried to argue that I had come back into the Army to be a crew chief, not a platoon sergeant, and I definitely didn't want to be in a slick platoon. "Put me in the scouts," I argued. "I know how to do their job."

"Listen," he replied, "you're on your second tour and an E-5. You're more experienced than anyone else in the lift platoon, so you're the platoon sergeant. Try it and I'll make sure you're promoted to staff sergeant in three months."

"Top, I don't want E-6. In fact, why can't I just transfer to the assault unit up the road? They have Charlie-model guns and that's what I want," I told him.

"You're lift platoon sergeant and that's it. Now get out of here and go find your platoon," he replied. He had verbally thrown me out of the orderly room.

Disappointed in my new job, I stoically resigned myself to make the best of it. I knew I would have enjoyed being a

scout because they were hunters, not killers. And I had a
bellyful of killing. I reluctantly reported to my platoon
leader, Captain Sayes, as his new sergeant. I hadn't been sure
what my duties would be as a lift platoon sergeant. I was expecting administrative duties, but I was pleasantly surprised
to learn that I was expected to fly as a crew chief with the
platoon. After drawing my flight gear from our supply room,
I spent most of the day lying on my bunk waiting for the
ships to return from their mission and wondering what the
hell I was going to do as a platoon sergeant. I had no idea that
for the next year I would shuffle more dead men than paper.
Riding the slicks of C Troop would break my heart, scar my
soul and open my mind.

Being made a sergeant meant nothing. As a Specialist 5, I
received the same pay as a buck sergeant and was only being
made an acting sergeant so the lift platoon had a real "platoon sergeant." Usually a platoon sergeant slot was an E-7
and was generally someone with at least a decade in the
Army. Making me a platoon sergeant indicates what shape
the Army was in during 1970. There is an old Army myth that
General Sherman had been asked by a newspaperman, "Why
was it that the Union had won the Civil War, but it seemed
that only the southern generals were famous for their war-
time exploits?" Sherman answered, "We had good corporals
and sergeants, and if you have good corporals and sergeants,
you don't need good generals." I don't think I was in the
same class as his sergeants.

I had arrived in C Troop just in time to go out on some of
the last missions across the border into Cambodia, before
U.S. policy officially stopped our "incursions" there. Following the official invasion, we still went into Cambodia, but
had to carry ARVN troops with us to refuel and rearm our
ships. As Americans, we were not really in Cambodia as long
as we did not physically touch the ground with our feet. The
skids of the helicopters could touch while refueling, and
civilian photographers hung around the refueling points hoping to take one picture of an American soldier standing on
Cambodian soil. It was fine if our bullets touched Cambo-

dian soil (and citizens), but not our feet. Who ever said war had to make sense? Crossing the border didn't really mean much, as our daily missions were similar in either country. After a few trips into Cambodia, I worked everywhere throughout the Delta: the villages, the vast Plain of Reeds, the mangrove swamps of the Forest of Darkness (U Minh), the Seven Sisters Mountains, the coastal swamps, the islands. If the Delta was anything, however, it was mud. Although the dry season baked the paddies and swamps into concrete hardness, when I recall my days in the Delta, I visualize warm, soaking monsoon storms, flooded fields and mud. If the word *patrol* really comes from the French word *patrouiller* and originally meant "to wade in mud," then the Army truly patrolled the Delta. The land was so fertile that the elephant grass reached our rotor blades as we landed and the soil was capable of producing several crops of rice a year. We were fighting in the Delta to protect Saigon's supper.

Our troop rarely worked with American infantry, usually ARVN draftees or Cambodian mercenaries led by American officers or NCOs. These local units with American advisers were generally based at a small compound or fort large enough to defend itself against an enemy attack of company size, but small enough for a larger enemy unit to overrun whenever they felt like doing so. Since we periodically resupplied both the Special Forces and the MACV soldiers at these compounds, we knew what they had to eat. The military rewarded their isolation with better rations than those served in our mess hall, so we always tried to eat lunch at their house. Their food and civilian help were compensation for their isolation. Their mess halls were spotless and the meals tasty. Usually next to the mess hall would be the compound bar, which typically had a large sign on a wall reading, "Kill them all and let God sort them out."

I naïvely thought the sign was extremely vulgar and cruel, considering these men worked directly with Vietnamese every day. At the time, I didn't know it was an old Christian saying from the Crusades. Supposedly, when areas along the borders of France and Spain would not send troops to join the Crusades (because the local Christians would not kill), the crusaders took a detour on their way to the Holy Land to punish the reluctant areas. When the crusaders asked how they were supposed to tell which villagers in the area to punish, they were told, "Kill them all. God will recognize his own." It's nice to know we were following Christian tradition.

Since the majority of our missions in the Delta involved ARVN troops, I had the opportunity to meet more Vietnamese soldiers than I had when I had worked in III Corps. Most South Vietnamese units seemed to have several soldiers who spoke English, and whenever it was slow, I'd sit around and talk with them while we waited for a radio call telling us to saddle up for another insertion. Like soldiers in all armies, we would talk about where we had been in the war and what we had seen and done. Most of the ARVNs seemed glad to be working in the Delta rather than up north, and most, having served in other areas, liked the Delta for two reasons: only a few mountains and no dragons.

Our ARVN troops, all "flatlanders" born and raised in the rice fields, didn't like working in the mountains, the homes of evil spirits. Anyone who has ever seen the mountains of either Viet Nam or Laos knows exactly what they meant by evil spirits. There are no friendly-looking mountains in these countries: all of them seem to give off a sense of evil that raises the hair on the back of your neck. The mountains appear malevolent, and it's easy to understand why very few Vietnamese live in the highlands. Old, old mountains unchanged since time began, their steep slopes wear a veil of mist made of lost souls. Few dare to trespass. It was not that the mountains hid the enemy that made us feel uncomfortable, but something much more basic. Something that gave everyone an involuntary shudder. Those of us who worked in the mountains soon became "born again" animists. A living entity sneered in your face when you looked at them. Even the Seven Sisters in the Delta, limestone monoliths towering a thousand feet above the surrounding thousands of square kilometers of cultivated flatlands, had impenetrable triple-canopy jungle on their plateaus. Peering into those isolated islands of vegetation in the clouds made me wonder what, besides the NVA, lived and hid there.

All of our English-speaking ARVN troops said they hated and feared the thick primeval tropical jungle, whether it was mountainous or flat. The jungle dragons especially frightened them, and every ARVN soldier I ever talked to claimed to have seen at least one dragon when he patrolled the jungles. Who knows? Maybe they did. When we couldn't find an NVA division of ten thousand men living in the jungle, how could we say the same jungle didn't hide dragons? They were right about the evil spirits; so they may have also been right about the dragons. There would never be any joking or laughing when discussing dragons. The ARVN soldiers knew they had seen things as real as the NVA soldiers hiding in the same terrain. Dragons just happened, quick glimpses appearing and disappearing in brief seconds, the fire of their breath as fearsome as any muzzle blast. No soldier went searching for a dragon. It would be suicide. Seeing one, the only prudent thing to do was to retreat. No one dared fire a shot. There were no Beowulfs in the Army of the Republic of Viet Nam.

In our opinion, most South Vietnamese Army or Marine units were overly cautious and didn't appear very interested in pursuing a fight with either dragons or enemy units. However, the ARVN rangers and Cambodian mercenaries we worked with seemed to perform very well and occasionally were too aggressive. Unlike most ARVN units, their rangers were disciplined and operated as a cohesive unit in the field. Their officers went out in the field with them and ruled with an iron fist. One morning, we had dropped three loads of rangers into an LZ and were heading back for more troops when a new pilot noticed his camera had been stolen. Obviously, someone on the ground had taken it, so he radioed the ranger lieutenant that one of the rangers had his camera. The ground commander called back that he had recovered the camera and asked the pilot to please return to the LZ for it. We turned around and landed back in the LZ to find the rangers standing in formation. As our skids settled into the mud, one man ran out of the formation and brought the camera back to the pilot. As he returned to his formation, the lieutenant stopped him and ordered him to stand at attention, then shot him in the head.

We were stunned. Talk about an Article 15. Leaving the LZ to catch our platoon, the pilot seemed to be in shock over the incident. He told us over and over how sorry he was he had even mentioned the camera. Too late for regrets; welcome to the Orient.

Our Cambodian mercenaries were tough and confident; they fought for a living and knew they were good at their jobs. Even though their families may have lived in the Delta for generations, they didn't look anything like their Vietnamese neighbors. They were taller and usually much darker than the Vietnamese, some of them almost black. While they generally dressed nearly identical to the ARVN troops, most of them wore a checkered scarf and a gold Buddha on a necklace. Wherever we worked, the local villagers seemed to hate and fear these mercenaries: they were ancient enemies. We often wondered what American officials thought of using Cambodian soldiers to guard Vietnamese villages. Doing so automatically forced the village males to back the other side. Every dumb ass enlisted man knew we were never going to win any local hearts and minds by using Cambodian troops to protect Vietnamese villagers from other Vietnamese. A few Cambodians would bluntly state that once they had killed all of the VC and NVA, the ARVN would be next. Their cousins living in Cambodia were the Khmer Rouge, who, after taking a village, immediately shot everyone who could drive, who wore eyeglasses or who owned a toothbrush. Any one of the three was a death sentence.

Even though the locals didn't like the Cambodians, they were good troops to work with and I always found them interesting to talk to. Once when working with Cambodians our scouts found a large NVA force resting in a swampy wooded area and our C&C, wisely deciding that our unit was too small to fight them, had called in artillery on the enemy position. The NVA forces were softened by artillery while we loafed on our parked slicks waiting patiently for the command to assault the enemy positions. We sat around the slicks with Cambodian infantry for half an hour, idly watching artillery shells blow spouts of water, mud and flesh into the air as they impacted on top of NVA soldiers hidden in the mangroves. We knew the survivors of the artillery were going to be mad as hornets when we dropped out of the sky and landed in their midst. Turning toward a tough old battle-scarred Cambodian sergeant who was leaning against my ship, I pointed toward the impacting artillery and said, "*Trung si,* it's going to be bad when we go in over there."

"Maybe," he answered, "but don't matter I die, I Buddhist, and I come back again."

Now, that statement opened my eyes. What faith! I had never heard a Christian soldier say that dying didn't matter as he was going to Heaven, unless of course there was no immediate chance of death. When dying seemed imminent, our men kept their thoughts to themselves and, while they may have prayed, I doubt if many really thought Heaven was a sure thing. If given a choice, most of our guys would have picked oblivion over Heaven anyway. Looking at this man, I could tell he was serious about what he had said: he was coming back. He looked closely at me and bluntly stated, "Don't matter if you die either."

"Why is that?" I asked, curiously.

"You have no soul."

"What? What do you mean, I have no soul?"

"You have gray eyes. No soul. Just like leopard."

Later on several Chinese girls would tell me the same thing, so I guess it must be true. We couldn't finish our religious discussion because we received a radio call to saddle up and load the Cambodian troops. We rose out of the paddies, gained altitude, then dropped quickly, gliding into the smoke and fire of the landing zone. I can still hear our AC singing, "I don't care if it rains or freezes, long as I have my plastic Jesus, riding on the dashboard of my car . . ." over the chattering roar of my machine gun. As we entered the smoke, flames and automatic weapons fire of the LZ, I glanced to my right and saw that my Cambodian philosopher, like most of his countrymen, had his gold Buddha clenched tightly in his teeth for luck. Like a lot of Americans who had been in country for a while I wore one too, but I didn't bother biting mine. There were heavy casualties on both sides in this anonymous, irrelevant battle. And I never saw this man of faith again.

XIX

Actually, there wasn't much shooting occurring during the summer of 1970. Maybe, as everyone claimed, the enemy troops were low on supplies from the cross-border raids of the Cambodian incursion. It seemed the quieter it became in the field, however, the worse things became in the base camps to the rear. Morale and discipline were disintegrating, perhaps because we lacked a mission, perhaps because of the certain knowledge that America's days in Viet Nam were numbered. It didn't help morale that massive troop withdrawals were occurring throughout the country, and many soldiers didn't want the honor of being the last American to die in Viet Nam. Everyone was convinced the Army of the Republic of Viet Nam would collapse when it was forced to face the enemy without American help. We were fighting for a lost cause. Withdrawing American troops conceded defeat. Most troops believed that we should go home if our government was conceding defeat.

Perhaps too many people had too much time to think. Those of us who were busy and out in the field didn't have the morale or discipline problems of the guys stuck at a base camp. We, at least, were seeing the country. And occasionally we got an adrenaline rush from automatic weapons fire coming at us. I can't say life in C Troop was harmonious and we were all "brothers in arms," but we didn't have half the problems that some units had. No one was throwing fragmentation grenades into hooches or shooting officers in the company area.

At Vinh Long we didn't have the hard drug problems that

275

were becoming common on other compounds, but our racial problems could match—or beat—those of other compounds. The black troops constantly provoked confrontations, knowing the white troops would not stick together, and that the whites would get no support from our leaders. Those in command appeared to be willing to ignore any act of insubordination by black troops rather than risk a black soldier filing a complaint of racial prejudice. None of our officers or NCOs wanted an investigation of alleged racial prejudice; it would kill their careers. Most of the black troops thumbed their noses at the military by growing beards or by not getting their hair cut. Nothing was done to them. The young black troops who were good soldiers were caught in the middle, unsure which way to turn. The military was letting itself be split apart on racial lines, and no one seemed to care.

While there were many small fights and racial incidents on the Vinh Long compound, one particularly violent incident in C Troop occurred late one evening after our scout platoon had refused to sell part of their private beer cache to some black troops. The scouts never sold their beer to anyone outside of their platoon no matter what their color, but apparently there were hard feelings about this particular refusal. Late that night a group of black troops invaded the scout platoon's hooch and beat the scouts severely with bunk adapters, the steel pipes that hold the top bunk above the lower bunk. Some of our scouts were hospitalized and there was constant talk of revenge. Our troop became a powder keg, waiting for the smallest incident to ignite an explosion. During the next two weeks, nothing happened on the compound, but several black soldiers who were known to have assaulted our scouts were found dead in the village of Vinh Long. At the NCO Club, MP sergeants said .38-caliber bullets had killed the dead men. Our scouts carried .38-caliber revolvers; the rest of us who carried sidearms used .45-caliber pistols. Most of us knew what was happening and were waiting for armed retaliation. The lift platoon and the infantry platoon had promised to back our scouts in any fight, and loaded weapons were kept next to our bunks at night. I wondered if our officers in the troop knew that the buck sergeants in C Troop had their men ready to fight an internal war. While the MPs often visited our troop area to shoot our pet dogs (because of a fear of rabies) in broad daylight, they never came around on those nights when we were ready to shoot each other. Everyone on the compound waited to see what was going to happen in C Troop, but the shootings in the village were warnings everyone could read. Nothing happened, but for a long time the nights at home were more tense and fearful than the days spent out in the field.

Besides the internal war among ourselves during these quiet times, incidents were frequently occurring that involved innocent civilians. One afternoon, I watched a guard on our bunker line shoot a Vietnamese woman cutting grass between the rows of barbed wire on the perimeter. She was part of an obvious group of civilians hired to cut the grass. And still she was shot. Probably the worst incident to occur in the Delta during the summer of 1970 was perpetrated by a group known as the "Dong Tam Eight." Dong Tam had been the sprawling base camp of the 9th Infantry Division, which had stood down and returned to the States. There were still a few units left at Dong Tam and they were bored and going stir crazy.

One September morning, two gunship crews of the 335th Assault Helicopter Company got drunk, climbed into their armed Charlie-model gunships and flew low-level for twenty miles along the nearby canals, shooting every Vietnamese they saw. It was said that they had become so intoxicated with bloodlust, they ignored their low fuel level alarms and killed until they were forced to land in open rice paddies with no fuel left. I could understand how it happened, because I knew from experience how the gun crews ran on adrenaline and how lack of action affected such crews. The Dong Tam Eight made the *Stars and Stripes* for a few weeks, then other stories made the news. Whatever happened to the four officers and four enlisted men who flew out of Dong Tam that quiet September day? Nothing?

The summer of 1970 was busy but relatively quiet. As the

monsoon season came to an end, most of us hoped that dry
weather would get the enemy moving and make our work
more interesting. On the tenth of September, daybreak found
C Troop landing in a flooded rice paddy near Tan Tri to pick
up an American infantry patrol that had spent the night on an
ambush. They had huddled together for seemingly endless
hours of mud and mosquitoes in the wet tropical darkness of
the monsoon season, trying to stay awake while waiting for
the enemy to walk into their midst. They had no luck—or
perhaps had been lucky, since they had not had contact with
enemy troops. Dropping out of the sky on our approach to
the PZ, we could see our infantry standing in six small
groups in the center of a rice paddy, muddy wisps in the
water showing the trails back to their night ambush position
in the wide tree line nearby. Losing altitude quickly, we
glided toward the PZ watching the numerous fighting positions and half-camouflaged bunkers that faced our touchdown site from the woods surrounding the field. A light rain
was falling as our three slicks hovered over the water, each
ship maneuvering to land between two groups of tired, dirty
men, standing waist deep in the flooded paddy. After coming
to a stop, each helicopter dropped down into the flooded rice
plants until the floor was even with the water. Our pilots were
trying to make it easier for our guys to flop on board rather
than having to climb up on the slippery wet skids. As our
ships settled into the water, the small groups of infantrymen
lurched through the water, struggling against the wind of our
rotor blades, trying to get on the ships. They were tired and
were having a difficult time fighting the deep water and mud
while encumbered by the heavy weight of their equipment
and weapons. Keeping my left hand on the machine gun, I'd
reach out and grab each tired infantryman who struggled to
my side of the ship to help him slide on board. I wanted to
get out of this PZ as fast as they did. We were taking much
too long to pick up the troops and were vulnerable sitting in
the open rice paddy surrounded by tree lines perforated with
bunkers and fighting positions. Our commander on the C&C
ship was yelling over the radio to speed up the extraction, but

there was nothing we could do. We had to have everyone on board before we could lift off. This patrol had seen nothing while hidden in their night ambush site, but that didn't mean no one was home in the bunkers barely camouflaged by the thick growth of vegetation forming a dull green wall around the field. The patrol may have been left alone all night purposely. The enemy was smart enough to know that the patrol would be a much easier target in the morning, when everyone was tired and anxious to be picked up by our helicopters.

As soon as the feet of the last infantryman were out of the water, I yelled, "We're good." Our AC lifted the ship straight up out of the water, momentarily stopping to hover a meter above the rice stalks to let the water trapped in the ship's belly pour out. Our three slicks, overloaded with water trapped in the bulkheads under the floors, were suspended at a low hover in front of the enemy bunkers, making ideal targets, the proverbial sitting ducks. Holding my machine gun pointed low on the brushy perimeter, expecting enemy gunfire to rip us apart, I had one of my rare feelings of impending doom and wanted to get moving. Our weight dropped quickly as gravity pulled the water from the ship's hollow belly. Feeling the ship getting lighter, the AC dipped the nose of our helicopter slightly and started forward. Skimming over the water at full speed, our platoon flew as fast as possible out of the PZ, all door guns firing streams of tracers into the brush and trees along our flanks. My ship was flying lead and we had traveled only a few hundred meters when the ship's nose started going down, while the rear of the helicopter lifted skyward.

Something was drastically wrong. Taking my eyes off the tree line, I looked to my right toward our front and saw our rotor blades reaching for the water. In slow motion, I watched the blades disintegrate into millions of small particles, as the rotor blades chewed water instead of air. The ship seemed to take hours to rise perpendicular to the paddy and then to descend slowly upside down past that vertical point. I knew we were doomed and said to myself, "This is it, Al." It sounds foolish, but that's what my last thought actually was. I had no doubt once we hit upside down, the ship would be torn apart and explode. I remembered watching Wilsher's ship explode in 1969 and purposely unhooked my seat belt. I grabbed my machine gun with my left hand and the seat post with my right and I distinctly recall hoping the gun wouldn't disembowel me when I was thrown out of the ship on impact. Moving at glacial speed, our ship had gone past the point of being perpendicular to the ground and was almost upside down—when everything went black.

It was pitch black for only an instant, and then suddenly I could see a soft diffused light, a delicate glow that appeared to be far ahead of me at the end of a passageway. I knew immediately what had happened; I was dead, killed in the crash. I was bodiless, a thinking, wide-awake awareness. A spirit? Possibly, but I don't know. What does a spirit feel like? This experience was definitely not a subconscious dream. I had never before or since experienced anything so absolutely real. Life may be an illusion, but this was real.

It was easy to see that the source of light was not directly at the end of the tunnel or passageway, but was an indirect light coming from either a room or a passageway to the right side of the tunnel's end. I was filled with an overwhelming feeling of contentment and gentle warmth. I experienced no fear or anxiety, but rather a feeling of "welcome home," a very comfortable "I've been here before and liked it" feeling. Everything was peaceful, and I felt so damn happy to be back again and finished with life. I somehow knew that I must make my way toward the source of light way off in the distance and started toward the soft, gentle glow. I didn't walk, but I didn't fly either. My mind or being moved toward the light with no exertion or any sense of actual body movement.

As I approached the light, I could sense that once I came to the tunnel's end and made the turn to the right, I would be in the presence of multiple beings. I don't know why, but I knew for certain that there was more than one being around the right turn. It is difficult to describe, but I felt that I was not going to learn something around the turn but instead was going to be given "knowledge." Whatever I did not understand would soon be made known to me. I understood that the multiple presence would enlighten me: the what, the why and the how of important and unimportant things would be given to me. As I moved to the light, I found that I now understood and knew the secrets of the oddest things. Irrelevant things to the dead, they were examples of the living not being able to see the forest for the trees. I felt amused, realizing the foolishness of the living. God, living human beings were so damn dumb! We had only had to find the lock securing whatever we had wanted as we had been given the keys. Life could have been so damn easy, but we all went out of our way to make everything difficult. There is a good reason why people don't come back from the grave; they are smart.

I was moving toward the light, eager to make the turn to the right, when suddenly I hesitated, knowing, or perhaps informed, that once around the turn, I would be questioned and would be held accountable. By accountable, I mean I would be held responsible for everything I had ever done in my life. This accountability, however, was not going to be a judgment. I felt no threat; it was not a Heaven-or-Hell situation. Rather I would be expected to have my life reviewed like an ongoing progress report. I knew one question was going to be, "Had I improved?" My past actions and inactions were going to be weighed by the group. I knew or could sense that my actions, with or toward other people, were high on the priority list. I don't know why, but how I had dealt with other people seemed to be important. I seemed to understand that all of our lives were intermingled for a reason. We interact with each other and our lives are mixed for a purpose. We learn from each other and rise higher by helping others. There was going to be an expectation that I had met certain standards, but more than that I knew that there was indeed a universal moral code. "Don't abandon your wounded and don't forget your friends" would have been how I would explain it in the words of a soldier. But it was much more than that. There had been no rights while living, only obligations and responsibilities.

There was no sense of hellfire for failing, but I felt that my failure would cause a collective disappointment: "You could have done better, but you let us down." While I could not think of any specific reason why I should be uneasy, I was very apprehensive and hesitant about being held accountable for my life. I recalled the two men at the bunker in 1969 and wondered if I could have done better. I knew I should have.

There was absolutely no implied religious connection with the accountability, and I knew it was not important to which religion I belonged or how religious I had been. My actions on a day-to-day basis and how I lived and treated others were important, not which religion I had followed. While religions might comfort some people and help the weak in spirit through life, they were not verity and were of no overall importance. My wearing of a Buddha on my dog tag chain meant as little as if I had been wearing a cross. Religion was irrelevant; it was only for the living, not for us on the other side. On this side of the fence, it seemed to be understood that there were in fact basic standards and obligations that were to be recognized and met while living. The group around the right-hand turn would not be asking where I worshiped on weekends, and henotheists would be much more welcome here than blind religious fanatics. No one played Pascal's wager with this house. It didn't matter what you bet, but why you bet.

Approaching the end of the passageway, I could almost feel the soft glow coming out of the right-hand passageway, but I had mixed emotions about making the right turn. There was no fear, but rather hesitation. I wanted to become part of the group and share their knowledge; but on the other hand, I felt unsure of my accountability. I knew I could have accomplished many things much better while alive, yet I didn't know exactly what standards I was supposed to have met. I wanted to find out what was around the turn, but I felt extremely uncomfortable knowing I was going to be held accountable.

I stopped moving toward the light. I somehow realized I didn't have to proceed. It was my choice: accountability and knowledge, or go back. I hesitated and thought, *I want to go back to try to do better.* I instantly regretted thinking that.

I was swimming in the rice paddy, weighed down by my heavy chest armor, but swimming nonetheless, ten or fifteen meters from the upside-down carcass of my helicopter. Stunned unarmed infantrymen, thrown out of the wrecked ship, were struggling to walk in the warm, muddy, waist-deep water. There had been no fire or explosion; the water had dampened our crash. If it had been the dry season and the rice paddy dirt baked to the hardness of concrete, we would have probably exploded in a huge fireball. "Crispy critters" was what we called those who perished in flaming helicopters. Trivia: Our medics advised us to quickly breathe in flames, blistering the interior of the lungs so that drowning occurred when the blisters broke. Better than life in a burn ward, they claimed. But how would they know?

Seeing the infantry walking around dazed and realizing the water couldn't be very deep, I stopped swimming and let my feet sink down into the mud. Wading over to the ship, I tried to get my machine gun off the mount but found the new gunner flying with us that day had bolted the gun to the mount, instead of using a spring-loaded "quick disconnect" pin. My training was taking over. I knew my primary duty when my ship went down was to take my machine gun and cover our left flank immediately. Somehow I managed to turn the nut off the bolt with my fingers and removed the gun from its mount.

All the time I was taking the gun off the mount, I expected machine-gun bullets to hit me in the back. I could feel the presence of armed men in the tree line, and a sixth sense told me that rifles were sighted on my back. Common sense was telling me to leave the damn gun and get on the other side of the ship and away from the bunkers behind me. But I was the only person with a weapon on my side of the ship. I knew I had to face the muzzle flashes that would soon erupt from the thick vegetation. After moving out in the paddy to protect our flank, I braced my feet into the mud, pulled a long loop of belted ammunition from my shoulder to feed the gun and stood facing the bunkers. I knew that by standing there with a machine gun I would immediately draw any enemy fire. But I didn't care. My stomach muscles tightened in anticipation of being ripped to pieces by machine-gun fire. Feeling vulnerable and exposed, I suddenly realized there was nothing to worry about. I had seen "the light at the end of the tunnel" and chosen to come back. Surely, I couldn't have been sent back just to be shot minutes later.

Our scouts arrived, zipping past me, then flaring to a hover between the tree line and me, while our Cobras flew circles above them. The cavalry to the rescue. Turning around, I saw our C&C ship coming in to hover on the other side of my wrecked ship. All of us in the muddy water were well protected then, so I waded back to the ship. I had a feeling of euphoria and was overwhelmed with emotion. Having been on the guns with the 116th, I knew our helicopters were acting as shields. When I had been with the Stingers of the 116th, we had done the same thing for others many times and had thought little of doing it, but no one had put themselves between the guns of the NVA and me before. I still believe that armed men sat in those camouflaged bunkers but chose not to initiate a fight that morning. It made me feel humble that the men of C Troop would risk their lives for me.

As I waded back to our wreck, I noticed that the AC was also out of the ship and standing in the water. He appeared dazed, but otherwise okay, so I walked around the nose of the ship to check out the other side. Lt. Eber Brown, our pilot, was still strapped in his seat, hanging upside down, trying to keep his head above water. He was losing his strength and, when his head fell under the water, bubbles would stream out of his mouth. The infantry lieutenant and I both stood next to his open door window for a long moment, alternately staring at Eber and then at the bubbles. Both of us finally realized we ought to help him. I reached into the open door window and pulled the toggle that released the door from its hinges. As I pulled the door from the ship, the infantry lieutenant reached into the ship, unbuckled Eber's seat belt and pulled him out. He was alive, but had almost drowned. Leaving the two lieutenants, I waded along the ship, helped the new gunner unbolt his gun from the mount, and then returned to retrieve the radios from the front of the ship. Carrying our radios and guns, our crew waded over to the C&C ship to find out what we were supposed to do next. I expected the gunner and I would stay there to guard the wreck until a Chinook flew out to retrieve it, but we were told to get on board with our pilots. One of our slicks would soon return to pick up our infantry passengers and our scouts would keep an eye on our wreck. C&C took us home to get another helicopter.

We were soaking wet, muddy, cut and bruised, but we smiled all the way back home. We had thought we were dead men and it felt great to be only wet, cold and sore. As I sat there grinning, I was thinking about the tunnel. What did it all mean? I felt so glad to be alive, but at the same time I was thinking I shouldn't have come back. I wondered if I had made the right decision in the tunnel. What had the other guys experienced?

We flew through the rain back to C Troop, where a jeep from operations waited for us on the flight line. We checked in at our troop TOC to find out which ship we would be taking back out to the field: three of us were told to hang around the troop area on standby for the rest of the day. The troop had a slick with an AC, crew chief and gunner waiting to go. Since the slick needed a pilot, Eber changed clothes and returned to the field. After the rest of the troop returned home that evening I went to see our platoon leader, and had my ass chewed for unbuckling my seat belt and getting thrown out of the ship. I was asked what I wanted to do about the new gunner and I replied, "Let's get rid of him."

"That's what I thought you'd say. He's going to A Troop tomorrow."

Our new guy hadn't been working out very well as a gunner, and bolting the machine guns to their mounts was the last straw. If there had been NVA soldiers in the tree line, we could have been shot to pieces while the gunner and I wasted time trying to remove our guns. That little error could have killed us. As the platoon sergeant, I should have noticed that the guns were bolted into the mounts and corrected his mistake, but I never thought anyone would do anything that foolish. He turned out to be a good gunner in A Troop. Perhaps he had a better sergeant there.

I was always tempted to discuss my experience in the tunnel with Eber, but I didn't. My experience had been vivid and real, but it went against everything I had been taught growing up. I had been raised a Christian of the "Jesus 'One Strike and You're Out' Christ" theology, going to church every Sunday. The episode in the tunnel didn't fit into any type of afterlife I had ever expected. Actually, I suppose, like most Christians, I had been hoping for oblivion—it sure beat Hell. I didn't know how to explain my experience to anyone else, so I kept my thoughts to myself. Knowing without a doubt I had truly seen the other side of death, I lost all fear of dying. I knew there was a reason why I was allowed to return, but couldn't remember what it was.

I really can't say that the episode in the tunnel changed my life. But perhaps it did and I don't realize it. I went back to my work, and life in the peaceful Delta went on. Several weeks later, while shut down outside of an ARVN fort, Eber would be radioed that we had landed in an unmarked minefield and would shout to warn me that I was strolling through a minefield. When he yelled, I stopped walking and stood still, ten long, long meters away from our ship. Assuming that the unmarked minefield had its mines laid in a preplanned pattern, I knew I had probably stepped over at least three or four mines buried under the hard sunbaked Delta mud. Thinking about the tunnel and the chance to try again gave me the confidence to turn around and calmly walk back to my ship. It was probably a foolish thing to do, because I might have lost my legs and still been alive. But I knew that I hadn't come back from the tunnel to step on a damn mine.

XX

Even though we weren't in contact with the enemy in the Delta as often as I had been when working in III Corps, it wasn't because our troop was trying to avoid a fight. As cavalry, we did reconnaissance almost every day, attempting to find the enemy and to make the initial contact. Out in the field, our troop was big enough to provoke a fight but not big enough to win one. Once we located concentrations of enemy, additional troops and artillery would have to be used to destroy the enemy. We were out all day, and some evenings and nights. We constantly inserted and extracted ARVN soldiers, randomly checkerboarding the vast Mekong Delta. On one busy day of doing quick turnarounds between LZs and PZs while checkerboarding, I recall making fifty-seven insertions into landing zones, each one with the potential for landing on top of an enemy unit. We knew the enemy was out there somewhere, and by maximizing landing zones it was thought we would have to eventually find the enemy. Sometimes we did, and brought our ships home full of bullet holes. The C Troop slicks did every type of mission possible in support of infantry operations in the Delta except one thing: haul prisoners. In all of my time with the troop, I never saw an enemy prisoner. Any NVA or VC who came in contact with our unit either escaped or died. Unlike the fresh NVA soldiers who had just infiltrated into the country from Cambodia and who sometimes surrendered up in III Corps, the hard-core guerrillas of the Mekong Delta didn't seem to *chieu hoi* very often. But I wasn't out in the field every day and didn't see everything that the troop did. Maybe they did take a prisoner one or two times: if so, no one ever mentioned it.

In the fall of 1970 we started doing combat assaults into the U Minh Forest, or Forest of Darkness, a vast flat featureless mangrove swamp on the Ca Mau peninsula and a well-known enemy stronghold. Being assigned to work the U Minh Forest was supposed to mean something special because it hadn't been the scene of many previous operations. It would be like hunting in a game preserve. In the past, the priority mission in the Delta was to protect and secure the populated areas; let the VC and NVA rot in the malarial swampland of the U Minh. Since the arms flow from Cambodia had been virtually shut off, however, it had been decided to use our cavalry to clean out enemy camps in the U Minh. We knew Navy SEALs had operated in the U Minh before us, but we had worked with SEALs and considered them to be tall ARVNs. They never accomplished much, but they did tell good stories. If there were NVA units in the U Minh, we knew it would be cavalry units that would find and fight them, not SEALs. We spent day after day searching for the enemy in this swampy refuge and, while we didn't find NVA soldiers everywhere, there were plenty of signs they were living there. Straw hooches were built on elevated mounds scattered throughout the marshland and elevated garden plots were strewn haphazardly to minimize their destruction by defoliants. Our enemy soon knew we were hunting them and they knew how we operated. The U Minh was their sanctuary. They would make us pay for trespassing.

On one typical day when C Troop was working the U Minh, our scouts and guns were busy hunting men while the slicks inserted and extracted small hunting parties of ARVN rangers. We were looking for the elusive enemy and had found nothing of interest. At midday, the scattered ARVN forces walked to a central point, regrouping for a long lunch break, and we were told to head for the nearest airfield and shut down. Our slicks were inbound to land at the local airfield when my ship received a call to leave our group and report to a nearby ARVN compound. We had to pick up a team of American advisers who wanted to spend the afternoon with our ARVN unit, observing their tactics. More likely, I thought, it was just a group of visitors who didn't want to go out on a normal mission, but since the day had been so quiet, they were willing to go for a walk to justify receiving the Combat Infantryman Badge (CIB). If they had really been looking for a fight, they wouldn't have waited until lunch to play soldier since early afternoon was when both Vietnamese armies forgot about the war because of the extreme heat and humidity.

After picking up the visiting advisers, we flew them to our morning's work site and found most of our allies were out of the mud and lounging around a large dry patch of raised earth. Judging by its size, I guessed that this piece of high ground was an old homesite several generations of farmers had labored to build and expand above the monsoon floods. We landed to let our passengers disembark in the muddy field on the north side of the low earthen mound covered with weary, wet soldiers. As soon as their feet hit the mud, our AC was lifting the skids out of the mud, moving forward and hurrying to join the rest of C Troop for lunch.

We had just passed the magical point of translational lift and were becoming airborne and starting to gain altitude when the shock wave from a huge explosion drove our helicopter sideways. The blast came from our left rear and pushed our ship violently toward our right front. In the instant that the shock wave hit, I thought that we were going to be spun over into the ground. Fighting the controls, our AC managed to keep us in the air and, as we straightened out in flight, we heard our C&C ship, high overhead, radio us to turn around. Our crew, stunned from the blast, had no idea what had happened behind us.

The local VC had realized that sooner or later, this flat, raised mound of earth was just the type of place that lazy ARVNs or Americans would pick for a break. Since it was a relatively high, dry island in a swamp of mud, troops would naturally congregate on it if given the opportunity. A command-detonated dud Air Force bomb had been buried in the mound. Somewhere nearby was a man who had been waiting for who knows how long for a patrol to sit and relax. When it appeared a maximum number of troops were near the bomb, he had turned a switch and triggered the explosion. The large group of ARVN soldiers was the target, and the American advisers were the icing on the cake. If the VC soldier hiding nearby had detonated the bomb just a little bit sooner, he would have had a helicopter, too.

Coming around, we saw that the low, earthen mound covered with resting troops had been turned into a smoking, blackened crater littered with mangled bodies and equipment. Several experienced American sergeants with a radio had wisely not joined the crowd on the dry embankment and were alive. They took control on the ground and, after finding another American still alive, called for us to medevac him out. Our C&C ship had also radioed for the rest of the troop to saddle up and hurry back to help us. While they would soon be airborne and returning to evacuate the wounded ARVNs, my ship was ordered to immediately land for our American casualty. As my ship gingerly hovered into the smoke and dust from the explosion, my muscles tensed. I waited for the VC to use their standard trick—setting off a second, bigger explosive for any rescuers arriving to help victims of the initial blast.

Anticipating a second explosion that would vaporize us at any moment, we landed to pick up our casualty: a sergeant with no arms or legs. In the words of our trade, he was a "baseball player," that is, the only job he could now do was serve as a base in a game of baseball. He was conscious and lay on the floor, calm and quiet, gazing up at me while we took off toward the nearest hospital. The letter *T* written in his own blood was on his forehead, the common mark used by medics to let others know that tourniquets were in place. Ordinarily a tourniquet was to be loosened every fifteen minutes to allow some blood to flow into the limb below the binding, but there were no limbs to be concerned about saving on this man. There wasn't a damn thing I could do for him, but silently murmur, *"Xin loi."*

After taking off and reaching a safe altitude, both the gunner and I pushed our guns forward into the barrel bracket on the gun mount and swung our legs around into the cargo area. The gunner was new, not used to combat casualties, and the sight of a real combat wound drew the color out of his face. This limbless man was his first look at what high explosives do to flesh, and it made him think about what war was really like. I suppose he may have just learned there wasn't any honor or glory in being blown into molecules while eating lunch. He might eventually learn there wasn't any honor or glory in being killed doing anything else, either. Trying to do something to comfort the man, he reached behind the AC's seat and grabbed my field jacket to drape over our limbless passenger. I immediately jerked it out of his hands. "Fucking asshole, new guy," I muttered as I grabbed my coat. I had told him earlier he had better bring a field jacket. It would get cold sitting behind the gun, flying through the rain all day, but a typical young, new kid, he hadn't listened to me. Maybe I was too callous and hard, but I knew that our passenger would soon be either dead or in a warm hospital. I, on the other hand, would be wet and miserable for long hours before the day was done, and I had no intention of wearing a blood-drenched field jacket. While I had also put my jacket on the wounded back when I was young, I had flown out of the rice paddies sitting alongside too many dead and dying boys to bother anymore. Too many shattered bodies had made it difficult for me to even say, *"Xin loi."*

Even though I wasn't willing to give him my jacket, I didn't ignore the old man lying on the floor. I knelt down next to his left side and, leaning over, spoke gently into his ear, trying to reassure him that he would be okay, but his eyes didn't believe me. Man to man, we looked into each other's eyes. We both knew that our positions could have easily been reversed if he had been standing somewhere else on the mound and if the bomb had been detonated sooner. Such are the fortunes of war. We were both old sergeants and old men; I was twenty-two and he appeared to be about twenty-six. We were old enough to know the work we did was dangerous.

Both of us wore unit patches on our right shoulders, an Army custom signifying that we had each spent a year in combat at some other time. We knew what we were doing and deserved whatever we received. Looking at him was looking in a mirror, and there was no sympathy or sorrow in the eyes of either one of us. Having been in the tunnel, I knew some secrets. Perhaps I should have told them to him but I think he already knew. He wasn't in shock and didn't seem to be in pain, but he didn't say a word. He kept looking straight at me and I could read his eyes. I knew what he wanted and it wasn't a field jacket. He was pleading for mercy—loosen the tourniquets. We delivered the dead sergeant to the nearest American medical facility.

In our absence, the rest of our platoon was busy hauling wounded ARVN soldiers. Twenty-six men died in the explosion and a lot more than that were wounded. My ship returned just in time to pick up the last of the wounded, a few litter cases and a lot of walking wounded, some carrying rifles whose barrels had been actually bent sideways by the blast. Looking at what the explosion had done to steel rifle barrels made me wonder how any human flesh had survived.

As always, we didn't count wounded. We just piled them on and flew away, no matter how overloaded. The few basket cases were put in the middle of the ship. The rest of our passengers squeezed into any spot they could find. At least the Vietnamese didn't police up the abandoned or forgotten arms, hands, feet and legs lying around and toss them on board, as was normally done with American wounded. It appeared someone had already done a medical triage and, this being the last load, we had picked up those least likely to survive as well as the walking wounded. The severely wounded men who appeared to have a reasonable chance to return to the battlefield again if treated had been given priority evacuation. The lowest priority for treatment were those who were dying, lightly wounded or missing limbs. The load on my ship were those certain to live or certain to die. Most of the soldiers hadn't even been bandaged. The man sitting next to me had a hole two inches in diameter in his lower left back that was oozing liquid meat. And the liquid blew all over me. I motioned to a wounded ARVN sitting on the floor behind our AC to grab the first aid kit on the bulkhead next to him, then pointed to myself, yelling *"Bac si!"* Telling him I was a doctor might help their morale a little. There wasn't much that I could do except bandage some wounds, but it was better than nothing. The soldier on the floor pulled a first aid kit from the doorway bulkhead, looked at the Red Cross on it, then threw it violently out of our ship. *You little bastard! I should throw you right out after it,* I thought, as I watched it fall to the ground far below us.

Using our intercom, I asked the gunner to throw me a bandage from the first aid kit on his side, then bandaged the gaping hole in the soldier next to me. Dressing his wound didn't do much good since a thick mixture of blood and liquid flesh oozed out along the bandage edges. It didn't matter, anyway. These guys were headed to a South Vietnamese hospital, where treatment would be minimal. Later that day, as we brought in the dead, this load of wounded would still be sitting in the rain and mud outside the hospital, ignored and not bandaged. If they had been dogs, we would have shot them. But they were men, and suffering is good for the soul.

During our medevac flights that afternoon, the blood of the dead and wounded pooled on the floor and dripped through the openings along the edges of the floor panels down into the compartments formed by structural members under the floor. The mixture of blood and body fluids congealed and cooked in the heat. In the warm humid compartments the mixture decomposed rapidly, filling our ship with the strong, warm, sickly smell of death. As the day went on and we went back to carrying other troops into other landing zones, the boarding troops would rush toward our ship but then pause at the doorways when the stench filled their nostrils. The smell of fresh death stopped them in their tracks. Soldiers are extremely superstitious. No one wants to ride into a fight on a ship carrying the ghosts of the recent dead. We were a bad omen, but there were no other buses coming so they reluctantly climbed on board.

Whenever we stopped to refuel, the gunner and I would heave ammo cans full of swamp water and mud onto the floor. We tried to erase the greenish-black bloodstains with a dirty rag in a vain attempt to chase death from our helicopter. I went through the motions, trying to clean out the carnage, but I had tried it many times before and knew our efforts wouldn't work. Swamp water and mud were not going to take away the smell of rotting blood under our floor. It was easier to throw mud on the floor to hide the bloodstains from other passengers. We spent the afternoon checkerboarding the U Minh, picking up soaking wet infantry from abandoned flooded fields and dropping them in identical flooded LZs. When they jumped from our ship in each new LZ, they left some souvenirs for us. Fat leeches, swollen with the blood of infantrymen and as big as hot dogs, would wiggle on the floor after they dropped from their hosts. Flying from each LZ, I would idly squish them with my feet, adding more blood to the tepid, dirty swill. That evening my ship picked up one last load of wounded from another isolated firefight, another ten or twelve severely wounded young men, quickly thrown onto the ship, where they quivered in pain while the filthy muddy floor abraded their raw gaping wounds. We lifted out of the pickup zone and flew through the fire of NVA automatic weapons. They were wasting bullets, trying to kill the dying. When I fired my machine gun, flecks of blood blew back from the dying and speckled my eyeglasses so all I could see was blood and muzzle flashes. It made me think back to Fort Hood, where I had been told I shouldn't be allowed to fly on a helicopter because I wore glasses.

After dropping our evening wounded at the ARVN hospital to join the lunch-hour group of casualties, we flew back home through massive monsoon thunderstorms. Lightning bolts flashed around us and the cool wet air of the storm soaked the gunner and me and flushed some of the odor from our ship. Only the guns and slicks were heading home. Our scouts had to stay behind at a small compound in the U Minh because their rotor blades might come apart if they flew in heavy rain. After landing at Vinh Long and refueling, our pilots hovered each ship into its revetment, then the crew chiefs and gunners went to work ripping out the floor panels. We had just finished cleaning out the bloody mess with soap and water when our scouts arrived home after flying around the storm. One of the scouts walked by my ship carrying his logbook to the maintenance tent. He stopped to ask why we bothered cleaning our ships so well when all we did was haul dirty infantrymen. I didn't bother giving him an answer.

At least we had taken those wounded soldiers to a hospital; sometimes we couldn't do even that much for them. On a bright sunny day of easy missions in the dry season, Lt. Eber Brown and I were using my ship as a taxi for several Vietnamese officers who were making inspections of scattered Ruff Puff compounds throughout the Delta. We'd land outside a compound, sit around and loaf until their inspection was finished, then fly to the next compound. We had visited several of these little mud forts the NVA destroyed whenever they felt like it, and had just landed at another when an explosion occurred in a field about a hundred meters to my front. At first, I thought it was only an incoming mortar round impacting, but it was a local Ruff Puff soldier stepping on a land mine. These Rural Force/Popular Force troops were a home village guard that generally patrolled an area close to their village, and in our opinion, never actively searched for the enemy. The man had stepped on a mine that had probably been buried by a local VC in the village, possibly by one of his friends or relatives.

Not bothering to tie our rotor blades down, in case we had to leave fast, I sat in the open doorway watching the members of the patrol pick up the soldier. Leaving his legs behind in the dirt, they carried the rest of him to a small refrigerator-sized bamboo hut used as the local bus stop. Someone from the group must have returned to the compound for his wife, as a distraught, weeping young woman soon came running along the road, trying to find her husband before he died. Our ARVN officers ignored the small drama occurring ten meters in front of them and nonchalantly walked down the road to inspect the compound. Leaving the medic at the bus stop with their wounded comrade, the rest of the patrol sauntered on, continuing the search for an invisible enemy.

As the small patrol walked out of sight, the medic and the woman started furiously arguing. Eber and I sat in the shade of our ship, idly watching them, not wanting to get involved. Screaming at the medic, the young woman turned and ran to us, grabbed my arm and started pulling me toward the medic. Holding back, I tried to understand what she wanted. Crying and sobbing, she spoke enough broken English that Eber and I finally were able to determine what was occurring. The medic (a local villager) had refused to treat her husband because she had no money to pay him for either his services or medications. An army of true capitalists trained by Americans, the wounded were charged for their bandages. For some reason, she was convinced I was a medic and begged me to treat her husband.

Before I could agree or refuse to help, Eber spoke up. "Sergeant, if you're willing to do the work, I'll tell you what to do."

"I'll do it, but are you sure you know what to do?" I answered, aware that usually when he addressed me as "Sergeant," he had something planned that I didn't want to do.

"I was a medic before I became an officer. I can't do anything now because American officers can't get involved in a local military matter. The ARVN officers we're carrying today might raise hell back at squadron HQ if I do anything. If you do it, they might get mad, but they won't raise hell about a sergeant sticking his nose into a local matter."

"Okay, what should I do?"

"Go over to the medic and get his medical bag. Take it over to the wounded ARVN and then I'll join you to talk you through whatever needs to be done."

"No sweat," I answered. I walked over to the medic and relieved him of his equipment. He wasn't happy, but that was too damn bad. We had paid for the medical equipment in his pack and we were just going to borrow it for a little while.

Walking over to the casualty, I looked him over and

thought, *This is hopeless.* His legs were gone and most of the right arm, his left hand was broken and dangling loose. His face was ashen gray, probably from both shock and the blast. *What am I going to do?* I wondered. His wounds looked hopeless. I doubted a surgeon could have done much to save him. While I was obtaining the medical supplies, his young wife had run over to him, cradled his body in her arms and wept. Looking down at the two lovers, I knew we had to try something for her sake.

Kneeling in the dirt, I started moving my hands over the soldier's body to determine the extent of damage. While his wounds were gruesome, he wasn't bleeding much. Eber had joined us and said that the blast had probably cauterized and sealed the massive wounds on his stumps. I couldn't find any holes in either his torso or his head to bandage, so Eber advised that I give him an intravenous solution of dextrose, the only IV solution in the medic's bag. It probably wouldn't help, but it wouldn't hurt, and we couldn't do nothing and walk away. I had never given an IV before, but Eber talked me through the procedure. After having a hell of a time finding a vein in his broken left arm, I eventually got the needle in and attached the tubing. Once the dextrose was flowing into his left arm, I taped the dextrose bottle to the roof of the bus stop, threw the medic's bag out into the land mines in the rice paddy and walked back to the ship with my lieutenant.

Eber asked our crew to chip in the money we had in our wallets and he gave it to the grieving young woman. He was planning to fly the young couple to the nearest hospital, and she would need the money to live nearby while her husband was being treated. I think she broke all of our hearts. It was obvious she loved this poor wounded man. I believe each of us might have been jealous of her dying soldier. Eber was married, but the rest of our crew were single with no ties to any woman, and we were awed by the sincere love this young woman had for her wounded soldier. It made me feel empty. I realized I was missing something important in life. While I didn't envy his wounds, he at least had someone to grieve for him; today or tomorrow, one of us might lie dying in some

anonymous rice paddy and we'd die alone and uncomforted.
On the other hand, none of us would ever want our loved
ones to be in her flip-flops. Our high-ranking ARVN officers
soon returned from their inspection and Eber told them that
he was going to place the wounded soldier and his wife in
our ship and fly them to a hospital. Glancing over at the piti-
ful weeping peasant girl cradling her dying soldier in her
arms, the senior officer just sneered and said, "No! We
go now."

Goddamned bastards. We were soldiers. Following our orders, we left. Lifting off, Eber pulled us to the right to lessen
the dust and dirt that would fly from the rotor wash toward
the couple. I watched them until they faded from view, thinking about our allies. No wonder ARVN troops deserted to
join the VC. I hoped these officers would find their own land
mines one day. I hoped they would die slowly.

I still think about a Delta assault conducted under the
command of ARVN officers, when we landed our troops into
a village blatantly flying VC flags. No supporting fire was
laid down by either artillery or gunships; we just flew down
from the dark monsoon clouds, beating our blades through
the heavy pouring rain to land in a wide, muddy street
flanked on each side by straw hooches. We were going in fast
on our final approach when the word came over the company
radio net to go in hot and shoot everything. Our AC glanced
back and said, "You guys hear that? Shoot everything." The
gunner and I acknowledged by pressing our intercom buttons twice. My ship was first slick in our line of three. As I
fired slightly to our front into the hooches on our left, I could
see we would be landing near a hooch with several people
standing on its porch.

We were coming down fast and I had mere seconds to decide if I would shoot the Vietnamese on the porch. Quickly
estimating our airspeed and approach, I guessed that my ship
would land almost directly in front of them. When I realized
the small group on the porch consisted of a young woman
about twenty years old, holding a baby in one arm while a
small boy held on to her left leg, I held my fire. Standing on

her right side was a large pig. A typical squad of hard-core VC guerrillas.

Should I shoot? The orders from the Vietnamese officers in our C&C ship were clear. Shoot everything. What if the woman and children were just decoys, standing there to ensure we didn't shoot so when we landed, her husband could hit us with an RPG? I had to decide quickly: shoot them or let them go.

I decided. My bullets tore away the top of the doorway behind and above her head. She was standing outside the radius of our rotor blades, our rotor wash blowing her long raven hair into tangles, but she braced herself and never flinched. We skidded through the mud, sliding past her home, while I anxiously watched for the man of the house to appear with an RPG launcher. Our AC had seen where my bullets had hit and complimented my marksmanship with "Good shooting, Sarge." He wasn't being sarcastic, but I replied, *"Xin loi."* I hadn't returned to the war to kill unarmed women and children. *Screw the orders from the goddamn ARVN commander. Let them court-martial me,* I thought, but I wondered if Americans were ever court-martialed for refusing an order from an ARVN officer. I had taken an oath to defend our Constitution and the United States, but I didn't recall offering to fight under a foreign command or obey orders from an officer of a foreign army. Who decides what is a lawful order given from a foreign officer?

Seconds after landing, our ships lifted out of the mud and, as we moved forward, I momentarily glanced to the rear. The ARVN infantrymen who jumped from my ship were shooting the woman and her children. Disgusted with everything, I slammed my machine gun forward into its bracket, lit a cigarette and thought to myself, *What a goddamn war.* The longer I worked with the ARVN in the Delta, the more I felt like painting swastikas on our ships—and not because they are symbols of good luck in the Orient.

XXI

Shortly before my year-long tour of duty in the Delta was over, I extended my tour for an additional six months. But I did not want to stay in C Troop. We had been ordered to inventory all equipment and requisition any items missing from our helicopters. We took this as a sign that the troop would stand down to return to the States and was preparing to turn over all aircraft to another unit. I wanted to extend to be in a unit that would likely stay in country for a long time.

A small unit of three gunships had recently been relocated from I Corps to hunt Delta guerrillas at night using the newest high-tech infrared wizardry available. I extended to fly on their gunships. The gunships had been stationed at Phu Bai in I Corps, but were sent south to get them out of the way of the massive relocation of helicopter units to I Corps for the invasion of Laos, officially known as Operation Lam Son 719.

The invasion was named after the village where a mythical Vietnamese hero was born; 71 was the year; 9 was the main highway into Laos to be used by invading ARVN units. Officially no American troops were involved. It was solely an operation of the South Vietnamese, but American helicopter units had been relocated to the old Marine base at Khe Sanh to carry the ARVN units into Laos. Their crews could die in Laos because our military had decided that helicopter crews were not combat troops. We were officially classified as non-combatants. Two hundred helicopters would be shot down and destroyed in the invasion. The ARVN would later blame us for their defeat in Laos because of our miserly concern over noncombatant personnel losses.

The small high-tech unit from Phu Bai had priority on replacements, and as soon as my extension was approved, I received my orders to join them. Late in March, I left C Troop to join the Forward Looking Infrared, or FLIR, platoon, and once more rode a gunship hunting men. I was a crew chief on a Mike-model gunship, just an old Charlie model with an engine from a Cobra. Our ships needed the extra power because they carried rockets, miniguns and a heavy load of infrared equipment. Every evening our ships would leave Vinh Long to hunt in the pitch-black tropical nights of the Delta. We were taking control of the night, ensuring that the VC and NVA would never again feel confident maneuvering men and supplies after the sun went down. On a typical mission we would arrive at our area of operations in darkness flying two hundred meters high, a Cobra above us and a slick full of flares above him. In order for the other two ships to be able to see us, our ships had special lighting installed on each side that could be seen only from above. Once we approached our area of operations, all normal lighting on our ship was turned off in flight, making us invisible to ground troops. It was thought the enemy, not being able to see us, would think that our rotor blade noise was coming from the lighted Cobra and slick to our rear and high above us. The plan seemed to work, because we would often spot columns of enemy troops walking or sitting on the rice paddy dikes, unconcerned that helicopters flew overhead in the tropical darkness. We were catching groups of enemy troops by surprise, and nightly kills of forty to fifty men were not unusual. Of course, there were plenty of zero nights, too, but on the nights when we found the enemy, I did not feel a sense of accomplishment.

There was no challenge involved. This was not like the old days with the Stingers when I had literally flown into the faces of NVA soldiers, close enough to see the buttons on their shirts as I fired my machine gun. On these night missions we watched television screens and, wherever the infrared camera pointed at men, the miniguns also pointed there. Whenever we saw men on the screen, the pilot pushed the button to fire the miniguns. We were basically doing the same thing bomber crews did: butchering people who couldn't fight back. "How could bomber crews live with themselves?" we had often wondered in idle conversation. I had read that in Great Britain there is a monument honoring every type of unit that served in World War II except bomber crews. I understood why.

After several weeks of working the night skies of the Delta, my ship was sent north to join the 1st Cavalry at Phu Loi in III Corps. While I expected to return to Vinh Long, I would never see Vinh Long or my old friends in C Troop again. I would learn later that, as my ship flew out of the early morning ground fog headed for Phu Loi, my old platoon of C Troop slicks was also taking off, on their way south to land on top of an NVA unit hiding in the U Minh. C Troop, who had always been the lucky guys that the NVA machine guns couldn't hurt, had nine cavalrymen shot that day. My old platoon took very heavy casualties, more than making up for all those previous LZs when enemy machine-gun fire missed us. Eber Brown's crew chief was killed and his pilot had his right hand removed by a .51-caliber bullet. I sometimes feel I should have been with Eber and my old platoon that day. But such are the fortunes of war.

At Phu Loi, we joined the 1st Cavalry Division and were assigned to work with another small unit using a different type of night-flying gunships. They were using Charlie-model gunships with an infrared system less sophisticated than ours and apparently were doing very well hunting NVA infiltrators and vehicles. Once we settled in, we expected to be going out on, near or perhaps across the Cambodian border. Well, we settled in and waited and waited and waited. Our 1st Cav counterparts went out every night, while we sat around Phu Loi. It was hot and boring. Our pilots told us we were being held in reserve for rumored enemy armor, and we loaded our rocket tubes with seventeen-pound warhead rockets. Every evening we'd lie in hammocks waiting for the call to saddle up and ride out to kill tanks. The call never came.

After vegetating at Phu Loi for a few weeks, we were told that the FLIR platoon had received orders to leave the Delta and move back to I Corps. The massive helicopter assaults on Laos were over, and most helicopter units were returning to their home bases. The FLIR platoon packed up our gear at Vinh Long and then moved up the coast by ship. We would stay at Phu Loi and join them later. We didn't do much at Phu Loi, but once in a while, we'd go out in daylight to fly around and familiarize ourselves with the areas where we assumed we would soon be flying in total darkness. We were trying to get a feel for the terrain in case we had to walk home some night. With all the expensive secret equipment on board, we knew the Cobra behind us would be ordered to destroy our ship immediately if we went down. Our ship wouldn't sit in a jungle clearing overnight waiting for a Chinook to sling it out. It would be destroyed before any enemy troops could get near it. And we'd better be gone when the rockets started coming down.

We wasted weeks of the war, idly anticipating a mission that never came. If there were tanks over the border, we weren't going after them. Bored and restless, we were happy when we were finally ordered to fly north and join our platoon at Da Nang. Disappointed that we had not been used to hunt NVA armor on the border, we were glad to be going somewhere we would be appreciated. In I Corps, we knew we wouldn't sit around. The morning after being ordered north, we stowed our gear in the ship, said farewell to our 1st Cav friends, then left for Da Nang, feeling we had not accomplished a damn thing at Phu Loi.

Moving north was a long flight but an interesting trip because there was quite a change in scenery from the flatland of III and IV Corps. Flying over miles of heavily timbered jungle, broken by waterways with churning rapids instead of the lazy looping channels of lowland streams, I had to admit that the country appeared to possess enormous economic potential. Someday, someone would be cutting the timber and developing the swift rivers for hydroelectric power. We took our time, circling waterfalls and following streams as they wore the mountains down. After working the silt-laden tributaries of the mighty Mekong, the clear mountain streams tumbling and churning through foamy rapids made me feel as if I had entered a different country. But the next ridge or two would show signs of fighting: artillery scars and abandoned fighting positions. We were never far from the war. The mountains and jungles below us sheltered thousands of NVA, waiting for their marching orders. Entire NVA divisions camped throughout this vast green wilderness, and our army stumbled upon them only by sheer luck. With all of our technology, we didn't have a clue where the northern army was located.

As we flew over miles and miles of thick vegetation, I realized that 90 percent of the population of the country must live either in the Delta or along the coast. Vast areas were devoid of hamlets or any other sign of human habitation. While scars of the war were evident along our flight, the vast majority of the land appeared untouched. We were fighting a losing battle, trying to protect the populated areas from the foe in the countryside. Given enough time, along with secure lines of supply, the lean, tough men living in these woods were going to wreak havoc when they streamed out of their hideaways. Men disciplined to function in these tree-covered mountains were not going to be stopped by the demoralized draftees of the South. I knew that America was going to be involved in fighting here for a long, long time. Perhaps not with infantry divisions. But advisers and helicopter crews were going to be needed for years. I could easily imagine spending a twenty-year military career in Viet Nam.

The farther north we flew, the poorer the villages looked, and the fields of rice didn't have the lush colors of the South. Southern fields cried "surplus," this land murmured "subsistence." Most upland villages seemed to be dirt poor, but along the coastal plains, there were burnt-out villages full of wrecked tile-roofed cottages, a sign of past prosperity. Most people along the coast seemed to be housed in thatched, straw hooches. Perhaps that was because Americans had destroyed their houses.

Reaching the sprawling military complex/refugee slum of Da Nang late in the day, we stopped to refuel at the Marine Corps installation at Marble Mountain. Looking at their large modern metal-sided maintenance hangars and Quonset huts, I thought the Marine helicopter units had it pretty easy. No mud, no dust, PSP planking everywhere. Our gunner, Lou Diantonio, pointed to their gunships and laughed—their gunners used mounted guns. We held our guns on our laps, proud to be trusted not to shoot our own rotor blades. When we learned later that Marine gunships didn't fly below an altitude of four hundred meters, we thought even less of them. Once our fuel tanks were filled, we jumped into the ship. But instead of lifting off, we maneuvered back along the line of Marine aviation units to where an Army company was stationed. Our pilot said that this was going to be our new home for a few months—we were now attached to the 282nd Assault Helicopter Company.

I looked around and didn't like what I saw. I had always mocked helicopter crews in the South flying VIPs, but it appeared as if we were joining their northern counterparts. The nearest slicks, parked alongside our gunships, glowed with wax, and I could see commercial airline seats installed for passengers. The shiny VIP ships made a very bad first impression. Another bad sign: the 282nd ships had stick figures with conical hats painted on the doors to indicate kills. I'd never seen that done before. I figured if the crews kept count of kills, they must not get many. Back in III and IV Corps, most slicks wouldn't have had doors to paint on. In the Delta with C Troop, we thought the Army was being soft when we were told passengers were no longer to sit on the floor and hold on to the cargo tie-downs: nylon seats had to be available. This unit looked too clean. We considered excessive cleanliness a sign of inexperience and idle bravado.

After finding our platoon and settling into our new base, we were happy to learn that we wouldn't be at Da Nang very often. We would spend most of our time working around

Hue, Phu Bai, Quang Tri and Chu Lai. I rarely saw the other people in our platoon during the first few months up north. My ship went as far north as the DMZ, flying during the day so we could learn the terrain and the location of refueling points. Lam Son 719 was officially an active campaign, with ARVN units still in Laos, and for a few days we flew as the "killer" with an LOH "hunter" along the border of Laos. Sometimes in Laos, sometimes out. I suppose, like everyone else, we were officially noncombatants.

The Laotian border area always gave me goose bumps. Flying over its brutal, steep hillsides, I could feel the terrain radiate death. Perhaps the spirits of the thousands of the recent dead wandered this landscape, silently communicating with us as we flew overhead. Whatever the cause, these mountains gave off evil vibrations, their sense of malevolence raising the hackles on my neck. Mountains, older than our gods, glaring with the sure knowledge that they will be standing long after we are gone. These are the secret mountains where the Buddhist temples obtain their sacred rocks with an indentation of Buddha's footprint. Men or gods walked these ridges when the surface rock had not yet solidified, leaving tracks much older than Buddha or Jesus. Laos made us devout heathens. When I looked at the rugged, mist-covered slopes, I could understand why ARVN soldiers in Laos hung on to our helicopter skids attempting to escape their doomed LZs. There was something worse than death, something evil, on those Laotian mountains that could eat our souls and spit out the bones.

The war in Laos made less sense than the war in Viet Nam. Flying overhead cover for an artillery unit pulling out of a firebase in Laos, I looked down at muddy vehicles carrying wounded soldiers wrapped with dirty white bandages. Our AC told us we were covering the withdrawal of an American unit and, since there were officially no American units in Laos, the wounded couldn't be evacuated by helicopter. I have no idea if he spoke the truth, but it would have fit our war—American helicopters flying into Laos to retrieve ARVN wounded, while American wounded, bleeding to death, bounced along for hours in trucks over the rough dirt roads.

We spent a lot of time learning the area surrounding Quang Tri, but were rarely given a mission to use our infrared equipment. Quang Tri was the northernmost MACV outpost in the country and had an aura that gave me a bad feeling. I had the sense of impending doom when I stayed there. The whole place felt like a graveyard waiting for the coffins to be delivered: it already had the bodies. If any place in Viet Nam had evil spirits, it was Quang Tri. In 1972, elements of the NVA would overrun Quang Tri and it would be totally obliterated in the largest one-day bombing mission of the entire war. Quang Tri became the graveyard for an estimated ten thousand troops from both sides who died in the fighting.

I probably spent more time stationed at Chu Lai than anywhere else in I Corps. Originally a Marine base, it was named for an American Marine, General Victor Krulak. The Marines told us that Chu Lai means Krulak in Vietnamese, but none of us believed it. The locals might have told him that, but we always thought it was some local pornographic expression. Once the base was named, who would tell a general the truth? The Chinese locals claim that Chu Lai means an opening in an enclosure. No matter what it meant, at Chu Lai our magical infrared equipment was wasted again. No one seemed willing to commit us to a mission in a free-fire zone. We ended up being used to find buried land mines, locating them by the temperature difference in the road surface where a mine was recently buried—on our monitors, freshly excavated cool earth covering a mine showed up as a dark spot on a white hot road.

Eventually our ships were recalled from their temporary duty stations and our entire platoon returned to Da Nang. Like numerous other units throughout the country in the fall of 1971, our unit was given orders to "Stand Down," and to ship all of our equipment back to the States. Once our helicopters and jeeps were shipped, there was nothing for us to do but wait for personnel orders. We would either be reassigned to other units or sent home. Most of us pulled guard duty at night and sat around reading or playing cards during the day. Every now and then, a few of us would hitchhike to China Beach to swim in the South China Sea or loaf on the beach.

Walking China Beach one afternoon, I found an old, chipped coin with a Roman profile on it. At the time, I guessed that some American or French soldier had carried it for luck and lost it on the beach. I wasn't aware that Roman coins had been found around the ancient city of Oc Eo and that a local museum in the Mekong Delta had a large cache of such coins found in the Delta. If the Romans made it to the Delta, they could have easily come up the coast to Da Nang, so maybe the coin is genuine.

I hadn't extended for six months to spend my time loafing on a tropical beach and was glad when we received our orders transferring us to working units. Our people were scattered to the winds, but I moved only a hundred meters, assigned as crew chief on a slick with the 282nd Assault Helicopter Company.

XXII

Like all soldiers who are reassigned, soon after joining the 282nd, I considered it home. When I had first arrived at Da Nang, I hadn't cared much for the 282nd after seeing the two or three slicks that were kept spotless as VIP taxis for generals. I soon learned, however, there were only those few VIP ships. The rest of the company did everything a normal assault unit did for a living. The flight platoons had good people and the platoon to which I had been assigned had an exceptional esprit de corps for that time of the war. Most of the guys had served in Laos and there was nothing in Viet Nam for them to be afraid of after their experiences across the border. While we didn't fly very many combat assaults during the time I served with them, we did enough for me to learn these guys knew their jobs. I knew I'd been lucky to become part of another good unit.

For a long time I had been leery about making friends with other people because I had learned in '69 it was damn hard to lose them. Perhaps, because the war seemed to be calming down, I found myself becoming a little more outgoing with others and found a good friend in Mike Meagher, another crew chief. Mike was a soldier who thrived on hard days and combat. His only regret in life was not being in country for the heavy fighting of 1968. Mike was the type of soldier I liked to be with.

At the 282nd company area we slept in Marine Quonset huts, had latrines with hot and cold running water, and even had flush toilets. Most of us who had grown accustomed to a much simpler lifestyle at other compounds didn't care very much for life at the Marine base at Marble Mountain. It was too soft and easy. I missed the normal hot, dirty hooches, cold water (if we were lucky), shit-burning day, rats, reptiles and mosquitoes. Most of all I missed the adrenaline rush of combat. It didn't appear any American units were actively searching for the enemy or attempting to initiate any contact. We were sitting at our base camps and firebases, doing nothing to win the war. We waited idly to see what would happen between the two opposing armies of Viet Nam and secretly hoped we would not get caught in the middle when they clashed.

At this stage of the war, our missions were mostly "ash and trash" missions, supplying the few scattered fire support bases still operating on top of the mountains around Da Nang. Occasionally, we would insert some infantry on one of the isolated mountain plateaus overlooking miles of jungle valleys that could hide entire NVA divisions. It was different assaulting a mountaintop by flying up from the valley, riding up mere meters from the trees and rocky outcrops while waiting to receive fire from above our rotor blades out of any one of hundreds of possible hiding places. Assaulting mountains from the bottom up didn't seem very smart since we couldn't fire our machine guns up through the turning blades, but what did I know about tactics. Occasionally, we flew way back into the mountains to the old French tiger hunting camps, flying over miles and miles of lush jungle carved by cascading rocky streams, and I would wonder where the enemy was hiding and waiting. We'd go south along the coast to scattered compounds, delivering men and materials. We went up to the DMZ doing the same thing. Everywhere we went, it was quiet.

It wasn't just quiet in I Corps. Everything seemed to be relatively quiet throughout Viet Nam. American units were standing down and returning to the States everywhere. The huge American compound at Chu Lai and the smaller bases north of Da Nang were being turned into ghost towns, populated only by small contingents of ARVN troops. Rumor had it that a deal had been made with the NVA. Let us leave in peace and there will be no trouble. Those of us who had been in country for a while didn't trust the situation. If the NVA made a serious attack, the Army of South Viet Nam was going to have to stop them. After Lam Son 719, no one seriously thought that the ARVNs had a prayer.

Even though everything was relatively quiet, the quiet never lasted. Eventually the NVA would leave their hidden base camps and the war would heat up again. While I was an old man of twenty-three in an army of nineteen-year-old soldiers, I could do my job in combat. It was my intention to stay in a combat zone as long as possible. Major military units were standing down all over the country, but I was optimistic the Army would be in country for a long time, much as it had been in Korea.

If I wanted to stay in the war, I realized I'd better find a way to be assigned someplace near Saigon. Since I Corps was being emptied of all Americans, I had to get out of Da Nang. But no matter who I talked to I got the same answer. "Where are you going to go? Everybody is standing down." I finally submitted a request to extend my tour for an additional six months in order to join the Third Brigade of the 1st Cavalry Division down country in III Corps. After thinking things over, I figured Saigon would have to be defended and, if any unit was going to stay until the bitter end, it would be the "Cav." I'd talked to the first sergeant of the 282nd and he agreed I was probably right about the Cav staying. He also said I might as well make myself at home until either my extension was approved or I received orders for another unit. The 282nd had been notified to stand down.

We were still flying some easy missions, but we weren't doing much. Helicopters were being readied for shipment back to the States. We knew our days were numbered at Da Nang. Soon there would be no missions. It wouldn't be long before we would pack up everything, bury our extra machine guns, and disband. Most of the men would be getting orders to return to the States, while others would be reassigned to units still operating in country. Soon after the company had received orders to stand down, an American Army captain visited those of us who were helicopter crewmembers. Since I had been involved with the stand-down of the FLIR platoon, I had talked to the captain and wasn't surprised by his visit. I was never sure just what his job was, but he always seemed to turn a conversation into the possibility of leaving the Army to serve as a mercenary on a helicopter along the borders of Israel. He always said that if flight crewmembers talked to the right people and agreed to a three-year contract as a mercenary, they would immediately receive an honorable discharge from the Army. The pay seemed excellent, but he was blunt. He told us mercenary helicopter crews were being lost in border clashes and no rescue attempts were made for them. I don't know if he ever convinced anyone to look for another job in Israel, but I wasn't interested in fighting another war on the wrong side.

I suppose we all thought that there was some truth to his stories, as half of our guys swore we were carrying foreign mercenaries into Laos. Periodically, we had hauled troops up to the Laotian border who spoke only German. While some people thought they were German mercenaries, most of us thought they were our own Special Forces who were speaking German to confuse the NVA. Perhaps they were mercenaries, however. One evening a ship went down with a load of these men and we were not allowed to attempt a rescue. The American pilots begged for help over the radios as NVA machine guns shredded our men while they waded for cover along a riverbank. All helicopters in the air were ordered *not* to attempt a rescue. That night, I drank a lot of whiskey while I sat and thought about how the Army had changed in a couple of years. I had flown with a lot of helicopter crews that would have ignored the order given that evening. I felt guilty drinking whiskey in the club instead of facing the NVA on that riverbank with the crew of the downed ship. It was a different Army now and different times. But we should have joined the fight, tried to save those guys. The Army was falling apart internally. I blamed our officers.

In late December, I saw something that made me realize the old Army I had loved had changed so much we were going to lose the war. On a dismal rainy day, my ship was sent out with a load of C-rations to resupply an American mechanized infantry unit. Rather than make two trips in the foggy mist, we had stacked cases of rations from the floor to the ceiling and managed to take the entire load by having the pilot, gunner and I hold the last of the C-ration cases on our laps. We flew southwest of Da Nang and located the company of APCs parked in a semicircle, guarding an insignificant piece of real estate. The weather had cleared a little and we dropped from the sky to land next to a smoke grenade thrown to mark where the company wanted their groceries delivered. As soon as our skids hit the ground, I jumped out to start stacking cases of rations on the ground and realized that something was different about this delivery. No one had run over to help the gunner and me unload the ship. I stopped unloading to look over at the APCs and saw something I had never seen before: an American military unit with segregated crews on the armored vehicles. Three APCs to my left had only black troops sitting on them, while mixed crews of white and Hispanic soldiers manned the rest of the vehicles. Neither group seemed willing to be the first to help unload food for someone else. Finally, a few black troops came over and took their share of rations from the ship. After the black troops had returned to their vehicles, several white troops walked over and carried the rest of the rations to their crews. I couldn't believe my eyes. What had happened to the Army? Why had their officers and NCOs let this unit disintegrate into two separate camps? I wondered if they trusted each other in a fight with the enemy: probably not. I went back to Da Nang feeling very unconfident about the southwestern approaches to the city being secure. If this unit couldn't even share the work of getting food, I doubted they would share ammunition in a fight.

As 1972 began, our company started standing down in earnest. The company lost people every day as individual assignments started flowing down from battalion headquarters. Most of the guys in our platoon would be leaving soon and a couple of them asked me, "When are you going to leave? Haven't you been here long enough?"

I'd just laugh and answer them, "Someday you'll be watching the news on TV and they'll show the last American leaving Viet Nam. When he walks up the stairway to get on the plane, the cameras are going to scan the crowd in the background. The six-foot-tall guy in the crowd will be me."

Soon only Mike Meagher and I were left in our platoon. Everyone else who had lived with us had received their orders and shipped out. Finally, at one of our small morning formations, our names were called to report to the orderly room to pick up our orders: Mike was going to the 1st Cavalry Division at Fort Hood, Texas, and I was going to the 48th Assault Helicopter Company, about three hundred meters away. The next day, Mike went to Cam Ranh Bay to wait for a flight to the States. I carried my gear up the dirt street to the orderly room of the 48th Assault. Since I hadn't received orders to go to the States, I was confident that my request to extend my tour for an additional six months with the 1st Cav in III Corps must have been approved. I didn't plan on staying with the 48th very long. In early February 1972, I was filling sandbags when a company clerk found me and told me to report to the company orderly room for my orders.

Running to the orderly room, I couldn't wait to get my orders and get out of Da Nang. Upon reading my orders, I felt doomed. They weren't what I had expected. My extension request had been denied and, instead of joining the Third Brigade of the 1st Cav in Viet Nam, I would be joining the rest of the 1st Cav in Texas. I couldn't believe it: Fort Hood again.

I had no intention of going back to Texas and immediately went to our battalion personnel office to try to get my extension denial revoked. The personnel clerks laughed at me. Said it was impossible. No extensions were being approved. Units all over Viet Nam were standing down, and the few units that weren't packing had plenty of troops being reassigned from other units. The Army in Viet Nam didn't need the troops that wanted to stay. Wandering back to my hooch,

I wondered what I had ever done that was so evil as to deserve the cruel and unusual punishment of being sent to Texas.

Several days later I joined the mass exodus from Viet Nam. Departing the 48th Assault, I turned in my rifle and field gear, keeping only my extra boots and my Roman coin from China Beach. Not much to show for the time I had spent in country, but they were enough. I left Da Nang by flying out of the huge Air Force base nearby and, as I gazed out of the windows of the C-130 on takeoff, I couldn't help but visualize the NVA overrunning everything in sight. While the ARVN were scattered all through the portion of I Corps north of Da Nang, they were there to guard the old imperial city of Hue. The NVA were going to come to Da Nang from the south and west, and I knew that the ARVN wouldn't stop them. I was glad to be leaving Da Nang, but flying down to Cam Ranh Bay, I seriously thought about catching another flight to Saigon, then hitching a ride to 1st Cav headquarters to beg to be assigned to them. But I knew it wouldn't do any good.

I was only at Cam Ranh Bay for a few hours before boarding a commercial airliner bound for the States. As soon as our wheels lifted off of the runway and we were no longer on the soil of Viet Nam, our plane vibrated with the shouts of two hundred jubilant departing troops. Apparently everyone on the plane except me was happy. I sat gazing out at the landmass of Asia, knowing I would probably never see it again. I sat and thought about what I had seen during two-and-a-half years in country. I doubted if anything we had done had made any difference. The war would continue without us. The wounding and the killing of Vietnamese and Americans, the heartaches in the homes of both sides; the widows, the orphans, the cripples; had anything been achieved worth the suffering?

How could we leave after what we had done to this country? How could we leave after what this country had done to us? The country was the mirror image of our national soul. The countryside was in ruins: abandoned fields and villages, defoliated hardwood forests and bomb craters everywhere. Prosperous peasants had been turned into refugees, crowding the cities to watch their children become thieves and prostitutes in order to survive. We had changed the Vietnamese and had changed ourselves even more. It was easy to understand why, throughout I Corps, we were told to watch for Marines who had changed sides. We never talked much about them, but we understood why they were fighting alongside the NVA. After a couple of months in country, smalltown farm boys would eventually stop and think, "What would I do if this was my home village?" I doubt many American farm families would have been grateful if government troops forced them into a secure, sterile settlement, then burned their homes and killed their livestock. It was difficult to comprehend that there were educated people on our side who developed such tactics and who actually thought the peasants should appreciate the wonderful things done for them.

Napalm, B-52 strikes, helicopters and tanks had been used against an opposing army of foot soldiers—without stopping them. Our military forces were leaving, but our technology was staying behind with the Army of the Republic of Viet Nam. Our equipment wouldn't make much difference. But it would delay the final outcome. Good soldiers know that determined men will beat technology. Technology might win some battles, but men would win this war. While I truly believed the ARVN was going to lose the war, I wished I could stay in the fight until the end. I had never regretted coming back to help with the fighting, and always wished I could have done more. Having learned warrior mysticism, I wanted to stay in the fight for the sake of the fight. While I had no love for the ARVN, I had been willing to fight their enemy for two-and-a-half years and was more than willing to stay until the end. With Americans pulling out, the end was not going to be far away. But orders were orders; I was a soldier and would leave the war.

I would return to the United States. But I would hold my thoughts and feelings about my time in Viet Nam forever. I was going to miss everything, even our enemy. I thought about the NVA and VC I had fought against for two-and-a-half years. I couldn't help but respect them for their determination and willingness to endure the hardships of jungle warfare for their cause. I had read that in the late 1800s, General George Crook had been asked if fighting Indians was hard work. He had answered, "Yes, it's hard work, but what makes it harder is knowing that they're right." I knew exactly what he meant.

Right or wrong, I knew it was really irrelevant which side I had served with. On a rainy morning in the Mekong Delta, I had been given a glance behind the curtain that hid the answers to the questions we all secretly asked. There were reasons for our lives and we had obligations to meet. If I had learned anything, it was that warfare was foolishness. But so was everything else. To those on the other side who would hold each of us accountable, causes meant nothing. We were all being tested individually to test our mettle. Combat was just another medium for testing. I knew from my experience in the tunnel that being a soldier was not a "minus," but was probably a "plus" when the score was tallied. Ever since the tunnel episode I thought I had returned from the tunnel to redeem myself for my failure to help the two wounded men at the bunker in 1969. I was bothered by my inability to find and recognize a way in which I had paid for my error. I believed it unfair for me to leave the war without wiping my slate clean. I knew I shouldn't be leaving. But I had no choice. Perhaps I had wished to stay in country only to hasten my death and return to the tunnel, but I don't think so. I wanted to stay because I knew it was, in fact, the honorable thing to do. I knew honor did mean something. Right or wrong, I knew I should be with the soldiers who were staying to face the big battalions that God so loves.

A thousand scenes of the country flooded my mind, but it wasn't the country I would miss. I knew I would miss our own soldiers more than anything else. After leaving here, where would I ever serve side by side with such men? Why was it so easy to find guys here who were so damn courageous and good? They surely weren't common anywhere else. The people I always feared being close to were the reason I wanted to stay in country. There was an indescribable sense of confidence that seemed to radiate from our men, and I wanted to brace my feet in the mud with those men being left to face the NVA. The more I thought about the troops I had served with, the more I realized *they* were the reason that I had come back, the reason I wanted to stay. There weren't any heroes in the States. I met them every day in country. I would miss the soldiers, not the war.

I thought back to my first days in country in 1968 and realized how much I had changed. I had been a scared adolescent in 1968; a hardened, unemotional old man in 1969. The years 1970 and 1971 had blunted some rough edges, but while time had tempered my desire to be in on the kill, it hadn't dampened the thrill of the hunt. I might have become more mature, but perhaps I was only callused. Had I wasted two-and-a-half years of my life? The fighting, the fear, the excitement and the boredom, all of it was meaningless. I couldn't really say I had accomplished much. I hadn't been in much of the war. I knew that I hadn't been a participant in the war, only an observer. I could easily sum up my war record with the common expression of our soldiers, "Don't mean nothing."

As our plane gained altitude over the South China Sea, I stared out the window watching the continent of Asia grow smaller and smaller until it faded from view. Leaning back in my seat, I almost wept. Choking back my emotions, I lit a cigarette and muttered softly to myself, "*Xin loi,* Viet Nam."

GLOSSARY

AC: Aircraft Commander, person in charge during flight; in other wars and other assignments, this person would have been called the pilot.

Airburst: Explosion of a projectile several meters above the ground.

Air Cav: Air Cavalry, a military unit that primarily uses helicopters to maneuver.

AIT: Advanced Individual Training.

AK-47: The basic infantry automatic weapon of Communist forces throughout the world.

AO: Area of Operations, the section of a war zone assigned to a unit.

APC: Armored Personnel Carrier, a lightly armored tracked vehicle.

Article 15: Company punishment or disciplinary action.

ARVN: Army of the Republic of Viet Nam.

Ash and trash: Term used by helicopter units to denote mission of carrying supplies.

AWOL: Absent Without Official Leave. A soldier carried on unit roster as AWOL is not considered a deserter.

***Bac si*:** Vietnamese term for doctor or medic.

Base camp: Field headquarters for a given unit.

Battalion: Unit consisting of four or five Companies or Artillery Batteries.

Battery: Company-sized artillery unit.

Berm: Any elevated piece of earth, such as a road or dike.

Bird dog: Small fixed-wing aircraft used as a forward observer to direct jet strikes.

C&C: Command and Control, the aircraft flown above all others in a battle and from which the commanding officer directed American forces.

Cav: Cavalry.

Chicken plate: Chest armor worn by flight crews.

Chieu hoi: Literally, "open arms," but used as a term to surrender and also used to denote one who had surrendered.

Chinook: CH-47 helicopter, a bus-sized twin-rotor helicopter.

Claymore: Fan-shaped antipersonnel mine normally command detonated.

CO: Commanding Officer.

Company: Military unit usually consisting of four platoons. Similar to a Battery or Troop.

Contact: Engagement with the enemy.

C-rations: Canned meals.

Delta: The vast Mekong Delta: IV Corps; any place south of Saigon.

DMZ: Demilitarized Zone, the border between North and South Viet Nam.

Elephant grass: A very tall, sharp-edged grass that grew in jungle clearings.

EM: Enlisted Man, someone who is not an officer.

Firefight: A usually short exchange of small arms fire between two opposing units.

FNG: Fucking New Guy.

FO: Forward observer; person who calls for and directs artillery fire.

Frag: A fragmentation grenade, a hand-thrown explosive that scatters ragged pieces of shrapnel.

Gunship: Any armed helicopter that was not used to carry troops or supplies.

HEAT: Type of artillery projectile; High Explosive, Anti-Tank.

Hootch: Any living quarters with partial walls and a roof.

I Corps: Northernmost military region.

II Corps: Central Highlands military region.

III Corps: Military region north of Saigon.

IV Corps: Mekong Delta.

In country: Republic of Viet Nam.

KIA: Killed in Action.

Klick: Kilometer.

LOH: Light Observation Helicopter used for scouting purposes.

LRRP: Long Range Reconnaissance Patrol.

LZ: Landing Zone.

MACV: Military Assistance Command Viet Nam.

Medevac: Medical evacuation by helicopter.

MIA: Missing in Action.

MOS: Military Occupational Specialty, a soldier's job title.

MPC: Military Payment Certificates; paper money used instead of normal U.S. currency.

NCO: Non-Commissioned Officer, a sergeant.

Nipa palm: A short palm tree that grows in thickets along waterways.

NVA: North Vietnamese Army.

Number Ten: Bad, horrible.

PF: Popular Forces; a village home guard.

PFC: Private First Class.

Pilot: The copilot of a helicopter, since the "pilot" was called Aircraft Commander.

Platoon: Military element of less than sixty men; usually consists of four squads.

Point man: The first man in a file on patrol; usually the first person to engage the enemy.

Poncho liner: Nylon insert for a rain poncho; it was used as a blanket.

R&R: Rest and Recreation; five-day vacation authorized to each soldier serving in country.

Recon: Reconnaissance.

Red Leg: An artilleryman.

RPD: Enemy light machine gun.

RPG: Rocket Propelled Grenade; antitank weapon.

RF/PF or Ruff Puff: Rural Force/Popular Force; local home defense units.

RVN: Republic of Viet Nam.

Sappers: Enemy troops trained to infiltrate American positions at night.

Slack: Second man in a file of troops on patrol; his duty is to protect the point man.

Slick: A UH-1 helicopter without armament equipment attached to its sides/nose.

Squad: Basic military maneuver element under the direction of a sergeant.

Squadron: A battalion-sized element of a cavalry regiment.

Stand-down: A period of unit inactivity meant to provide time to refit equipment.

Troop: A company-sized element in a cavalry unit.

VC: The Viet Cong; enemy guerrilla forces.

Viet Minh: Guerrilla forces who opposed the French forces.

WIA: Wounded in Action.